When the Norns Have Spoken

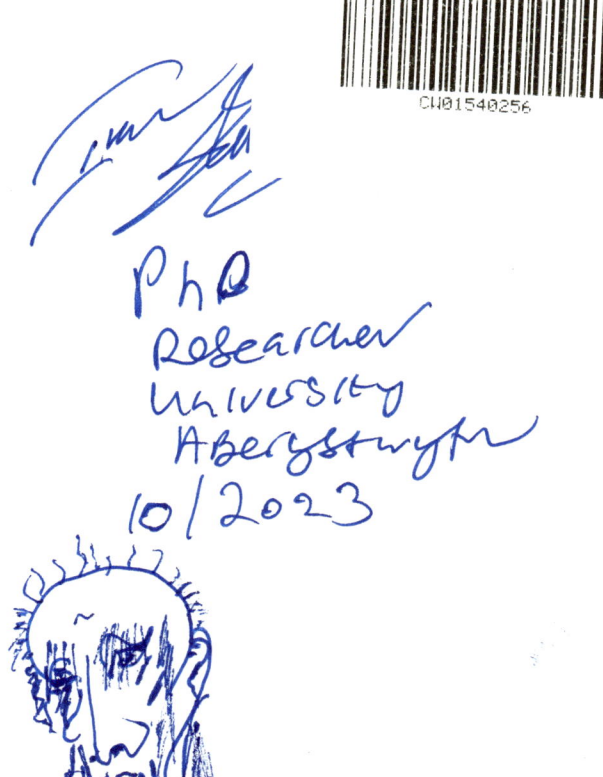

PhD Researcher
University Aberystwyth
10/2023

When the Norns Have Spoken

Time and Fate in Germanic Paganism

Anthony Winterbourne

Superscript
The imprint of Cyhoeddwyr y Superscript Ltd,
404 Robin Square
Newtown. SY16 1HP

Copyright 2004 by Rosemont Publishing and Printing Corp.

First paperback edition published by Superscript, 2007, by kind permission of Associated University Presses

All rights reserved. No part of this publication may be reproduced, stored in a retrieval system, or transmitted in any form or by any means without the prior permission of Associated University Presses, 2010 Eastpark Boulevard, Cranbury, NJ 08512. USA.

Cover by Oisin Little, featuring a marble bust of one of the Fates, attributed to Antonio Montauti, reproduced by permission of the National Gallery of Scotland.

ISBN 97809550028
A catalogue record for this book is available from the British Library.

Typesetting by Fairleigh Dickinson University Press
Printed and bound by CPI-Antony Rowe, Eastbourne.

"What reaches you could not possibly have missed you,
and what misses you could not possibly have reached you."

Abu Hanifa (from the *Fiqh Akbar*)

Contents

Introduction	11
1. Paganism in Myth and Cult	20
2. Mythical Space and Time	42
3. Cosmogony and the World-Tree	60
4. Spinning and Weaving Fate	84
5. The Logic of Fatalism	104
6. From Pagan Fate to Christian Providence	120
Notes	146
Bibliography	170
Index	183

To Nicola

No *daimon* will cast lots for you,
but you shall choose your own *daimon*.

Introduction

It has been said that in planning any essay it is essential to begin with a bibliographic inquiry in order to decide whether or not it is worthwhile exploring the subject in question. On this criterion, even a cursory examination of the available literature related to the subject of Germanic mythology, in so far as this reveals anything of the conceptual framework of our ancestors, would reveal a corner of scholarship that would seem to be in robust health. In fact, this secondary literature is now so vast, both in scope and detail, that anyone intruding upon another's special field—as I am here—risks being overwhelmed. And yet in undertaking my own preliminary research, it became increasingly clear that certainly in so far as fate in particular is concerned, although the subject can hardly be said to have been overlooked, the attention devoted to it has tended to treat it as more of a contextual "given" than as a philosophical issue meriting detailed examination in its own right. It is the purpose of this inquiry to confront the question of just what fate means, or what it meant to those people who employed over centuries a range of cognate terms in the Germanic languages for it—"Urðr," "wurt," "wurd," "wyrd," etc. While attention has been given to the concept of fate as an overall feature of the cosmographies or cosmogonies, it seems that as a properly philosophical question, the fundamental nature of fate (and time) has been unnecessarily neglected. Yet the absolute centrality of the issues involved is undeniable (and, indeed, acknowledged), for the Germanic view of the world is saturated with the effects of the belief in an all-powerful destiny. It has to be conceded that there has been rather more interest in the nature of time—and, indeed, space—as it is represented in (mostly) Scandinavian cosmographies. Now since it is invariably assumed that time and fate are somehow or other inextricably related, not just for the Norsemen but for ourselves, it is somewhat surprising that these often elaborate and ingenious reconstructions of space-time models do not thereby nourish a concomitant analysis of fate. It seems sometimes that fate as such is either too easy, or too obscure, to inspire analysis. This relative neglect of conceptual issues, even in the wake of a clear interest in the nature of time with which it is supposed to be intimately connected, is somewhat paradoxical in the light of what follows; for it is part of the aim here to examine that connection and to break it, or at least to loosen it.

Before proceeding any further, some justification for the terminology employed here would seem to be appropriate. I have already used different terms to refer to what is a broadly similar cultural phenomenon: I have used "Germanic" (given also in the book's title), "Norse," and "Scandinavian," and we can easily add "Icelandic" or "Northern" to the list. It is a historical fact that most of what sustains our interest concerning the beliefs and mythology of the Northern European peoples comes to us in the form of Scandinavian and, even more precisely, Icelandic (Norse) literature. The Eddas, skaldic verse, and the sagas, are the primary resource for any discussions of this nature. Yet since this is not intended as a commentary on these very specific sources, and since we sometimes must give some weight to alternative material—Anglo-Saxon, or "mainland" Scandinavian, for instance—in what follows the terms most often employed in the literature, whether "Icelandic," "Northern," or "Norse," have been nudged underneath the umbrella term "Germanic." "Teutonic," strictly speaking, might also seem accurate enough, but suffers now from seeming an archaism. In fact, we will require all of these terms at different points in the argument: but for those not entirely familiar with the field, the choice of "Germanic" as a generality seems to be the most appropriate. More narrowly, much the same considerations apply to those terms used for "fate" itself: it would be cumbersome to constantly remind the reader that, for example, "*Urðr*" was the Old Norse form, and "*wyrd*" the Old English, with Germanic "*Wurt*" and Old Saxon "*wurd*" also relevant. I have therefore taken the decision to move somewhat more freely between them than would be permissible in a strictly literary or philological context. Since the focus here will be, in the main, upon conceptual issues, some lability is preferable to a clumsy repetition of etymologies at every point.[1]

What follows is offered as a philosopher's interruption of what is, quite clearly, an already vigorous and healthy conversation.[2] But this is not a commentary on Norse literature: the reader will find many excellent such commentaries elsewhere, some of which are plundered here as the philosophical argument unfolds. This is an essay in the history of ideas: it is a reconstruction of one way of understanding an issue that is, apparently, all too easy to misunderstand.

One of the most prominent of contemporary scholars of Norse literature, Margaret Clunies Ross, has remarked that for the people of ancient Scandinavia, some knowledge of the mythic world and how it worked was an expected cultural resource and point of reference. As a fundamental part of their conceptual framework (even after the conversion to Christianity) it formed part of the means by which ideas were communicated—ideas that were themselves integral to their culture.[3] The assumption will be made throughout this study that in Eddic poetry and the sagas, no less than in other yet more ancient texts, used in what follows as contrasts to the Germanic case that is the primary focus, that these are works not only of considerable literary merit, but that they are works embedding sophisticated and reflective manifestations of a recognizable philosophical impulse to grasp the meaning of the world around them. It does not matter that they were one and all wrong about their cosmology—for we are likely as not wrong about our own, too, for all that we asymptotically approach (or think we do) the nature of things as they are in themselves.

Ross also remarks that "there is always a contrast in Icelandic writing about indigenous subjects between pagan and Christian times," a contrast that, she says, touches almost all medieval Icelandic literature.[4] It cannot be overstated how important the concepts of time and fate are to understanding both this contrast and the manner in which the eventual triumph of Christianity was achieved. For time—and, especially, fate—were not merely philosophical abstractions, but parts of the very fabric—the weave—of the culture's experiences of life. If we think of time, for instance, only as that which clocks measure, we have thereby understood little of its meaning, even for ourselves, let alone for cultures for whom time was measured for different purposes than making appointments. We may still feel that there is "a divinity that shapes our ends, Rough-hew them how we will . . ." and that this is a power that is forever hidden from us. Oswald Spengler called destiny "the organic logic of existence," yet since it is beyond time it can neither be measured nor fully analyzed, but only suggested, implied, and, for our Germanic ancestors, lived.[5] And while causality—that sometime imposter of fate—can be understood through reason, destiny, at least according to Spengler, can be expressed only through art or metaphor or poetry. "We know what destiny is by letting ourselves sink into the meaning and sound of such words as fate, doom, chance, submission to providence, predestination. To know what is meant by providence, grace, or original sin, is to know much about the Western soul. Similarly, we gain a glimpse into other cultures by immersing ourselves in their destiny ideas—Moira, Ananke, Tyche, Kismet."[6]

Of course we are concerned here not with souls only, but with minds. One scholar, Steblin-Kaminskij, in writing a book called *The Saga Mind,* perhaps raises expectations that we will find there some "topography" of such minds. His approach is not without its critics, but it does have the merit of taking seriously the very idea that through the literature, their conceptual framework might be explicable. He sees an almost impenetrable barrier, however, in the inevitable fact that the symbols by means of which these frameworks are communicated—words—are never transparent to us at this distance. This lack of transparency is at its most acute, he thinks, in relation to the elementary words of any spiritual vocabulary—words like "soul," "truth," and "good."[7] It is not entirely clear why he thinks this, except that these are obviously abstract concepts, and unlike terms for denotable objects in space, are bound to provide innumerable opportunities for misdirection and ambiguity. Translations, especially contemporary ones, can help (he concedes), but even those provide a further barrier to comprehension. And yet this seems a counsel of despair. Given that contemporary philosophers are prepared to argue over whether or not one can ever logically know what is going on right now in another's mind (their behavior, even their words, being subject always to systematic ambiguity), it is neither very surprising nor, frankly, very interesting that we should have to concede that our knowledge of minds so far from us in time, space, and concept is and must always be at best partial and conjectural. That is the position from which we start: it is not a conclusion that ought to merit any special attention. We are not ancient Icelanders, or Semnones, or Goths, or Egyptians. And what of it? What then? For we are not all contemporary Inuit either—nor are we Saamis or Hopi or even Englishmen.

Steblin-Kaminskij's thesis is that the literature of remote ages is inseparable from the spiritual world of those among whom it has its origins. He does not say how he could know this, given the "insuperable barriers" that he has identified between us and them in terms of language. And this certainly sounds like something he claims to know quite independently of his own strictures on how we come to know anything at all about ancient cultures. He then goes on to say that in order to understand this literature it is essential for us to understand this spiritual world, thereby neatly closing the circle around us: for if the literature is what provides us with the primary evidence for understanding this spiritual world, and the spiritual world is a necessary precondition for understanding the literature, we move forever in a cloud of unknowing. Of course, in a sense, he is correct. It is the literature that provides glimpses of the minds of those who composed and read it. And for all the uncertainties of translation, commentary, exegesis, and etymology, the literature is closer to us than the mind of the poet, if only because some kind of continuity can be established, albeit never definitively.[8]

Another assumption on which this essay proceeds is that it is not necessary to have a definition of myth prior to investigating its contents with confidence. No theory of myth is either presupposed in this discussion or argued for in its course, and if one wishes a definition, then there are any number of good dictionaries available. Definitions record usage. They do not constrain intelligibilty, and they should not limit debate. A definition may be one of the aims of a philosophical inquiry: unlike the example of mathematics, it should not be a premise from which other propositions are deduced. This point has been put with admirable directness and clarity by Mary Beard, when she says that problems will certainly follow from the "insistent modern practice of first *defining* myth, then *judging* the surviving material against these fixed criteria. 'Myth defined,' in other words, becomes a weapon not merely of classification, but of *exclusion* and *closure*." She adds (in a neat phrase) that whatever does not quite fit the bill gets put into the "*salon des refusés,*" and asks us to consider the significance of distinctions as between such categories as "myth," "legend," and "folk-tale." No technical definition distinguishing these is wholly plausible, since matters of technical definition are not really the issue. "For these are value judgments masquerading as professional jargon; they are justifications of neglect—the dustbin categories for all kinds of mythic thinking that we would rather not treat as 'myth.'"[9]

It is possible to identify within the literature of Old Norse studies in particular a distinction—sometimes quite explicit, but more often implied—whereby the content of the sagas is treated as being very different, from the mythic-philosophic point of view, from Eddic and other poetry. This differentiation is perhaps at its most clear-cut in relation to the ideas of time and fate. Mythical time and "saga time" may occasionally interact in the latter, but they are clearly distinguishable. Put crudely, "saga time" is mythic time plus causality: it is this awareness of causality that, according to Cecil Wood, makes the sagas seem so very "modern."[10] The assumption seems to be that the causal nexus is absent from myth. This is correct because myth is time*less:* what is being described are not events *in* time, but sometimes events that give rise to historical time in the first place. It is not sensible to try to connect the sequence of events as expressed in a mythical account with the sequence of cause and effect in which human time, and human consciousness, is delineated.

We will see below how central a role is played, for an understanding of fate by a number of terms in many different languages, by images of "turning": verbs that imply this kind of movement describe a "temporal" gestalt that cannot be apprehended simply as succession. It seems almost as if the primary verb—German "*Zeitwort,*" that is, time-word—for the time that is involved in fate is not strictly a "time" word at all, but one that is closely allied to spatial concepts. Some primitive languages could make distinctions only between what was either "now" or "not-now," while others made no distinction between the remote past and the remote future—time was conceived as an individual, single substance existing "out there" in its totality. Something moves, yet at the same time it does not move. Events follow one another, but they do not cause one another. This is causality as Hume, rather than Kant, would like us to understand it—it is just one damn thing after another. And this is not at all unexpected, since the Kantian conception of cause is that it is a category put into the phenomenal sequence of events by us—put in, so to speak, "after the events." Causality as a principle is a category that Kant thinks is a necessary presupposition of logical, scientific, and philosophical thinking. It is not somehow "read off" directly from phenomena. This is partly what makes the structure of the sagas seem to us so very remarkable and, indeed, so very modern. For not only do we find there a "historical" narrative in which the idea of a causal nexus is crucial, but—much more remarkable—this narrative moves against the temporally static backdrop of mythical fate. Fate is never overcome, because causality, in providing a direction for time, propels man always into the future, the "not-yet," while fate, as grasped by ancient man, was a function of the past—his past. *Man cannot overcome what has already been written*— "nor all thy Piety nor Wit, Shall lure it back to cancel half a Line, Nor all thy Tears wash out a Word of it." He can only go to meet it, in the form, ultimately, of his death: something in his future, but decided in his past. Fate has nothing to do with time, for time is causal consciousness, not mythical consciousness.

This challenge to fate, this defiance in the face of it, was precisely what was involved in the Greek concept of hubris: and there, in Greek myth, man was brought down by just this defiance—in this case, of the gods. It is interesting that such hubris has no obvious parallels in Norse myth, nor indeed in the sagas, where defiance of fate (a fate to which even the gods were subject) was a heroic quality. It may be precisely because challenging destiny was not at the same time defiance of the gods that permitted this relative absence of hubris. By disconnecting fate from the gods, men could "defy" the former without in any way challenging the latter. That there are different—if not necessarily alternative—world-pictures within Old Scandinavian literature in particular is therefore to be expected. Rosalie Wax offers a tripartite division, where at one end of the mythology (which includes for these purposes folk-tales) we are presented with an "enchanted" view, where the universe is "morally responsible"—where acting well brings rewards. At the other end there are the sagas, in which there is a putative relationship between what a man does and his fate. And between these two there are the heroic poems idealizing the men who act out of a sense of honor, and do "what they are fated to do."[11] However, it is not clear that we are really presented in the mythology with any such "morally responsible" universe. The latter involves freedom of will and action, which in turn implies the belief in an open future: yet the mythology is suffused with fate, not freedom. These three categories therefore appear to collapse into one—that radical notion (with sufficient longevity to have become a cliché in the modern Western) that a man must do what he must do when his honor is at stake. What we see so often in Norse literature is something that is perhaps unique in European paganism: an attempt to escape fate *by living up to it*—the near-opposite of hubris. In other words, the acknowledgment of fate provides the necessary presupposition for facing the challenges of life, which far from being made nugatory by fate's eventual and inevitable victory, are precisely made meaningful by it. It is, in some respects, a hugely impressive humanistic vision, and it would be abandoned only in favor of a God who promised them a second chance.

The relationship between causality, fate, and time cannot be said to be in any way conceptually transparent. Together they constitute what might be thought of as a philosophical "three-body problem." Thus, while some coherence can be given to the inner relationship obtaining between any two of these concepts when taken together—causality and time, time and fate, fate and causality—when the three are juxtaposed, the complexities multiply by several orders of magnitude, making clarity almost impossible to achieve. Mythical thought can accommodate inconsistencies, even contradictions, that are denied to symbolic thought as it is achieved through science and philosophy. And yet it is still possible to detect a certain tension in the connections between these ideas even for myth. Causality, for example, far from being a strictly "scientific" category unknown to mythical thinking, will very often suffuse it. For myth, causality is a kind of "anti-fate," for the world in which cause and effect is given prominence is itself delineated as a way in which man can be protected from its vicissitudes. But since causality, even for mythical thought, has a lawlikeness that can be recognized by man, it speaks of a world that is logically independent of fate, whose workings are in principle opaque to us. In the sagas, for example, a feud is clearly understood as a sequence of events with causes; a sequence of events set in train by an act of killing that must have consequences running into the future. A feud is a social vector whose origin is a single act—a cause—that has effects that give direction to further actions. There was human control over the prosecution of a feud such that (as we shall see below) counting of men—their deaths, even their wounds—becomes crucial. At any point in the prosecution of a feud a score is kept and a calculation is made. This is precisely what cannot happen in the case of the future as fated. Fate cannot be calculated, although it was often thought that it could be divined: for it has to do with intuition, not calculation. Fate stands outside of all comprehended nature, and hence outside of time: "Time may show,/But cannot alter, what shall be./Events will take their way. Even as the prophet's words foreshadowed all."[12] This is the message that we will find confirmed again and again in what follows, no matter that our first intuition is to believe that time and fate must be related by some inner necessity. That fate is, however, a supratemporal concept, seems to have been understood implicitly by many mythologies. Since causality itself has nothing to do with time but instead gives *directedness* to time for human consciousness, the "three-body problem" reduces to no problem at all: for time ≠ fate, causality ≠ time, and fate ≠ causality. Causality's concern is *that* something happens—not *when* it happens: "the distance between cause and effect belongs to a different order."[13] Time is a discovery made only by thinking: Kant called it an "intuition" (*Anschauung*), rather than a concept, and insisted that it was a condition of human sensibility, not a property of things-in-themselves.[14] Causality is a category used to bring order—lawfulness—to the sequence of phenomena.

Nordal has written in relation to *Voluspa* that for some commentators it would seem that "the difficult is often not worth the most consideration." Those verses of the poem richest in spiritual content—and here we must add also "philosophical"—are precisely those too often not considered in need of comment. "There is a danger that the ancient writings will become only chewing-bones and shooting-targets for the sharp wits or ingenious folly of the commentators."[15]

The following discussion is offered in order that at least one of those difficult aspects of ancient Germanic pagan and mythological material is given just such proper consideration. The extent to which any of it represents yet more ingenious folly, I must leave to the judgment of others.

1
Paganism in Myth and Cult

> Now entertain conjecture of a time
> when creeping murmur and the poring dark
> fills the wide vessel of the universe.
> —Henry V

WHEN AN ATHEIST CONFRONTS THE MATTER OF BELIEF IN A POWER OR powers supposedly beyond the sphere of human knowledge, whether the latter has been obtained through science, philosophy, anthropology, or whatever else, there is no distinction to be made, logically speaking, in terms of the validity of, on the one side, any of the many forms of paganism to which humankind in all places and at all times has been wedded, and, on the other, the (ultimately victorious) monotheisms that still form the core beliefs of much of the world's population. If one does not believe in God, then one does not believe either in gods, and the claims of the former over the latter can be no more valid by virtue of having been either victorious or longer lived. This is a point that is not often made: perhaps it is too obvious. The point is, I think, that we do not get very far in our understanding of paganism by patronizing it, nor by making the implicit assumption that Christianity—and it is Christianity that will mainly concern us when in the following pages we make contrasts with paganism—is somehow philosophically superior. For the atheist, one cannot speak of an "advance" from paganism in any strict sense, and even if one could, that would not assist us to grasp the nature of just what it was that, for example, the conversion to Christianity in Iceland in the year 1000 was a conversion from. The precise character of that conversion, at least in so far as it illuminates our preoccupations with the concepts of time and fate, is the subject of a later chapter. Our concern for the moment is with paganism as a system of beliefs: to speak exactly, with the Northern cosmography and cosmogony as we find it in the Eddas, sagas, and other literature. We cannot assume that the ideas found in these and other texts sprang unaided from the imagination of the Northmen, and we therefore inevitably find ourselves asking questions about sources and influences. And while it is true that we possess no primary "liturgical" text for Germanic paganism that is in any way comparable to the Hebrew bible, we forget too easily that that text is itself a collection gathered together many years after the events described in it. We nevertheless witness over centuries the Christian tradition rejecting the wisdom of the pagans, and denying absolutely its equality of status with biblical revelation. As Heinrich Zimmer reminds us, those "divinely inspired" books are gospels coming from the early Christian community, pamphlets "addressed by St. Paul to certain small, ex-Jewish, heretical communities . . . minor letters to other communities composed by other apostles . . . together with the cryptic, somewhat delirious Book of Revelation."[1] These—"and only these"—we deign to accept as the all-comprehensive source of guidance for the human soul. "And yet there has been a semi-liberal, timid, and guarded acknowledgment that in pagan tradition also there may be found some light, the 'natural light,' a kind of be-dimmed reflex of the truth of revelation."[2]

These comments of Zimmer's are made in the context of a work on Indian thought, and they serve to remind us that any attempt to interpret the Eddic mythological poems compels us to confront non-Christian traditions, notwithstanding that they were, almost certainly, given their present form by Christian scholars. Yet even here there is debate, for sometimes any presence of Christian influence in, for example, the *Voluspa,* is denied, and the assertion made that what we are presented with there is an accurate picture of pagan beliefs. Finnur Jonssen takes such a line, while others—Olsen, for instance—regard the *Voluspa* as essentially a Christian document: Turville-Petre, on the other hand, says that the truth must lie somewhere between these two extremes.[3] But why must it? There is no logical reason why it should: either view (extreme or not) may be the correct one. There is no law or scientific algorithm that demands a third, compromise option living comfortably between extremes, likely as this may be from an empirical point of view. The point is that we will learn, sometimes, by taking what we see at face value, as a working hypothesis, as evidence for paganism as it was lived and understood.

Yet is it not clear from the *Voluspa* that those passages dealing with "heaven" and "hell," for example, reveal both a subject matter and a terminology that is Christian inspired? It is—yet the regeneration of the world following the Ragnarok has no parallel in Christian eschatology, at least as we find it in Old Norse religious texts. Even the distinction made by Viktor Rydberg between the realm of Hel and that of Niflhel, which might at first sight seem to have little in common with the Christian concept, turns out to be a clear parallel. Rydberg argues for the idea of a "second death" within Norse cosmogony; for when the dead arrive at Urd's Well their "final" doom is not yet sealed. "They have not yet been separated into the groups which are to be divided between Asgard, Hel, and Nifelhel"—a distinction echoed in the Christian concept of purgatory.[4] Since key passages in *Revelations* leave no traces in Old Norse literature, it is difficult to affirm with any confidence that these are the source of the cosmic restoration as we find it in the Eddic poems. Considerations such as these should make us more sensitive to the possibility that the eschatology of the *Voluspa* almost certainly echoes other sources—Indian, or Iranian perhaps—that can also be identified in Germanic ideas. There is indeed a mythological-cum-philosophical neatness—if not an airtight logic—in the recognition of a thread of influence that takes us from Indo-European legend, to Iranian mythology, to the *Voluspa*, via Christian eschatology.

Paganism was both more and less than a religion. It was more than a religion in the sense that it was part of—perhaps much of—an extensive social system, where communal life was suffused with religious rituals and cult practices. And it was less than a religion in the sense that in virtually all of its manifestations it possessed no dogma; indeed, in Old Norse there is no word for religion as such, but instead there is the term *"sidr"*—custom—while expressions for "belief" and "believe" (*tru, trua*) are loan words.[5] This kind of consideration has compelled some scholars to deny any beliefs to paganism at all, from which comes the often-repeated idea that therein lies the essential distinction between paganism and Christianity. In the context of ancient Egypt, for example (and for these precise purposes it does not matter what the context is, since the point is a conceptual, not a parochial one), Jan Assmann pleads that "surely, one did not first encounter the divine and then cultivate contact with it."[6] This idea will be discussed in more detail in a subsequent chapter, but for the moment what we can say is that if such was the case, it goes some of the way to helping us to grasp the significance of another claim that is almost as often made as that one distinguishing paganism from Christianity in terms of beliefs, viz., that paganism was a very tolerant religion, system, or whatever. Unlike the Christian God, the pagan gods were not jealous, "and the Halls of Valhalla were open to more or less any god who wanted entry."[7]

This tolerance inevitably involves also a certain looseness. Free of dogma as it was, paganism—at least as we find it in Germania—also tended to broaden and divide as the number of its votaries increased. What was an essentially local deity might well tolerate a "new" god, and the cult associated with it might take on functions that it had not previously enjoyed. But pagan gods could accommodate different functions with ease—a god of war could also be a god of poetry. Only by becoming very specific would some pagan deities escape functional absorption into rival gods, which might account for some deities restricting their activities to very precise locations—trees, water, stones, etc. When threatened with extinction, a pagan god could specialize. But the overall result of such absorption was, for many societies, pantheism, where a single god comprehended all of nature and not just a part of it. Polytheism, and pantheism, can thus be very different religious outcomes of broadly similar impulses. If a deity became "merely" an aspect of a supreme being, the practical, idolatrous worship of such a god might coexist in a culture that was, in effect, approaching monotheism—as in the case of Syria.[8] Whether monotheism is an inevitable logical outcome of paganism qua polytheism is a very difficult question to answer, as it seems almost as if the latter instinct is turning against itself: yet such was clearly the case in the Aryanism of the *Rig Veda*, where the god Brahma inexorably retreats into the background of the pantheon. We see this process too in Germanic paganism, as Oðin takes over from Thor in the popular consciousness. But polytheism does not have to collapse into monotheism: it can stabilize, as it did in the example of Hindu "universalism," where we can see among other manifestations an art "inspired by the monistic view of life that appears everywhere in Hindu philosophy and myth. Everything is alive. The entire universe is alive; only the degrees of life vary. Everything proceeds from the divine life-substance-and-energy as a temporary transmutation. All is part of the universal display of God's Maya."[9]

We begin, therefore, with the assumption that Germanic heathenism, just like its counterparts elsewhere, functioned as a religion, and we agree with the judgment of Jan de Vries that the psyche of our Germanic ancestors in the time of paganism was through and through tinged with religiosity.[10] But is there truly any evidence for Germanic paganism as such, or is it entirely a literary-cum-philosophical construct that is connected in only the loosest fashion with the lives of those ancestors? Was this "Eddic multitude" of gods always likely to simplify into deism (as Spengler seems to have thought) rather than proliferate still more into an impossible multiplicity, as in the Classical world, "where every tree, every spring, every house . . . is a god . . . [and where] every tangible thing is an *independent* existence . . . [where] none is functionally subordinate to any other."[11] Was the dynamic movement of Eddic cosmogony centripetal—where the vortex of forces issues in the end in a single, massive object of power (the Christian God)—or, like the Classical polytheism with which it shares a history, centrifugal, where the fragmentation of deities could just as easily have been replaced by another polytheism as by monotheism?

Ernst Cassirer understands myth to be but a primitive form of symbolic thought, an early groping toward science. Rather oddly, much the same could be said for Snorri's picture of the pagan religion as expressed in the Prologue to *Gylfaginning,* as his pagan ancestors fumbled toward the truth of Christianity. What commonalities we find there between the two views are likely, therefore, to be conscious attempts by Snorri to explore the common ground between them; this is not evidence of "syncretism" either on Snorri's part or on the part of the traditions with which his work is concerned. Yet it is here, and some say only here—in the Prologue—that we can identify a truly philosophical account of the origins and development of pagan Scandinavian religion.[12] Skeptics will argue that it is impossible to eliminate from analysis the Christian influence on what sources there are available to us, such that we can never be certain in any one case that we are indeed dealing with beliefs that are authentically pagan. This view is now so widely held that we can in justice think of it as the prevailing orthodoxy. Richard North, for example, argues that the overall tendency so far as paganism was concerned was simply to cast off a way of life and then, with that life lost beyond recovery, "reinvent it for the imagination." He insists that "genuine knowledge of paganism recedes in inverse proportion to the ever more imaginative attempts of writers to reconstruct it."[13] But we must ask: How could anyone *know* something like this to be true? How could anyone know that such "genuine knowledge" has receded unless he already knows some things essential to paganism—knowledge that is at the same time being denied to others? And in any case, some of those imaginative writers, being themselves Christian scholars, must be considered fertile sources of information: they may have been prejudiced against their subject matter in questions of belief, yet ironically, they can still assist us in the task of reconstructing aspects of that idolatry that it was sometimes their intention to destroy or undermine in those very writings. In the parallel example of Old English literature, J. Niles argues that "one can scarcely hope to comprehend it without reference to both its Christian themes and forms and its pagan substrata of popular belief." He suggests, quite plausibly, that the collective memories of a people, "encompassing values, ethics, hopes and fears" lived on after the conversion to Christianity not only in a residual paganism, but in "deep-set patterns of belief."[14]

It has to be conceded that it is often in the matter of cults, rather than recognizable core beliefs, that we are on firmer interpretive foundations. We may see only a "dim reflection" of pagan religious ceremonies and, like "profane outsiders" hear but echoes of the sacred songs—"since not even in imagination can we attend the celebration of the mysteries"; but we are often no worse off here than we may be in trying to penetrate the original meaning of those monotheistic religions that have bequeathed to us, through texts that have enjoyed two millennia of interpretation, philosophical and moral precepts that for all we know are connected only by the most fragile of links to their origins. Monotheisms such as Christianity (assuming that it is properly so described—one is, after all, required to believe in the existence of God the Father and Christ the Son with equal conviction) exist for us as a constantly changing effect of interpretation and exegesis; paganism as a constantly changing reconstruction from allusions, incidental remarks, and ecclesiastical assaults. We may never know that we are right in any particular case about the precise nature of pagan beliefs: that does not mean that we have always been wrong. In the specific example of our Germanic ancestors, the centuries in which much of our source material was written is indeed at a remove from the heathen deities that appear therein, and no doubt much that we see suffers from distortions. We cannot know whether the elements that survived to be "reinvented" truly represented the religion as it was lived three or more centuries earlier. Such reconstruction of belief from isolated fragments is not like reconstructing an entire pot from the contours of a single shard. But I shall argue throughout this book that in the case of the concepts of time and fate in particular, the fact that key aspects of them were carried over into Christianity says much for their importance, as well as for their resilience.[15] We should not, therefore, limit our ambitions too much at this early stage. Instead, we should examine the material that is available to us, and then ask at the end of the journey what kind of land we have traversed, and where we have come to. We should follow Kant in thinking of skepticism as a useful place to rest on such a journey, but no place in which to establish a permanent settlement.

We noted above that it has become a commonplace to distinguish the Christian from the pagan in terms of the idea of belief: the Christian has it, the pagan does not—the pagan has only cults and rituals—"surely one did not first encounter the divine and then cultivate contact with it." Yet it stretches credulity to think that every cult practice, every ritual, was expressed in complete psychological independence of belief: that there was, in effect, nothing "inner" of which such manifest behaviors were the "outer."[16] Otto Höfler suggests that we are bound to ask ourselves what lies at the roots of cult activities, and that the only kind of answer that presents itself is something anchored in the spiritual life of man. He goes further, and identifies a "genetic" sequence as follows: the causal/historical connection between "vision" (inner) and "cult" (outer), starts with vision as an inner experience of the human soul. This vision can be shared—presumably through language—and it comes to be believed, even by those who have not shared it. The individual experience is thus transcended and subsequently realized in the ritual. In a sense, this sequence gives us both the inner experience as primary and the cult experience as secondary, but occupies a space for the group as a whole. It is not now necessary for the content of the beliefs to be part of everyone's experience—some, perhaps most, share the beliefs without having first had the experience, just as a Christian may come to share the beliefs of a mystic without ever having had the same vision that led to the expression of the beliefs in the first place. It seems to me that it is possible that our Germanic ancestors did not think religiously without acting religiously through the cult: we can never be certain that they always acted religiously without thinking religiously. Cassirer may be correct in saying that the mythical explanation merely represents in the form of a narrative what is present as immediate reality in the sacred action, but this tells us little of the reciprocation that must have occurred "from vision to cult" at some time in the mythical past, and which set the cult onto its path in the first place.[17] The two positions therefore come in quite distinct and extreme versions. On the one side there is that view expressed by those such as Cassirer, who insists on what he calls "the cardinal truth of ethnology," viz., that rite precedes dogma, and hence that the cult practice precedes—both in time and logically—any explanations for it. Such a view is entirely consistent with his support for Levy-Bruhl's views of "primitive" thinking as a logically simpler form of ontology recapitulating phylogeny—the development of individual thinking must be a microcosmic recapitulation of the development of abstract thinking taken in the round. For Cassirer, the action is the beginning and the mythical explanation comes later, as if the logic is somehow put in afterward, by no means, of course, an implausible state of affairs. On the other side there are those—sometimes, but not always, adherents to what has come to be known in ethnology as "primitivism"—who take a very different view of the nature of primitive thinking. The primitivist thesis is that our ancestors were as cerebrally capable as we are: what distinguishes us is our wealth of information, our education—not our power to think. And presumably, also, not our power to experience, our capacity to confront the world around us and be moved by it, and to find in it the reflection of something other, something numinous. This experience—this inner experience—provides the stimulus for thought that takes a cultic or religious form. In this regard we take the view, pace Cassirer, that every custom must, in the end, have its foundations in something spiritually inner.

What then, is a pagan? A pagan is someone who is not a Christian. This is not intended facetiously. Latin *paganus* meaning "rustic" came to be used as simply the opposite of "Jewish" or "Christian," and was allied with words having a legal connotation, such as *superstitio, crimen,* and *insania.* And since "pagan" thus means simply "of the countryside," just as "heathen" means "of the heath" (both being terms implying "remote from civilization"), the category "pagan" is to be defined entirely negatively.[18] But this gets us nowhere. What we wish to know is what such a person believed, for it is simply not credible to imagine that he believed nothing at all, and merely acted out rituals and engaged in cults without having the least idea of why he was doing it. And while in this case we totally reject the "philosophy by etymology" that lies behind the idea, it does help us to focus on a real question: since the pagan qua pagan was the "invention" of Christianity (and the other monotheistic religions) what, if anything, did the pagan call himself? When a pagan encountered another—say, from a distant part of Germania—would an answer to the question "What religion have you?" or "What do you believe?" have led to some answer that did *not* involve belief in some specific deity? "I am a follower of Oðin" sounds suspiciously like a sensible answer to such a question, and to insist that such an answer could have no reference whatever to beliefs is unconvincing.

Can anything be learned in this context from what we know of other paganisms, and in particular from any that, like Germanic heathenism, were coming under strain as a result of an encounter with alien beliefs? The example of Roman paganism (as analyzed by Franz Cumont) offers us some interesting parallels. We can certainly note in passing that much more research could be done on the place of magical texts in our general understanding of paganism, for in the Roman case these are, says Cumont, "almost the only literary documents we possess."[19] No doubt much the same might be said of Germanic magical "texts" (such as they are available to us) and in both examples there is the advantage that magical rites and customs were very likely to persist—especially in the private context of families or individuals—long after the official conversion to the new religion was an established fact. People do not so easily give up their faith in charms, for example, which may in themselves very well be witnesses to paganism. In the Anglo-Saxon case, Branston suggests that it is the very fact that such charms may have in them elements of Old English, Latin, Greek, Celtic, Hebrew, and Norse that attests to their resilience.[20] In the example of Rome, where one paganism was abandoned in favor of another from further East, faith in the old gods persisted, and even continued to find its way further afield through the army, where perhaps such cherished rituals as there were served as a reminder of home. For instance, Syrians in the Roman army practiced the religion of their Baals (originally Phoenician gods) in the neighborhood of the camps; and at Hadrian's Wall there is an inscription in honor of Hierapolis (a Syrian town on the Euphrates). Its author, Cumont informs us, was a prefect, probably of a cohort of Hamites (North African tribes with likely ancestry from ancient Egypt) stationed there: while Jupiter of Doliche (a town in Syria)—"an obscure Baal"—found worshippers in Roman provinces as far apart as Africa, Germany, and Brittany.[21] Originally just a local "storm-god," he was elevated to the rank of divinity of the Imperial Armies. Of course, paganism's well-attested tolerance would frequently absorb the new gods into its own pantheon, a strategy found almost everywhere, and this tradition did not die altogether with the coming of a more jealous God, as we see in an inscription in Britain assimilating the Syrian goddess to "Peace, Virtue, and even to the sign of the Virgin."[22]

It may very well be the case that this tolerance, this openness to gods from outside, became a major contributing factor in paganism's eventual supercession everywhere. Whether we are talking about

Germanic paganism, or Roman, or Egyptian, the analysis is the same, and so was the conclusion. Without a principle of contradiction even between different (though not always strictly speaking "competing") cults, no systematic dogma can be formulated. "All the heterogeneous beliefs that ever obtained in the various districts [of Egypt] during the different periods of a very long history, were maintained concurrently and formed an inextricable confusion in the sacred books." The gods were everything and nothing: "they got lost in a sfumato."[23] Of course the principle of contradiction is itself the creature of an ontology essentially Greek, and the absence of it in one domain of thought—here, religion—does not tell us that what we would call rationality had no hold on the ancient Egyptian's imagination. Indeed, they were capable of a subtlety of thinking that evades precise expression within the framework of our formalized logical systems, wherein there are the categories "true" and "false," with no space whatever between the two—where the logic-gate, in other words, is either open or closed.[24]

It is true that in the Egyptian case in particular, ritual and cult played an absolutely crucial role in the absence of those dogmas already alluded to. Cult, in Egypt, unquestionably possessed a power deemed to be quite independent of the intentions of the officiating priest—a function that was, in any case, passed from one individual to another, rather like an English Lord Mayor. This did not mean that no one *believed in* what was happening—only that what was happening was independent of their beliefs. This is not so very different—from an atheist's standpoint—from what is supposed to be happening each Sunday at a Catholic Mass, where wine is routinely transformed into the blood of a man who died two thousand years ago. For the ritualistic Egyptian, the efficacy of prayer did not depend on the inner disposition of the believer, but on the correctness of the words and gestures being made (an idea that would later form the core of a specifically Christian heresy). The sacred words were an incantation compelling the gods to obey, regardless of the priest's inner purpose. In other words, the connection between the ritual and the outcome was direct, and neither mediated nor attentuated by the officiating priest. "The ritual that conferred such superhuman power developed in Egyptian into a state of perfection, completeness, and splendor unknown in the Occident. It possesses a unity, a precision, and a permanency that stood in striking contrast to the variety of the myths, the uncertainty of the dogmas and the arbitrariness of the interpretations."[25]

Even when we are confronted with the extraordinary complexity of Germanic cult practices, scholars are often at pains to point out that there, still, we have to do with experiences and rituals that seem firmly anchored in—and indeed, exhausted by—practices of various kinds, where the issue of transcendent beliefs simply does not enter into the analysis. It was not just that Egyptian religion was lacking in holy scripture, but that shamanistic visions or mystic experiences as such played little or no role. The heart of Egyptian religion was the cult, the daily routine of an endlessly differentiated service rendered to the gods in their local forms.[26] Jan Assmann is one those scholars noted above who emphasizes cult at the expense of belief, yet in describing Egyptian cult activities insists that they must have been "emotionally charged" in a way we can describe only as a reaction "to the prior occurrence of a spontaneous manifestation of the divine."[27] But what is that if not a belief? What is that if it is not a ritual performed in order that a belief in some god or other may not be consolidated in the here and now? Assmann holds to the view that action and experience are both the heart and origin of religion, and rejects the idea—which he attributes to "phenomenology"—that at the beginning stood the religious experience of the individual that, when theologically elaborated, gave rise to ritual *and* the accompanying ideational world. On the contrary, like many others, Assmann insists on the primacy of cultic acts: *rituals precede deities*.[28]

For the moment, this issue must be left to stand without further comment; it will be confronted in a later chapter when the specific question as to the nature of the conversion of the Germanic pagans to Christianity takes center stage. The reason for introducing themes from Roman and Egyptian mythology at this stage is twofold: first, to provide a context for the very idea of paganism from outside the Germanic "theater," and second, to lead into a discussion of possible influences on Northern mythologies and beliefs. Just how far have these myths traveled, before crystalizing into the unique and vigorous forms that we find in Eddic poetry, in the sagas, and elsewhere? For all that we must continue to harbor reservations about the ultimate reliability of any source material available to us, Eddic poetry remains the closest we shall ever approach to the pre-Christian beliefs of the Germanic peoples. And although the specifics of the Anglo-Saxon experience in England is (mostly) outside the frame of reference of this discussion, we can certainly agree with William Chaney's judgment in that context—and see its relevance for our own—that while no Anglo-Saxon work can provide us with the comprehensive evidence on pre-Christian religion that we would wish, "almost no poem from before the Norman Conquest, no matter how Christian its theme, is not steeped in it, and the evidences for pagan survivals and their integration into the new faith go beyond even the literary sources."[29]

Since the Eddic texts are not per se religious, but more in the nature of dramas where the pagan gods teach—at least by implication—pagan beliefs, it is essential for us to reach beyond the literature of Scandinavia for those influences that can with some degree of plausibility be identified within them. Such influences come from far and wide, and the connections and commonalities that we find—whether from philosophical, mythological, literary, or philological evidence—lead us to the delineation of a network of Celtic, Sanskrit, Greek, Roman, and other sources. Certainly even the most casual perusal of the Norse material would encourage us to accept that the literature, the cosmogony, of our Germanic ancestors contains treasure that must, like other Viking booty, have its origins elsewhere. And it is only to be expected that much of that treasure will sometimes have Indo-European (and other) hallmarks stamped upon it.

At this stage we should also put to one side any patronizing notions we might have that much of this material carries little or no intellectual weight (compared, for example, to the Greek), and that therefore we will have done the job of penetrating to the heart of Norse beliefs once we have catalogued artifacts, and perhaps drawn Oðin's family tree. If it is true that some of this material—from non-Nordic Germanic religious sources—might impress us more with its charm than with its weight, we should nonetheless follow Ursula Dronke in her insistence that "in interpreting the richer poetic material from the North, we must beware of underestimating the cerebral powers of *nordische Kopfe*." As she quite justifiably adds, "we need all the powers we have ourselves to keep up with them."[30]

Although it is well understood that there were some Irish settlers in Iceland when the Norsemen arrived to colonize it—they were, in all probability, eremites or religious heretics of some description, possibly gnostics—the role of the Celts in the founding and development of Icelandic literature is usually underplayed. The Icelandic language itself, thanks to its remarkable capacity to have remained—largely speaking—pure over centuries, and which thus may be unpicked for foreign influence with some confidence, shows in fact only the slightest traces of Celtic influence. Those Irish words that have been identified in Old Norse are a curious mixture, and when aggregated offer scant evidence for systematic infiltration.[31] All the same, Turville-Petre thinks that some of the intellectual and imaginative qualities that distinguish the Icelanders from other Scandinavians could possibly be traced to this very early contact with Irish Celts. The lack of available raw materials—which had they been present would probably have led to a continuation of the astonishing visual art found elsewhere in Viking lands—primed instead a nascent literary imagination. In Turville-Petre's opinion, this is probably a further sign of Celtic influence, for though the Irish artistic tradition included visual art that was outstanding in its own right, they could also draw upon an advanced literary culture. In this way, it might be a happy confluence of accidents that led to the invention of verse forms and prose, so that stories, and particularly legends from the heroic past, might help to settle the colonists in their new land. Whatever the extent of such Celtic influence, this alone could not account for the fact that scholars believe that some of the poetry contained in the Edda is very ancient indeed, and has its roots in a period that long predates the settlement of Iceland. Of these, the heroic lays are almost certainly the oldest, and compare with those preserved in Old English and Old High German.[32]

How were such tales transmitted from one place or society to another? Some, no doubt, would have been spread orally, with changes occurring in both formal (dialect changes, for instance) and informal fashion: stories may have been embellished, truncated, and in various other ways altered. But in most cases such transmission seems unlikely, although Axel Olrik has suggested that some, admittedly narrow, aspects of Persian eschatological myths found their way westwards in a crystalized oral form.[33] More plausibly, such stories may have been carried, literally, by travelers, during whose peregrinations they would have been sold, or traded, then rendered into the local dialect, with concomitant modifications to take account of local geography, etc. Given all such possibilities, it is still more remarkable that themes and concepts of power and precision were preserved, any Chinese whisper effect barely impinging at all, for example, on the central cosmogonical concepts of time and fate. Such, however, is not the view of Turville-Petre. For by making a distinction between the heroic lays—which, he concedes, represent a branch of literature common to all Germanic peoples—and mythic lays—which he says show no commonalities with comparable poems from other Scandinavian tribes—his analysis leads him to the conclusion that the Edda is a product of the Norwegians and Icelanders. Yet the conceptual links with other groups—far removed from Iceland—are very clear, as we shall see. The precise contours taken by particular myths may be uniquely Norse, but the substantive philosophical content was not, I believe, plucked from the head of the Norsemen unassisted by a rich and variegated Indo-European mythological heritage. Even more surprisingly, Turville-Petre wishes us to believe that, for example, "the mythical origin of *Skirnismal* has *no more relevance to the poem* than has the history of the Goths to the *Hamðismal*." This is because, it seems, that "it is doubtful whether the authors of them considered the origins of the stories which they retold."[34] Yet while the origins may not have traveled with the poems, the meanings certainly could have. What Turville-Petre says may be true of the retelling of the legends in the thirteenth century, but for those for whom these were reservoirs of belief, not yet attached to or absorbed by Christianity, the poetry and the meaning would not have been so easily disconnected.

We have already noted that so far as the *Voluspa* is concerned, interpretations of its religious significance can oscillate between the idea that Christian influences are clearly present, and the alternative view that it is a more or less faithful expression of paganism. While it is true enough that Eddic poems in general by no means come to us stamped with their country of origin—Norway, Iceland, or farther afield—it seems equally true that in its present form the *Voluspa* at least, in Turville-Petre's words, "can hardly be other than an Icelandic poem."[35] But though the reasons for this assertion are quite clear—for example, that the landscape alluded to in it is indeed a near-treeless land like Iceland, not a densely wooded Norway—it also serves to remind us of the point made above that the *meanings* inherent in the poem must have a very long history indeed. To take a single, but telling example: in the *Voluspa* mistletoe is described as "a beautiful, slender tree towering above the plain." The incongruity here reveals an idea taken from elsewhere and incorporated into an Icelandic context. Even the precise form that the poem takes refuses to be held down to a place, for not only do some of its passages contain references and resonances that deliver fragmentary images from Old Irish, and Sanskrit, and Avestan, but in the manner of its vocal delivery it also offers links with its Indo-European past. Mary Niepokij argues that the protolanguage carried an expression that was highly characteristic of the poetic genre, in which—just as in the opening stanza of the *Voluspa*—the assembly is asked to "give a hearing," as the poet states his intention to begin a recitation: this was achieved through a formula that had a ritual function which told everyone, in effect, that this was to be information that the people needed to have.[36]

All such considerations raise one of the fundamental issues of ethnography and mythology—issues that are far too complex to be engaged appropriately here, but that should be remarked in passing. As with language, so with mythology, we are confronted, broadly speaking, with two alternatives when faced by similar forms of life and literature from widely separated places and societies. We may argue for separate development, and insist that it is the universality of the human condition in the face of life, death, natural disaster, etc., that generates such superficially similar forms. Or we may opt for the alternative of a migration, hypothesising protolanguage, or even protomyths, which follow the transmission lines of tribes, probably radiating from a single source (region or tribe) and retaining (as we suggested) substantive elements of the mythological model through many otherwise different manifestations. Broad themes are indeed easy enough to identify across mythologies, but even there the themes seem too specific to be accounted for on such a separate development model, unless one makes further—almost Jungian—assumptions about the psychic life of all peoples at all times in history. For example, the struggle between the gods and certain monsters of chaos is attested in many mythologies, and gods such as Thor assume the role as personifications of primitive agriculture in the constantly waged battle against an unruly nature—a theme mirrored in such legends as those of Bel-Marduk, Indra, Mithra, Zeus, and Heracles.[37] But it is the more precise examples that seem to testify to this idea that a myth has migrated, as when in Norse mythology we are told of Ymir's dismemberment in the creation of the world, and we compare this with the *Rig Veda*, where the giant Parusha is sacrificed to create the world; or in Persia, where a primordial bull is killed by Mithra: the bull's members then "give birth"—in this case to cereals and medicinal plants.[38] Other thematic materials, crucial to the Norse cosmogony, are witnessed in many other cultures. We will return to the precise nature of one such theme—Yggdrasill, the world-tree—later, but it is well-enough understood that trees and tree symbolism take on mythical significance almost everywhere, and that this is evident as far away from Old Europe as in the mythologies of Native Americans. Just as "Yggdrasill" means "Oðin's steed," so in the *Rig Veda* the universe is often represented by the image of the "tree of Brahma," such that the god, the tree, and the cosmos are inextricably linked. As Dronke says, "Oðin's steed" is a remarkable name for the world ash-tree: for here the god and the horse somehow coalesce into the world-tree. Yet even here there are Indian parallels, as in the legend in which Prajapati wished for his body to be made fit for sacrifice, "whereupon it swelled up and became a horse; while the fire-god Agni made himself into the form of a horse and lived for a year in the world-tree." The great Saxon tree Irminsul has many parallels in Indo-European cultures—and also in Egypt in a *conceptual* sense, at least, where it connects with the idea of a "world-axis."[39] And we would expect, I suppose, that for our barbarian pagan ancestors, various blood cults would be common across tribes. There are references in the sagas to sprinkling of men with sacrificial blood "according to ancient custom"—a ritual notably present within the religion of Mithras.[40]

We can pursue such trails still further, for there is something yet more precise—though to an extent also more obscure—in the widespread mythical association of such cosmic trees with serpents or snakes, or dragons. Yggdrasill, of course, has at its roots, according to *Grimnismal,* an ever-present enemy in Niðhoggr, gnawing at it. In India the cosmic tree *acvattha* has a nest of snakes at its roots, the tree of the Hesperides is guarded by a serpent—and of course there is the serpent, the Tree of Knowledge, and the Garden of Eden. Also in Indian mythology, a huge cobra—Muchalinda—lives in a hole among the roots of the Bo-tree.[41] And since Indian symbolism was in its turn influenced by the culture of Mesopotamia, we are thrown westward again, into the orbit of the Indo-Europeans from whom the Germanic peoples trace their ancestry.

We will see more of such parallels as the story unfolds, but even these few examples should make it clear that, without necessarily agreeing with the judgment that so far as Norse religion and mythology was concerned, "only Barbarism was once native," our understanding of Norse myths simply cannot proceed *at a philosophical level at least,* independently of such influences. It is not that cult practices in themselves somehow express definitively polytheistic religions (hence paganisms) such that these can be used to identify an earlier stage of religious belief. Certainly that is the implication of much comment on the probable manner by which polytheisms are transformed into monotheisms. The example here of ancient Egypt is instructive. The Egyptian scholar Jan Assmann acknowledges that monotheism is the measure, the yardstick, against which other religions are assessed. It is seen as an evolutionary—and to that extent inevitable—development from polytheism.[42] The facility of the

Egyptian language to accommodate more than two "truth-values" for the same state of affairs at one and the same time meant that Egyptian religion was able to run monotheism and polytheism in tandem, at least for a time. This was possible because in place of—perhaps as a precursor to—true monotheism, there was belief in the thematic idea of unity—a concept that is spoken of by some scholars as a clear monotheistic tendency. God's unity could be referred to by priests despite the clear acceptance of many gods elsewhere in the system. Assmann sees this tendency as expressing a distinction between a "practical" and a "speculative" religion, "between popular belief and priestly philosophizing, between a polytheistic facade and a monotheistic core."[43] He regards this idea of the unity of god as a way of externalizing what was otherwise an esoteric belief in a single god, which in turn generates the distinction between monotheism and henotheism. While the former denies the existence of other gods, the latter understands a monotheism of "emotion and mood" (*"Affekts und der Stimmung"*). Monotheism "in the strong sense" means belief in one God, from which the very idea of other gods is excluded. Against this, Assmann argues that this monotheism is "cosmologic," while henotheism is "politic."[44] His central point is that a religion such as this, which at one and the same time believes in the unity of God and in many gods, must apportion its beliefs accordingly into "foreground" and "background," "public" and "secret"; and the means of mediating between such a contradiction within a religion is *secrecy*.[45]

It seems to me to be entirely possible that insofar as we can speak of a transition period during which Germanic paganism had not yet yielded completely to Christianity, yet was under increasing strain from it, then it would be characteristic for this background to consist primarily in the perseverence of cult practices, particularly those that could be prosecuted in private rather than in public arenas. The historical fact that Iceland, at least, converted all at once is not a counterexample, since even there certain of the old practices were permitted under certain circumstances. We cannot know whether those who did, indeed, continue with the old ways took these (often) public rituals into their homes, or whether they retained their commitment to the public sites, for there were many such places in Germania, as is well known.[46] The point about this is that, as public places, they presumably achieved this status either by collective recognition or priestly sanction, neither of which would be available to any pagan wishing to maintain his faith after the conversion. And so if there is any plausibility in the idea that the two faiths could, for a time, co-exist, there would be an interesting inversion of the Egyptian example, where it was the monotheist case that had to remain hidden, while the public face of the religion remained staunchly polytheist. In the Germanic case (as we shall see later) it was the power of *wurt*—a power to which even the gods were subject—that facilitated the transition from pagan polytheism to Christian monotheism; it was the bridge from one to the other, just as in ancient Egypt "One-ness" bridged polytheism and Amarna monotheism.[47]

It is unlikely, however, that many cult practices were able to long survive the conversion, since most cults (in most places) had the aim not simply of making contact with the sacral world, but of affirming solidarity with the group—a function now lost.[48] We have already noted that paganism *in general* involved collective acts linked to religious rites, creating a kind of collective soul. And for many pagan societies, the most important of these collective acts of engagement with the sacred was the sacrifice, both animal and (sometimes) human. Among the ancients, it had been the Semitic religions, according to Cumont, that practiced human immolations longer than any other, "sacrificing children and grown men in order to please sanguinary gods."[49] There is plenty of evidence that Germanic tribes also practiced it, the grove of the Semnones being a place for such activities, to celebrate the first sacrificial killing of the primordial body out of which the world was to be shaped by the gods. The term found most often for sacrifice is *blot*, a verb that in West Norse later came to mean "curse" or "swear"—"presumably because the invocation of old gods (or new devils) stayed strong in it."[50] There were other verbs meaning "to sacrifice," such as *soa, senda, forna*. The first of these, according to Foote and Wilson, may have originally meant "stab," and came to be used for the act of ritual killing. *Forna* means "present" or "give," and was adopted by the Christian church as a translation for *offero, oblatio,* and used particularly in relation to Judaic sacrificial practices.[51] This *blot* might take two forms: as a votive sacrifice that could be either a private or a public offering, or the convivial sacrifice—in other words a ritual meal in which those present partook of a communal meal offered as a sacrifice to the gods.[52]

Reference to the Semnones connects us, via Tacitus's account, with another religious concept, namely atonement. Ursula Dronke's analysis shows us that the only Norse god with whom the heathen term for atonement—"*son*"—is associated is Oðin. The word *son* is related to the German word for sin—*Sühne*—and is the name of one of the vats of mead that Oðin drinks in the giants' cave; while the skald Kormakr refers to Oðin as "*haptsoenir*"—one who provides *son* for the *hopt,* "atoner for the gods." When Oðin delivers his "liquid theft" to the gods, he enacts a ritual that in many different cultures is associated with religious cleansing and expiation—he vomits his winning for the gods.[53] And of course the primary act of atonement involves Oðin's *self*-sacrifice, hanging himself on the world ash-tree. Atonement is, in effect, an individual's linking himself to god—it is an "at-one-ment"—or, as in this case, to the entire cosmogony as represented by Yggdrasill. This self-sacrifice for the sake of secret knowledge has been taken by some as clear evidence for the existence of Germanic shamanism. Edgar Polomé, for example, says that "as supreme magician, Odin had to add the runes to his domain when they came in . . . [the runes] are a specification of his secret science. Gothic *runn* means 'secret,' 'mystery' . . . [and] the early Finnish loan from Germanic, *runo,* applies to magic songs. So what Odin . . . acquired by hanging on the tree for nine days, starving and thirsting as in a shamanistic initiation rite, was a powerful secret lore, of which the runes later on became merely the tool."[54]

And so Oðin fetters himself as a means of obtaining wisdom and atoning—echoing the Greek tradition where both Hera and Prometheus atone for their guilt in fetters. In fact, one of the Old Norse names for the gods was "*Bönd*"—the binder of bonds, and in many languages the general notion of magic is expressed by the term for binding—an idea still found in the English word "spellbound." Binding was the commonest manner by which someone was thought to be bewitched. Although we are not concerned here with all of the details of the magical beliefs of the Norsemen, some general remarks are in order, since these touch on the central theme of this book insofar as there is often taken to be an inherent contradiction in systematic appeals to the efficacy of prophecy and divination on the one hand and an overarching belief in the power and inexorability of fate on the other.

The Icelandic sagas often mention magical devices, but most interestingly for our purposes here, they also frequently have recourse to prophetic dreams as a means of prosecuting the narrative. The content of such dreams has nothing of the psychoanalytic about it, for they are not fantastic (or erotic)—they are premonitory. They are not at all the vehicle for transmitting messages to a febrile mind, but are instead "voices from destiny"—conveyed through the individual's *hamingja* or guardian spirit.[55] This *hamingja* carries three main characteristics—shape-shifting abilities, "fortune" as such, and the guardian spirit. Each of these has links with the original meaning of *hamr*—"skin," or "shape," presumed to be some kind of fluid image, which was able to be molded into different forms. The term *hamr* assumed distinctly magical qualities in the Norse context.[56] If the *hamr* of an individual was injured in any way, the normal physical body would receive the same wound. This conception of the *hamingja* was almost abstract, having more to do with particular qualities that would cleave to someone throughout their lives—having good luck, for instance. In this sense it is not so very different from aspects of the soul concept; however, unlike a soul it can be transferred after death to (usually) another member of the same family. In this respect it is unlike the related concept of the *fylgja*, or "fetch," which is conceived more as a kind of ghostly doppelgänger.[57] The *hamingja* was very often associated with a person's name, so that a child might be called after, say, a father or grandfather, in the expectation that the *hamingja* would be automatically inherited along with the name.[58]

We have seen that shamanism is usually attached to Northern mythology through the figure of Oðin. The shaman's journey through the different parts of the cosmos is symbolized by the *hamingja* concept of the shape-shifting soul, and gains another symbolic dimension for the Norse soul in the accounts of Oðin's ravens, Huginn and Muninn. These two are sent out by the god in order to report on the state of the world: and what is said of them has a philosophical resonance that has been largely overlooked.

> The whole earth over, every day,
>   hover Hugin and Munin;
> I dread lest Hugin droop in his flight,
>   yet I fear me still more for Munin.[59]

What does Oðin mean when he says that although he fears for both, he fears more for Muninn? Why should this be so—what significance does this concern carry? The explanation is not obvious, and is very interesting. We will see in the following pages that the Norse concept of time is not so much chronological as *genealogical*. Family histories perform the function of objectifying the passage of time and enable one to locate oneself inside the cosmogony in significant ways. And we can see now why *memory* (the "real organ of history," according to Spengler)—in the image of the raven Muninn—is more important, or more of a loss to Oðin, than *thought*, in the image of Huginn. The cosmogony is held together by such genealogies and could, *in principle at least,* be reconstructed by memory, but not by thought (judgment) alone. If memory were to fail (if Muginn failed to return), the cement of the Norse universe would fracture. Memory is the human (and godlike) command of the past, and hence of the only aspect of time about which there could be knowledge. Thus relating the deeds of one's ancestors and even, often enough, simply the iteration of their names—as in the sagas—is not merely space-filling by poets and myth-makers, but is part of that fundamentally important process in which the present is made continuous and contiguous with the past, as, for instance, in *Beowulf*'s opening lines concerning Scyld. The future is already in the hands of fate; to lose memory also would be to lose any grip on the past. Rudolf Simek thinks that since these names were not given to the ravens much before the ninth or tenth centuries, attempts to interpret them "philosophically," as I have done here, are of doubtful value. But such speculations as are offered here simply strengthen the conceptual significance made plausible by other features of the mythology. In any case, attention is focused here on Oðin's response, rather than the issue of the names, and that still demands more explanation than is usually provided. Nor is it especially convincing to see in this only some matter that is private, somehow, to Oðin, as in this from Richard North: "[the] speaker whom Snorri but not the poet of the *Grimnismal* named Odinn, is afraid of losing the birds he sends out each day as aids to his mind, and then of losing his mind itself—his memory, or some faculty unexplained, even more than his reason." North sees Muninn's greater value as that of "prophecy over conventional intelligence."[60] Paradoxically, there is a connection between prophecy and memory—and thus between North's interpretation and my own—that comes from a fuller understanding of the relationship between time and fate, described in the following chapters. A purely shamanistic view of the two ravens is offered by Mircea Eliade, who asks (rhetorically) whether they do not represent "in highly mythicised form, two helping spirits in the shape of birds, which the Great Magician sent (in true shamanistic fashion) to the four corners of the world."[61] While this is plausible enough, it provides only the "internal" meaning as it concerns Oðin (as in North's view) and makes no attempt to account for Oðin's very different attitude to the possible loss of one of the ravens. We will see in the next chapter that only by knowing the past can we know the true workings of fate which, though we cannot avoid it, can be confronted in each man's struggle with himself.

This image of ravens on Oðin's shoulder has been linked to Gallo-Roman tradition, with figurative examples found on a relief sculpture at Compiègne, where two ravens appear to be speaking into the ears of the central figure. Such a representation may have its roots in Hellenic-Oriental culture, and in the first century following the Germanic conversion. Jan de Vries informs us of the ninth century *Adamaan's Vision,* where *three* birds sit at the throne of God, named for the 'Augustinian' trinity *Memoria, Intelligentia,* and *Voluntas.*[62] While the first two are clear parallels with Norse mythology in the figures of Muninn and Huginn, the absence of the third—*Voluntas,* "will"—is almost equally significant, for not only must this appear within the Christian context, but it equally must not do so for the Norse, where fate has prominence. This concept of *Voluntas* cannot simply be understood in terms of Christian ethics, for at bottom it also speaks of the Christian cosmogony. As has already been noted, the transition from paganism to Christianity demanded the transformation—but not the destruction—of the idea of fate. The Christian church had to find some mechanism for allowing *Voluntas* without challenging the power of God to dispose of the future. This came in the shape of God's providence, and it proved to be the undoing of the pagan concept of fate—if not quite once and for all, then with sufficient power to mortally weaken it.

2
Mythical Space and Time

> Nothing puzzles me more than time and space;
> and yet nothing troubles me less,
> as I never think about them.
> —Charles Lamb

THERE ARE OF COURSE A NUMBER OF WAYS IN WHICH THE SPATIAL AND temporal conceptions of our ancestors can be distinguished from our own, but in the broadest of terms these can be seen to reduce to two thematic ideas. First, there is the idea that in some sense "primitive" space and time is fundamentally magical. And second, there is the view that mythical space and time is diametrically opposed to our scientific conceptions since what characterizes the latter is that they are each infinite, homogeneous, and isotropic (that is, the same in all directions), and that mythical space and time is finite, heterogeneous, and anisotropic. And yet one has only to state the distinction in such a fashion to wonder about its general validity, not least from the standpoint of modern man. Indeed, it is very much to be doubted that modern man, in general, entertains (even should he fully understand) his space and time in this way. In any case, the advent of relativistic theories of space-time (where, mathematically at least, time becomes the fourth dimension of space), throws into confusion any sense of tidiness that the earlier Newtonian picture may have offered to the modern manner of seeing things and, curiously, may even propel us back to consider conceptions that we were only recently pleased to call primitive. We shall have to look at all of these claims in turn, as well as some others, before we can begin to feel any sense of confidence that mythical space and time have altogether vanished from our thinking.

Let us look first at the claim that mythical time is never abstract, but is always concrete; that time as an abstract *process* plays no role whatsoever in the mythical cosmogonies with which this book is concerned. We should note at once that, although the idea of time as an abstract process—that is, as independent of objects or events—might be assumed to have its origin in the invention of mechanical clocks, the very precise, and not at all simple, notion of time (and space) as infinite, homogeneous, and isotropic, did not receive its classic scientific formulation until the seventeenth century, when Newton defined "absolute" time as follows: "Absolute, true and mathematical time of itself, and from its own nature flows equably without relation to anything external, and by another name is called duration."[1] This famous definition, with its spatial "container" counterpart, provided the framework for an entire system of physics that would dominate scientific thinking until the early part of the twentieth century. Yet man cannot really be said to have quite overthrown more anthropocentric ideas, where time is taken as having a sensory content. Such an interiorized point of view had only the vaguest connection with any idea of time as an object—even an object supposedly being whatever was measured by our clocks. And in addition to the qualities that time (as nonabstract) supposedly possessed of finitude, heterogeneity, and anisotropy (that is, as nonuniform), it would have had, at least for some mythologies, the quality of being reversible. Man would have to wait until the second half of the twentieth century before popular (and to that extent mostly wrongheaded) conceptions of Einsteinian space-time, along with its mathematico-physical model quantum mechanics, merged, spawning science-fiction versions of reversible time, before such concepts once again entered the general consciousness.

We must start with some notion of abstract time, and contrast it with mythical time as its supposed negation, putting aside for the moment any reservations we might entertain concerning the post-Newtonian transformation wrought by physics and quantum theory on this conception, and keeping in mind also that the time (and space) of physics has *always* been disconnected from the spatiotemporal experiences of man, being an idealization of that experience, not a description of it. That is partly why the Newtonian definition given above has nothing of the intuitively self-evident about it.

First, Newtonian absolute time is infinite: if we have abstracted time from bodies *and* events, such a concept of time implies that even if time had a beginning, it is still conceptually infinite since it cannot have an end. Newtonian infinite time simply ticks away all by itself, unchanging, relentless, for all eternity. Mythical, finite time requires us to acknowledge no such fairy-tale: time not only began with the creation of the world (which it could have done for Newton), but it will cease to be at its destruction—a remarkably modern-sounding conception, where time and events coalesce. Second, Newtonian, infinite time is homogeneous. This means that every single moment of time is qualitatively identical to every other such moment—there is no characteristic marker possessed by one moment of time that is not possessed by every other moment. They cannot be distinguished. For mythical time, there are moments that *are* different—there are moments that have a sacred character that sets them apart. This is not to say that mythical time could not incorporate conceptions akin to this modern notion of homogeneity—it is simply that time is much more of a complex gestalt than it is a series of identical units placed alongside one another in an infinite series. Mesoamerican mythology, for instance, denies this idea of moments of time as somehow strung together "like beads on a rope"; instead, "time is more like the rope itself, in which many fibers of differing lengths spin together. Now some fibers overlap and others do not; now others overlap that before had not."[2] And these different qualities can be *re*-created—not simply represented or celebrated—through various priestly or magical or shamanistic ceremonies. Third, Newtonian infinite time is isotropic; it is uniform and equable—the instants that together constitute abstract time are not only qualitatively identical (homogeneous) but quantitatively identical; instants cannot be stretched, or collapsed, or otherwise changed. An instant of mythical time, on the other hand, may last as long as it must, as long as a mythical narrative (for example) calls for it to last. Mythical time is elastic, and significant or critical dates may also fracture its continuity. The calendar in many cultures is an ordering of the periodicity of certain rites, and the earliest calendars were always, in effect, almanacs presenting a day-to-day reminder of magico-religious obligations.

    H. Hubert and Marcel Mauss argue, as does Ernst Cassirer, for the idea that objective, quantitative time was "achieved" through progressive abstraction from the "semi-concrete" qualitative time of religious enactments of many different kinds.[3] Time and space, on this view, were not concepts at all, and certainly never a priori concepts existing before or outside of experience; they were sensory givens. Time was not so much understood as directly experienced, and some moments of time were intrinsically sacred and protected by divine forces, just as some places were intrinsically sacred. Space and time were perceived, nevertheless, symbolically.

It is Cassirer who perhaps gives us the clearest expression of this symbolic view of time and space as we find it in mythical thinking in all cultures, insofar as they can be seen as standing at the beginning of a process that would, through an inexorable process of abstraction, lead at last to the symbolic forms that are science and mathematics. For Cassirer, the mythical intuition of space and time occupies a transitional position between the space and time of mere sense-perception, and the space and time of pure cognition, the latter being realized in geometry (and for some, arithmetic) and—eventually—in science.[4] The key to understanding what Cassirer sees as this relentless and inevitable march from one symbolic form (myth) to another (science) is the transition from "substance" to "function," from what is meaningful only when seen as one *object* set over against another, to that of one *relation* set against another. And it is this reciprocal relation that exhausts the reality of the points of a homogeneous, infinite, Euclidean space; and this reality is purely functional, never substantial.[5] Such a space can never be encountered in sense experience. It is constructed, not given—an idealization, not a description. From every point in such a constructed space it must be possible, as a matter of the strictest definition, to draw similar figures in all directions—this, as we have noted, is the meaning of the homogeneity of space. On the other hand, every position and direction of mythical space is endowed as it were, "with a mythical accent, the division between the sacred and the profane."[6] For Cassirer—and the many writers who share his view—mythical space and time is *structural*, not functional, as is the space and time of mathematics. We cannot "grow" mythical space genetically in accordance with some general rule; what we find instead is *"a purely static relation of inherence."*[7]

It is this very nonhomogeneity of space and time that allows the religious and mythical world to be constituted, for only this—only by experiencing the differences between one space and another, and between one time and another—only via these intercalations, these tears in the fabric, can the *truly* fixed point, the central axis—the world-tree or world-pillar for instance—be revealed for all subsequent orientations. It is in this way that sacred space obtains its existential value, for nothing can begin, and nothing can be done, in the absence of just such an orientation. As Eliade expresses it: "if the world is to be lived in, it must be *founded,* and no world can come to birth in the chaos of the homogeneity and relativity of profane space."[8] In other words, without such sacred points of reference, the world has no meaning, and a homogeneous space—the abstract space of mathematics and physics—furnishes no such points. For where one space (or time) is as good as any other, no space (or time) carries significance—and the world is deprived of meaning. This goes some way toward explaining why all territory previously unknown must be consecrated in some way, for such organizing of a space to some extent is a repetition, a reenactment of the paradigmatic work of the gods. We find an echo of this in the Norse tradition whereby a piece of wood from an erstwhile dwelling was cast adrift from a boat, and the new dwelling built where the wood came ashore. The wood carried the merits of the old structure and helped in the true foundation of the new one. Settling in a territory thus amounted to founding a world, and the new land would be provided with a religious or cultic focus just as the old one had had. There is no paradox in that the world might thus possess many such centers, for we are dealing here not with geometrical space, but with lived, sacred space. As such, this mythic view of space-time has a completely different structure that permits an infinite number of such breaks, and thus permits, also, an infinite number of links with the transcendent.[9]

This break, constituted as a sacred place, fractures the homogeneity of space. But mythical space needs to be complete, not continuous. This break could be symbolized by some opening by means of which passage from one cosmic region to another might be effected. Since such a journey might be undertaken only by a shaman, it does not have to be marked by a continuous path from one to the other. The images used to express this break invariably referred to it as the axis mundi—whether this was a tree, a vine, a mountain, a ladder, or a pillar. Around this axis lies the world, of which it is perforce located at its absolute center—"at the navel of the earth."[10] In this way we can account for other beliefs and other images, for instance, holy sites and sanctuaries also taken to be the center of the world, or temples seen as models of the cosmic mountain, where the foundations reach deep into the lower regions and the topmost parts of which reach into the heavens. In Norse paganism, structures representing this religious imagery (such as the ziggurat) are rare, but the powerful and central image of the world ash-tree, Yggdrasill, resonates with just such significance, as we will see in a later chapter. What is important is that the world—this world, and the next—be *organized* into a cosmography. Mircea Eliade argues that religious architecture itself took over and developed the cosmological symbolism present in the structure of primitive habitations. *All* symbols and rituals concerning temples, cities, and houses, "are finally derived from the primary experience of sacred space." In this way, he says, every "spatial hierophany or consecration of a space is itself a cosmogony."[11]

Many mythologies are able to accommodate the multiplicity of systems that this kind of thinking is almost bound to generate, for the universe was often seen as a system of systems—a connection of systems, where each one was somehow separate and distinct in some respects, and linked often only by the possibility of shamanistic journeys, with very similar conceptions applying to the objective against the shamanistic lapse of time. The other world possesses its own time, which does not need to dovetail with mundane time in order to be part of a comprehensible whole.[12]

It is implicit in what has been said so far that it is often possible to employ similar conceptual arguments for thinking about time as are used in thinking about space; and indeed the language of time will itself often be analogous with, if not parasitic upon, the language of space. That they somehow belong to one another from a logical point of view is an assumption so often made as to scarcely require either comment or justification. Yet it does not demand too much additional reflection to acknowledge that time presents different and largely irreducible, sui generis philosophical challenges that are of a character that are themselves so profound and so deeply puzzling as to defy description, let alone complete explanation. In this matter it is easy to sympathise with St. Augustine's frustrated assertion that so long as he did not much reflect on the matter, he knew perfectly well what time was, yet as soon as he put his mind to it, he seemed to know nothing about it at all. Certainly the problem of time has challenged and defied the greatest of minds, from Aristotle to Kant and beyond, and anyone who believes that our contemporary mathematical/ physical account of it as the fourth dimension of space—as the fourth coordinate by means of which every point in the universe may be uniquely identified—anyone who believes that such a definition has somehow resolved all puzzlement and eliminated all mystery and unclarity has clearly not been paying attention to the statement of the problem. And we must take great care not to understate the problem.

The relationship between time and fate as expressed in myth is the central theme of this book. Indeed, Cassirer points out that in its basic signification, *mythos* is itself temporal *as such,* for the concept of myth embodies not so much a spatial as a temporal view. True myth begins, he says, not with images, but with something having a life *in time*—as the expression of a becoming into which these images may be placed: "Only . . . where the human consciousness takes the step forward from the figurine of the gods to the history, the narrative, of the gods—only then do we have to do with 'myths' in the restricted, specific meaning of the word."[13] This is a very important point. It tells us that, for example, it is not the "goddess" images found across old Europe that can speak to us as part of an authentic pagan world-picture, as part of a mythology. It is instead some account of them that plausibly locates them inside a narrative that embraces birth, change, fecundity, the seasons, etc. And we can note in passing that it is the very absence of any such coherent narrative that makes one of the best-known of such figures seem yet more mysterious and opaque. For in the case of the so-called Venus of Willendorf we know of no such account that would include reference to her face, hidden completely by its strange headdress or coiffure—a face that, unlike all other such images, even those where the features are merely suggested, is not stylized, but deliberately omitted.[14] A god of myth is thus constituted *only* by its history. It is the *past* that is the why of things, while the past itself—hence time itself—has no "why." Mythical time is differentiated from historical time in that for the former there can be no absolute past, no past, that is to say, that is not some*one's* past, that is for the mythology and for some gods. Indeed, time as history may erupt into the world as a result of some event in the life of a god—or more often, in the death of a god; just as death is brought into the world when Seth murders Osiris, so the world becomes subject to historical time when Horus takes the place of Osiris. "The atrocity committed by Seth brought evil into the world. This is evidently the point at which cosmogonic primeval time turns into historical time"—a pattern that we see repeated in Norse mythology at the death of Baldr. In the Ragnarok, we see the world's end as Spengler was to describe it—as "completion of an inwardly necessary evolution."[15]

If no events are taking place then, for Eddic mythology as for others, there is no time. In the *Voluspa*, for example, names are attached to units of time in accordance with what happened within them, rather than according to their relation to any other units of time, as in the "age of axes" and so on.[16] Steblin-Kamenskij writes that in the heroic time of the Eddas, events qua portions of time are ranked in the past, such that a grid is laid over it, even though the squares of this grid are not units of measurement, not Cassirer's "functional, reciprocal relations," *but links in a genealogical chain.*[17] This device is particularly prominent in the sagas, of course, and we shall return to this below, when the claim will be supported that, in place of any abstract chronology, Norse mythology presents us with *time as genealogy*. This is an idea that assists us in understanding how it is possible that in Germanic mythology the past becomes more powerful through the flow of time; it does not recede in significance, because the past is, paradoxically, fullest *now*, in the present. This is not ancestor worship, as we find it, for instance, in Shintoism. As Hubert and Mauss put it, the rejuvenation of myths is not a different phenomenon from that of their localization in the past, but a special form of the same phenomenon.[18]

It is through the power of fate, seen as inviolable and inexorable, that the actions of men, and the actions of gods, are provided with their richest context of meaning. But just what is the relationship between time and destiny? We have just noted that it is the fullness of the past *in the present* that marks Germanic mythology. It will be argued in what follows that it is the characteristic of fate to mark the present that contributes in a unique fashion to its essence. But the question must be raised: is it not obvious that the essence of fate must have something to do primarily not with the past, but with the future? And how can it be otherwise?

The primary response to such a challenge is to suggest that, contrary to almost everything that is written or, more often, assumed, in relation to this subject—whether by mythologists or literary historians—*fate is not a temporal concept at all*, although it has to be conceded that it frequently makes some sense to treat it as if it were. But if that is so, just what kind of concept is it? Cassirer points out that mythological thinking (especially when it is in cosmogonical mode), is often concerned with the fundamental tensions obtaining between two ideas, namely, destiny, and creation. There is, he writes, "a peculiar dialectical opposition between destiny, *which though manifested in time is essentially a supratemporal power*, and creation, which must always be thought of as a single act in time." He goes on to say that wherever "almighty time" and fate enter the stage, they spell the end (eventually) for the polytheistic gods. The gods endure and are worshipped not for themselves, "but as administrators and guardians of the universal order of destiny, to which they are themselves ultimately subject."[19] We have already noted the primitive concept of a mulitiplicity of worlds coexisting, even coinciding and overlapping each other. This kind of coincidence and superimposition can only occur *outside time.*[20] And following Parmenides, Cassirer says that it was in this exclusion of all temporal determinations that the mythical concept of fate for the first time passed into the logical concept of necessity.

We find in Plato the conception of the Fates as "daughters of necessity." This leads us directly into a demand that we take account of a number of different sources and influences upon the Germanic idea of fate that is our central theme. The fact that the crosscultural parallelisms are frequently so striking—to be acknowledged on a profound as well as a superficial level—makes such comparisons natural. Even if we may never be quite certain in any one case whether we are confronting direct influence, or a remarkable example of separate development, the very different ways in which other mythologies have developed their ideas of time and fate can hardly be less than important or illuminating for the Germanic case.

One of the problems we face in confronting either very different cultures and mythological traditions from our own, or simply aspects of our own mythological traditions seen, as it were, through the wrong end of a telescope, is that there is an ever-present temptation—as with metaphysical thinking, with which there are sometimes connections—to regard certain ideas with which we are confronted either as trivial or absurd. For when an idea accords in a general fashion with one of our own, we easily dismiss it as trivial, lacking, as it must, the scientific rigor that we are quite sure grounds *our* conceptions so much more convincingly, as we see it. On the other hand, when such an idea contradicts our views, it will just as readily be regarded as being absurd, and as the product of "merely" primitive thinking, or primitive but prescientific thinking, and therefore inferior. The concepts of space and time in particular—though fate often suffers equally—are so easily taken for granted within a tradition or culture that they hardly seem like presuppositions at all, so fundamental are they to ways of thinking. Indeed, their role as presuppositions, their validity within the system, may escape detailed examination altogether. Which of us, for instance, knew anything of Newtonian ideas of space and time (as expressed in the definition given above) until they were overthrown by the Einsteinian alternative? Space and time are such all-pervasive aspects of our experience that they will evade all reference within the everyday, such that "[we] are contained within them and caught by them, unaware of their character.... They are the texture of our experience. Hence the time and space conceptions of India, for example, may seem unsound and bizarre."[21] What Heinrich Zimmer says for India is certainly true not

only of other cultures with which we share a mythological history—
the Mesopotamian, the Egyptian, the Babylonian, and the Vedic,
among others—but of much of what is clearly our own culture (insofar as we are Germanic), and particularly as this was expressed
through pre-Christian myths. For while Christianity did not change
everything, at least not all at once, it did change much that related to
the overall view of the cosmos and man's place within it; and when it
did not overthrow it, it changed it in its own image, molding it in ways
that make it formidably difficult now for us to recognize any original
meaning. Perhaps this is an example of Spenglerian "pseudomorphosis," insofar as in the case of the concept of fate in particular, the
Christian employed pagan means to express something quite different, as the appropriation of the heathen *wyrd* made the task of conversion of pagan Germania that much simpler.[22]

The concept of fate is often seen as philosophically crude and
somehow likely to be the possession of cultures that lack a whole
range of characteristics that we take for granted as being the essence
of enlightened, rational, and scientific thinking, such as free will, ethical responsibility, autonomy, and so on—such that it is all too easy to
dismiss it without further serious examination. And yet it is at least
debatable as to whether a Germanic tribal leader of the first century
A.D., or a Babylonian prince—or pauper—from a thousand years earlier was not aware that he had, for instance, just *freely chosen* a wife, or
a horse, or a pitcher of wine; and it is debatable also whether his sorrow at the death of this same wife—or horse—was not the occasion
for weeping rather than resignation in the face of inexorable fate. Yet
it may have been that it was just this kind of circumstance that would
lead him to be resigned in this way, for the link between fate and
death is made in many cultures. This link is often so close that the
two ideas sometimes threaten to collapse one into the other, as in the
Christian poem *Heliand,* where *wurd* means the spirit of death, or
death in the abstract as the fate of man. In India, too, more than one
word for "fate" also meant "death."

Although we cannot be certain of the precise influences that impinged on the Northern conception of fate, it would be quite implausible to pretend that the idea was in every respect native. This makes
it desirable to consider how the ideas of time and fate have been expressed in other mythologies. Although the concern here is with
those key concepts, it should be remembered that these influences
may sometimes be illuminated through small details and incidents
within a mythological tradition, since the chances of such details be-

ing randomly and similarly produced within traditions far apart in time and geography seems vanishingly small.[23]

Almost every culture presents in its mythology a shifting relationship between fate as abstract and impersonal on the one hand, and fate as a personalized god or, more usually, a goddess, on the other. It is sometimes argued that belief in the latter can produce authentically religious behavior in a way that the former cannot, and that therefore the impersonal concept must logically precede and presuppose the personal. One cannot, so it is said, enter into any kind of relationship with an abstraction *simpliciter*, one cannot with any sense of plausibility pray to an idea or indeed offer sacrifices to it. Yet the situation is rarely so simple as this. If destiny is regarded as something given, as some cosmic sense of order—in other words, as something natural—this could easily be taken as a manifestation of a higher level of philosophical sophistication than belief in a personal god. It would seem to be at the very least at less of a remove from Cassirer's idea of "natural necessity," which is supposed to be a later (and higher) stage of symbolic concept formation than belief in gods. Some scholars will insist, indeed, that belief in fate is actually incompatible with belief in gods. The idea that one's hour has come, that one has lived out one's time, does not necessarily imply (on this view) that this precise hour has been fixed by a higher power; it merely acknowledges that the general conditions of life are such that every man has his certain time span allotted to him. Yet this is *so* obvious that it is hard to believe that, on its own, this idea would be causative for a belief in a power such as destiny.[24]

As we proceed, many points of contact in how fate is described in different mythologies will become obvious. One way of representing the operation of the power of fate—which is clearly just such a point of contact, and with which we will be occupied later—is in the idea that it expresses an allotment or portion. Pre-Islamic Arabs, for instance, like the Germanic races, preferred to use passive verbal forms for such ideas, as in "it was allotted to him." The noun form in Arabic—*qadr*—derives from *qdr*, which has the primary meaning of "to measure" and thence "to assign specifically by measure," and as though God "measured out" his decrees. Persian has the word *bakht*, meaning "fortune," which is the Pahlavi word meaning "something allotted," (with its root *bhanj* = to divide). In the most ancient texts we find *bagha*—a divine epithet meaning "the Allotter," which seems to offer support for the thesis that the personalized concept *precedes* the abstraction.[25]

We can see also how frequently words for time become identified and sometimes conflated with words for fate. This is particularly clear in the Arabic example, where the Koranic theistic concept of predestination is in sharp contrast to the pre-Islamic near-identification of time and fate. The pre-Islamic Arabs seem to have held time to be the actual source of whatever happened in the course of men's lives. Generally, however, this was restricted to certain critical aspects of life— a man's span of life, or day of death, for instance. But it has also been regarded as incorrect to render "time" by "fate," since time as such was the determining factor, rather than as itself being determined by some other power. "But it must admitted that the Arabs themselves do not always clearly distinguish the power of Time from that of Destiny pure and simple."[26] Such an identification occurs also in Iranian religion, where it is said that at a given moment, finite time comes into existence out of infinite time, moves in a circle until it returns to its origins, whence it merges once again with infinite time. Superficially, this could be seen as a cyclic conception, but it has to be said that in that case it is a very bizarre one, since this cyclic process seems to occur only once—it is not endlessly renewed or repeated. The regeneration of the world following the Ragnarok could be interpreted in a similar fashion—not so much a cycle of events that will be infinitely rerun, but as a single cyclic cosmic event, from which conception one can completely understand both the Northmen's fear of Ragnarok's approach, and their anxiety to avoid its consequences by embracing the Christian message of salvation at world's end. Bauschatz says that in Iranian thinking the principle of time exists "within and without the creation" and is boundless: the creation generates time that is finite.[27] This is probably not as obscurely metaphysical as it is made to sound. It says, in effect, nothing more opaque than that finite time is a proper part of infinite time—which though mathematically false, is a commonsense commonplace.[28]

In spite of the frequent identification of time with fate (and the related identification of time with death), the impulse we have noted to personify fate in so many cultures is not matched, curiously, by an equally widespread impulse to personify time. The most striking counterexample of this generality occurs within the mythological tradition of India. Indian mythology teaches about four aeons—*Krita, Treta, Dvapara,* and *Kali*—that together comprise a *kalpa*.[29] At the end of this there is a cosmic holocaust, followed by another cycle of creation, in the same order—a catastrophe followed by renewal which reminds us of the *Voluspa* and is reflected also in these words from *Vaf-*

pruðnismal: "In Vanaheim Vanir begat him,/ and gave him as hostage to gods;/ at the world's last weird he will end again/ home to the wise Vanir."[30] Although the Indian concept above is an unambiguously cyclic conception, *within* each *kalpa,* time is linear and regressive, the latter because there is gradual ethical and physical degeneration. This destruction of time (and *by* time) is crystalized in the figure of the god Kali. This idea of the inexorable course of time—Time as destroyer—symbolizes the inescapability of fate, not just here, but in Iranian religion, pre-Islamic Arabia, and Israel, among other examples. On its own, this does not offer any explanation why time and fate have so often become identified with each other; that requires analysis of a different kind. If the concept of time was always and everywhere identified with destiny, we would quite naturally expect to find that time was as frequently personified as fate, which it clearly is not. It seems more likely that such personification occurred only after fate had itself become identified with death, thereby touching life in more direct ways than the abstractions involved in making comprehensible the experience of the passage of time.

There are some significant counterexamples to this idea that fate as personified is somehow conceptually consequential to the notion of fate as an abstraction. In the Babylonian tradition, for instance, the very earliest conception of fate is that it somehow emanates from the mother-goddess Tiamat, and that fate is hers to do with as she pleases: "Great are her commands, irresistible are they. . . . She gave him [Qingu] the Tablet of Destinies, fastened it on his breast." Fate in this example is embodied in this Tablet of Destinies, given to Qingu with the words "your command shall be unchangeable."[31] In this example there is a curious hierarchy of fate—Tiamat and Qingu over the lesser gods of the pantheon—and, still more curiously, the power of fate as something transferable. The Tablet of Destinies (something written, of course, at a "here and now," a theme that will recur throughout this discussion) was the emblem of supreme power, which would attach itself to whoever was the lawful keeper. The lot of humanity, by stark contrast, was finitude and death. As the *Epic of Gilgamesh* puts it, "When the gods created humankind, they assigned death to humankind, but held life in their own keeping."[32] Death is the one fated phenomenon that by its nature limits all others for humankind. *Simtu*—destiny—thus became at this early stage of civilization a metaphor for death. This Akkadian tradition is also a counterexample to subsequent mythologies—especially Scandinavian—that, far from handing to the gods the power of fate to be used *against* humankind, makes the gods themselves equally subject to it. This is reiterated in the Akkadian myth of *Atrahasis,* where the goddess Ninmah boasts that she holds the clue to man's fate, which she controls absolutely. In this theology, fate qua goddess is accommodated within the pantheon.[33]

An ancient Lithuanian proverb says that "time passes even in an overturned pot." Such a conceptualization of time as a process in ceaseless onward movement (in effect, Newton's "equable time, flowing in and of itself") is, as we have noted, often seen as a precursor to the logically more complex idea of necessity, via its link with the idea of a cosmic order or power that cannot be gainsaid and that leads ultimately to death. But just how is it that a primitive mind (any mind, for that matter) can move from the acknowledgment that time must pass even in the absence of events—time as Newtonian container, passing "even in an overturned pot," or as in the Arab version of the same idea, that "God shaped two vessels, Time and Space,/ The world and all its folk to store,"—to the idea of *necessity,* that is, from the necessity of time's passage, to the acceptance of fate?[34] In effect what we see here is an ellipsis, for this transition from fate into necessity can occur only when man sees himself not as the plaything of destiny, but more as a random piece moved around by chance. Turning *fate* into necessity (or turning time into necessity) pushes two quite different kinds of category together. What was required was something, some mechanism, by which *chance* could be evaded on an everyday level—chance that nullifies man's actions if believed in absolutely—in ways that time could not. Fate could then be seen as what intervenes between chance and necessity, taking on a dual characteristic. On the one hand it *orders* events that would otherwise be merely random and perhaps chaotic; and on the other it connects man's absolute knowledge—that he must die—to a power over which he has no control.

There is a Lithuanian legend involving one Gegutė, a goddess of fate who appears as a cuckoo. In a way that is reminiscent of the Indian system of *kalpas,* although on a much more intimate scale, Gegutė "knows" time and is responsible for it. Time is cyclic, yet organized into yearlong intervals. Even though the years repeat, the cosmic order established through this repetition cannot be guaranteed at the outset.[35] In the legend the uncontrollable powers of Winter "open the gates," freeing all of nature's elemental forces, "ruining time," and threatening to bring chaos. The cuckoo, with her first song, freezes the actions of humankind, "like the projectionist who suddenly stops the rolling of the film," changing chaos—chance—to fate. Here, fate intervenes only when time has stopped. It thereby becomes that supratemporal concept that we introduced earlier. Such legends as this may cleave to the notion that time and fate are coextensive, if not actually identical, but conceptually there are different implications to be drawn from them when taken separately. Both destiny and time were taken largely as an unchanging backdrop divided into periods of good and bad. Another Lithuanian deity, Laima—also a goddess of fate—determines the relation between events and the passing of time. By recording such chance events as birth *into* time, she gives meaning to man's life. Chance is overcome by being inscribed into the order of the universe. Laima looked down upon men from a hilltop, from where she distributed both rewards and punishments to men: "My Laima sits on a hill,/On a silver pedestal,/Musing of a spot for me!" Laima is probably the same figure as Lauma— Goddess of the Earth—who is also a deity of the same cultures. The Christian conquerers made her a sorceress—the Roman Lamia, a she-devil, night-hag, or nightmare—not retaining the indigenous idea that she was a protectress of women in childbirth. As Mother Earth, Laima was the source of fortune and prosperity.[36] The legend is more complicated still, for a third goddess of fate, Perkunas, oversees and executes the fate forecast by Laima. (She is the guardian of all types of boundaries and borders—in itself a fascinating idea.) Laima, so it seems, legislates, allotting man his share; Perkunas executes the laws thus laid down—a metaphor that will occupy us much more below.[37]

Although there is much dispute among specialist scholars concerning the influence on the *Voluspa* of Hesiod's *Theogony,* even those not willing to push any perceived analogies very far often concede that *Voluspa*'s renewal conclusion probably has its source there.[38] A clear connection with Germanic mythology is the clash of the gods with fate, as we find it in particular in Homer. Sometimes the varying Greek concepts of fate within Homer are interpreted so as to show no real conflict between them. Certainly "Μοιρα" can be regarded in a number of ways: she is an agent who brings death, and therefore "stands for" death. But Μοιρα was also an *impersonal* power that decided death. "Μοιρα," of course, is one of those Greek concepts of fate that became personalized and embodied, although one scholar sees the boundaries of human conduct civilized only when Μοιρα remains impersonal.[39] In Homer, although linguistic usages frequently overlap (as they surely must for any poet), for Dietrich at least, there is in any case no "true fatalism" to be found there, since men become responsible through their own actions both for their own welfare and for their undoing: "every man is the maker of his own fortune."[40] It is not surprising that in many languages one finds overlapping usages for the idea of fate—English being relatively poor in this respect, retaining only two, "fate" and "destiny," with indistinguishable connotations. "Kismet" now seems somewhat arch, and in any case refers us to an Islamic concept that was not an impersonal power at all, being more akin to an aspect of God. In as much as the concept has been personalized within a mythology, we often find the functions of fate distributed among more than one deity. In fact, we find that in neither Sumer, Akkad, Assyria, Babylonia, Lithuania, nor Greece, is there just a single god capable of expressing all the various aspects of fate seen as touching men's lives. One cannot really insist that Germanic mythology offers any exception to this pattern, since while it is true that the Norns represent the whole of destiny, their functions are also divided, and this would seem to have been a feature of them that can be regarded as native in Germanic paganism. Certainly in Latin, all, or most, of these Greek conceptions seem eventually to coalesce into the unitary idea of *fatum,* absorbing the Homeric conception of Μοιρα—the allotted portion—the will of Zeus, "and the further distinctions given through *Ananke, Heimarmene,* and *Pronoia.*"[41] What connects Indian, Greek, and Germanic mythology is that their goddesses (and gods) of fate are quite distinct from the remaining pantheon. Whether the Norns are a later interpolation into the *Voluspa* or not, in respect to their being given different names—names modeled almost certainly on the Roman Parcae or influenced by "speculations about the time-references of the three fates"—does not concern us for the moment.[42]

> Thence wise maidens   three betake them—
> under spreading boughs   their bower stands—
> [Urth one is hight,   the other, Verthandi,
> Skuld the third: they scores did cut,]
> they laws did make,   they lives did choose:
> for the children of men   they marked their fates.[43]

However, it seems plausible that the essence of this stanza of *Voluspa* is the same whether their separate names is a later addition or not. There are three maidens possessing great knowledge, who established laws and laid down the fates of men. This conception seems to have been extant independently of that naming process—the names fitted, in other words, the originary idea, and the conception did not simply arise out of that naming.

The remarks made so far should have made it clear that few of the issues in relation to time and fate are simple or straightforward, and that they are by no means to be dismissed as merely primitive. However, it has been easy for some scholars (particularly philosophers) to dismiss fate—and fatalism—out of hand, as being the product of just such merely primitive thinking, a product of crude mentality properly swept away when man's sense of himself as the focus of action, ethics, and responsibility, finally comes to fruition. But when, exactly, would that have been? Was it when polytheism and paganism fractured and disintegrated before the great monotheistic religions of Judaism, Christianity, and Islam? Does fate have no meaning, then, for a Jew, or a Christian, or a Muslim? Are these truths all that was required to banish fatalism from the minds of men forever—this fatalism that apparently "stems from man's total ignorance and apprehension regarding what befalls him"? Did fate then offer "none but pseudo-explanations to mundane anomalies, social discrepancies, injustices and oppressions"?[44] Is fatalism *so* easy, then, as a doctrine? If we assume—as I think we must—that man was confronted with what befalls him, in apprehension certainly, and perhaps also in ignorance (if not quite total), does it not matter whether we should ask *why* he should choose, in just about every culture on earth, to opt for fate? Why not opt for an open future? Surely *that* impulse could not have been entirely absent from the minds of our ancestors. We need to ask many more questions about the nature of fate before we can begin to recognize an appropriate answer to such questions. But we can be reasonably confident of this much at least. In the Scandinavian example—and in all probability in other mythologies as well—the acknowledgment of the power of fate not only did not lead to spiritual and moral atrophy, but seemed in fact to act as a spur to man's religious sense of himself. Fate was a challenge, a force to be confronted—not a power to be meekly accepted in inaction and Stoic resignation. To know that one is fated to die in a particular battle, or in a particular place, did not make a man fight less hard, less bravely. Instead it seemed to encourage in him a sense that human significance could be achieved *in spite of fate*. There is therefore a profound and challenging contradiction at the heart of this that admits of no easy explanation, for it is quite plausible to argue that our Germanic ancestors (among others) never permitted their acknowledgment of the power of destiny to transmute into resigned fatalism. The tensions of a life proscribed by fate could be redeemed by men acting well; they were a source of strength in ways that we have almost totally forgotten—we, who insist that we create ourselves on a daily basis, and yet live, many of us, in permanent fear of one thing or another, from the imagined to the real and cataclysmic. Can we truly say that belief in fate was an easy way out?

3
Cosmogony and the World-Tree

> We don't ask to be eternal. What we ask is not to see
> acts and objects abruptly lose their meaning. The void
> surrounding us then suddenly yawns on every side.
> —Antoine de Saint-Exupéry

Attempts to reconstruct the spatio-temporal cosmogony and cosmography of our Germanic ancestors are made a good deal more difficult by the fact that by almost everyone's account, the literature describes two systems that simply do not admit of easy reconciliation. It is almost as if one attempted to provide a single map embracing Creationism and the theory of evolution by laying one over the other: there will be occasional points of contact, perhaps some broad similarities, but in the end the contradictions, inconsistencies, and anomalies between their respective dynamics will make mutual coherence impossible. The problem we face is compounded by the fact that there is every reason to think that these contradictory systems of Norse mythology (in particular) were indeed accepted together, and that the evident tensions did not produce such fractures in one as would undermine belief in the other, as frameworks for their respective narratives. We shall see as we proceed that there is little reason to imagine that any such broad systematic failures played any role in the eventual overthrow of paganism by Christianity. We cannot say with any confidence that the Christian cosmology, insofar as it would have been apprehended and understood by Germanic pagans, seemed preferable to the Norse—although there is evidence that the eschatology at least did indeed strike the Northmen as significantly different and somehow more comforting.

Mythological accounts of the beginning and end of the world are rarely products of explicitly literary endeavors alone. The fact that they are invariably expressed in poetic form is readily explained by pointing out that such forms performed the dual function of embodying metaphysical beliefs, while being accessible to everyone capable of listening to a good story, even if (and sometimes especially if) they lacked the ability to read one. If we then include cosmologies in our frame of reference—theories of the universe taken as a whole—we see still more clearly that such poetic models often performed the role of what would later come to be called "natural philosophy," as well as the metaphysics we find in the cosmogonies. E. H. Meyer remarked that behind all of the cosmogonies of ancient times—the biblical, the Platonic, and Germanic—lies what he refers to as the *"Mutterkosmogonie"* of Babylonia. And just as Babylonian cosmogony was no product of simple minds, but was instead a learned and priestly vocation, just as this model of the birth, life, and death of everything that exists was not merely mythical but also *speculative* (in an inquiring, scientific sense) so we must acknowledge similar characteristics for those systems influenced by it.[1] Cosmogony is the outcome not simply of poetic fancy, but of profound reflection; the narrative literary form is the medium, not the entire message. The origin of such cosmogonies is more likely to be the temple, not the homestead.[2] I see no reason to disagree with Meyer's judgment here. It is a presupposition of this essay that Germanic mythology merits consideration as the precursor of philosophical systematizing, no matter how distant it is from an Aristotelian *Metaphysics* or a Leibnizian *Monadology*. The fact that its vehicle of expression is literary achievement of a high order is one compelling reason for continuing to study it. Philosophy *in* poetry is a higher achievement (taking one against the other) than philosophy detached from it on principle.

We can see this at work on a number of levels, but a single example will establish the point. The Norse distinction between Midgard (the realm of men) and Utgard (the realm of the Giants) is directly reflected in their legal system. "Midgard" means "middle yard," "Utgard" the "outer yard"—that which is outside the fence, or whatever is uncultivated. From this distinction come two analogous legal terms: *innangards*—inside the fence; and *utangards*—outside the fence (nicely resonant in such a context as London's "Inner" and "Middle" Temple—divisions of the Inns of Court). In this way the contrast between Midgard and Utgard embraced both legal relationships and central ideas about the cosmos.[3] The estate of the gods—Asgard—was completely surrounded by a world liable to slide into chaos. This cosmos/real world reflection was manifested further in the Norse idea that settlements were *centers* around which the entire rest of the world was situated. We have already noted Eliade's observation that for ancient religious thought there could be many such centers. Indeed, even the names given to Scandinavian estates reflect this concept of a localized universe.[4]

Ernst Cassirer insists that there is perhaps no cosmology, "however primitive," in which the contrast of the four main spatial directions does not in some way emerge as the cardinal point of its understanding and explanation of the world.[5] In trying to understand Norse cosmogony we are faced with problems involved with interlocking—or superimposing—one model onto another, where what we are told of these cardinal directions and what is contained within their compass resists any such superimposition. The complexities and contradictions evident in the different versions are such that overall coherence seems unattainable. But the systems have been described, often in some detail, independently of one another, with claims occasionally made that something definitive has been offered. Not the least of the difficulties for the interpreter is that the elements are so widely scattered throughout the mythological literature, where some aspect of the model may be emphasized while another plays no role at all. Synthesizing these fragments seems formidably complex—but a number of intriguing attempts have been made, which will be reviewed here.

A distinction can be found in most of these reconstructions that, if not obviously of crucial significance for comprehending the supposed relationship between gods and events, is probably the single most confusing aspect for any attempt made to bring these different pictures together. This is the distinction between a "horizontal" and a "vertical" model for Norse cosmography and cosmogony.[6]

For some scholars the primary model is vertical. The most compelling argument for this is the fundamental significance of the world ash-tree, Yggdrasill.

> An ash I know, hight Yggdrasil,
> the mighty tree moist with white dews;
> thence come the floods that fall adown;
> evergreen o'ertops Urth's well this tree.[7]

Through the Norns, this model is governed by fate. The Norns sustain the tree, and decide what is to happen both to men and gods. Time is irreversible. For some, the irreversibility of time, and the inexorability of fate, are related necessarily. It is the very fact that fate is operating that leads to the conclusion that once fixed, the future as decreed by the Norns is unchangeable. Time cannot run back-

3: COSMOGONY AND THE WORLD-TREE 63

ward. In this cosmogony fate, like time, is a vector. We must note immediately in this context that no argument is ever presented linking time and fate *logically:* it is presumably so self-evident as to require no such argument. The reasoning involved is simply that *if* fate operates, *then* the future is fixed and inexorable *and* time is irreversible. Much of this will be challenged in due course.

The horizontal model, by contrast, stresses the reversibility of time. It has been suggested that it is this aspect that provides the appeal to modern readers of those myths contributing to the horizontal model, since somehow they imply a kind of extended narrative with which we find it much easier to cope than with the more obscure myths in which the vertical model seems more comfortable. We can, it is suggested, fix these myths more securely onto a horizontal axis, while in fact the myths on this axis are just as implicated in the determination of the course of history of the supernatural world as are those on the vertical axis. The horizontal axis is seen as one in which there is a constant cosmological order—the world has a certain permanence, for there was no change in the cosmic situation along time's direction; there was, in effect, permanent balance, represented in the battles between the various orders of beings involved.[8] None of the parties—gods or giants—achieved any ultimate victories. However, it is not entirely clear why this should imply reversible time. The idea seems to be that if the world of gods and giants is stable, any change within the system must be regarded as minor and does not bring about significant development—it has no ultimate telos. In that sense time is reversible. Yet this seems to imply the very curious thesis that the reversibility of time is a function of the *importance* of the events occurring within it, which is certainly incorrect. A much more telling point, confirming that the temporal order of some myths is not reversible, is the widespread use of a genealogical model to express time-depth in Norse mythic and saga society.[9]

The Edda is often seen as an integrated version of the horizontal and vertical models. According to Margaret Clunies Ross, the picture that emerges from a comparison of the Eddic poems *Voluspa, Vafþruðnismal, Fafnismal,* and *Hyndluljoð* is one that divides elapsed time into five separate periods, the transitions of which are marked by significant mythical events.[10] A cyclical view of time is identifiable here (the final stanzas of *Voluspa* are often taken, somewhat unconvincingly, as giving plausibility to such a view of time), but what we see more clearly is the expression of time as linear, time, indeed, seen in human terms. Ross describes these five periods in the following terms: Although Norse myth begins with chaos (as indeed do most myths, even many that are not truly cosmogonic), it is more accurate to think of this first period as lacking direction. The gods would subsequently give it that direction, setting time in motion, so to speak. But in this first period the nine worlds and the world ash-tree are not themselves evidence of any formlessness or disorder. Since the giants already existed (and indeed the sybil tells us that she was raised by them), it cannot be accurately described as a formless age. In the second period of activity, earth is brought into being from the parts of the primeval giant Ymir, and the gods create Midgard. Fate pervades the world in the third period, bringing both mortality and death to gods and humans alike. This third phase is the mythic present experienced by gods and men. In this phase the gods lived with giants, dwarves, and humans, and made efforts to establish and maintain order. The Vanir are incorporated into divine society in this period, which precedes the Ragnarok. For the *Voluspa*, the events that characterize the mythic present are the war between the Aesir and the Vanir, the pledges of Oðin's sight and Heimdall's hearing, the activities of the Valkyrie, and, perhaps most important, the death of Baldr. Valholl is also established during this phase as preparatory for the coming conflagration. In the fourth period Surtr leads an assault on the gods—an event "causally" prepared in phase three, but still only the near future. The fifth and final period is everything occurring following the Ragnarok.

Clunies Ross makes a very interesting remark in the course of this fascinating analysis. She says that there is *a very strong sense of entailment* in Norse mythology, appealing to the Eddic poems' use of *ragan roc*—fate, or doom of the divine powers, as evidence.[11] But entailment is *causal,* and since causality is temporal (which is in turn directional) what has happened here to fate? The point about fate for those who take it to be intimately related to time is that fate is *not* causal, otherwise an event would be caused twice. If Baldr's death is *caused by* Hoðr's arrow, then it was not *caused by* the Norns. If one tries to circumvent this by insisting that Hoðr's arrow was in turn fated— that is, *caused by* fate—*all* causes become aspects of fate and the notion of entailment collapses *into* fate, which is not, it seems to me, the conclusion Ross supports. Fate is supposed to be *in* time—it is not supposed to *be* time itself. In fact, on such a view, fate has become cause *and* time, rather than cause operating *in* time, which implies that fate is causally efficacious, collapsing the distinction between time and cause (time, and events *in* time) altogether.

3: COSMOGONY AND THE WORLD-TREE

There have been a number of attempts made to integrate the horizontal and vertical models. Whether one believes that either version was somehow primary depends very often on the role given to fate. One of the most unusual (and detailed) interpretations comes from the Swedish scholar Viktor Rydberg who, by taking Snorri's introductory remarks in the *Gylfaginning* at more or less face value, suggested that in that place an entirely foreign cosmography had been interpolated into Norse mythology, producing all of the various tensions and inconsistencies that have troubled scholars ever since. Rydberg says that a careful examination of this text demonstrates that the entire cosmographical and eschatological structure which Snorri builds out of fragmentary mythic traditions "is based on a conception wholly foreign to Teutonic mythology—i.e., on the conception framed by the scholars in Frankish cloisters and then handed down, that the Teutons were descended from the Trojans. This conception found its way to the North, eventually into the Younger Edda."[12]

The cosmography developed from this assumption has the Aesir's origin in Troy, which was the center of the earth, just as Asgard would become in Northern mythology. Bifrost then becomes a bridge from Troy to the heavens, with Urd's Well located at the other end. As Rydberg points out, this means that when the Asas (Aesir) ride to the heavens, they must be riding *upward,* not downward. Now according to *Voluspa,* Urd's Well is beneath one of Yggdrasill's roots. Since Urd's Well is in the heavens, it must be "further up," and if the placing of the root "is done with consistency," Rydberg says that we end up with a series of faulty localizations: on the earth is Asgard-Troy; thence upward, via Bifrost, to the heavens. Above Bifrost, there is Urd's Well, and still farther above this, is one of Yggdrasill's three roots—"which in the mythology are all in the lower world." Since one of these roots is placed far up in the heavens, a second root had to be placed on a level with earth, while the third retained its position in the lower world. "Thus was produced a just distribution of the roots among the three regions constituting the universe—heavens, earth, hell."[13] Two myths, says Rydberg, were in this way pressed into service in relation to the remaining roots of Yggdrasill. One was taken from *Voluspa*—Mimr's Well is located below the tree, as we have seen: "evergreen o'ertops Urth's well this tree."[14] The other was taken from *Grimnismal,* where we are told that the frost giants dwell under another of the three roots. "The manner in which *Gylfaginning* has placed the roots of Yggdrasill makes us first of all conceive [it] as lying horizontal in space: this gives us the following picture":

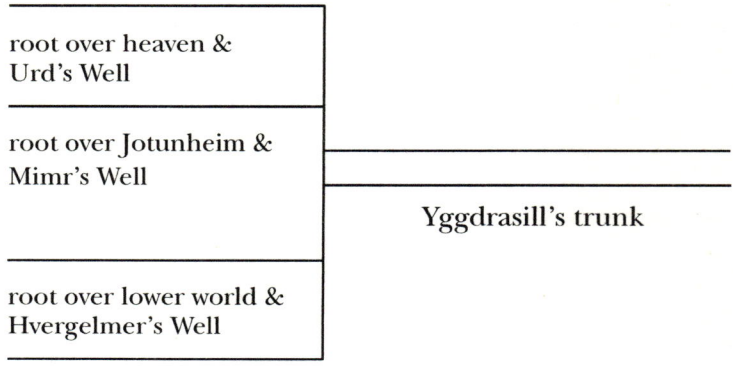

But as Rydberg points out, *Gylfaginning* does not draw this conclusion, since it insists that the world ash-tree "stands erect" on its three roots. He says that *Gylfaginning*'s "pretended account" of the Norse cosmography, because of its making Troy its starting-point, "and doubtless as a result of Christian methods of thought, is *a monstrous caricature of the mythology.*"[15]

And so here we have a very strange picture indeed. If we insist on trying to superimpose the cosmography of the world ash-tree onto that model of Bifrost, Mitgard, Asgard, and so on, from other sources in the mythology, we can make little sense of it as a two-dimensional *mappa mundi*. Even with Yggdrasill laid on its side rather than erect—as the *Voluspa* tells us it must be—we have to manipulate and rethink natural directions to accommodate the topography of its roots. It is clear that the tree should be upright; from that we then do the best we can to fit the other accounts into this structure. There are other options. One of these is to introduce into this picture of Yggdrasill a dynamic, shamanistic component. In other words, we add time to space. The Germanic folkloric tradition and the associated mythology each contribute something to the idea that ecstatic techniques were known and used, though how widespread this was is not clear. There are certainly elements of the mythology with obvious shamanistic implications. Yggdrasill linked worlds together, thereby offering a path for shamanic journeys. Such world-trees linking one realm to another can be found in many Asian mythologies, and some have suggested that this is the likely source for the Germanic case—for Cosmic trees are related to so-called world poles (as in Amerindian culture, and the mythologies of parts of Australasia). These poles are routes to the sky for shamans, not unlike Bifrost. "Shape-shifting, binding and blinding, voluntary mutilation in return for the gift of prophecy, are all traits found in shamanic traditions, especially Asia."[16] Oðin's self-sacrifice, and his hanging on the world-tree for the magical nine days, has all the hallmarks of shamanistic behavior, as indeed has the very idea of a cosmic tree connecting the various parts of the universe. We can therefore remove some of the problems of the spatial incongruity seen above, by incorporating that model into a framework of shamanism—shamanistic journeys being both spatially and temporally disconnected from everyday mythical space-time. For example, if we focus on just a very small subsystem of the cosmography, we can represent the horizontal axis—the "steady-state, permanent, reversible time-axis" as follows:

We can now superimpose a vertical axis in which cosmos versus chaos is prominent, thus:

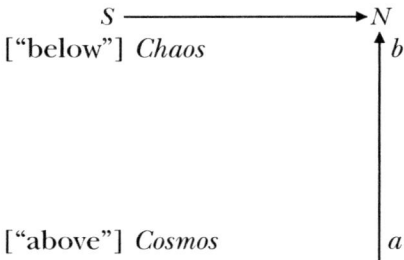

North in the horizontal model and the underworld in the vertical model are linked by the same *semantic* content. But at this nodal point N, Hermoðr (on the horizontal axis) has to go *North* and then *down* to reach Hel. Thus:

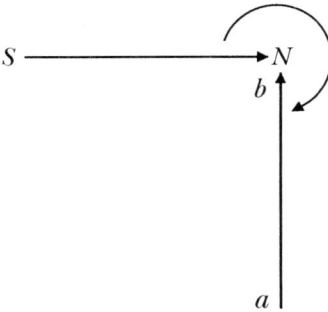

By the same reasoning, when Oðin acquires the sacred mead, this involves his transition from the horizontal to the vertical axis—"Odin qua culture hero turns into the first shaman"—the first Norse shaman, that is.[17] The point is that we are told in *Gylfaginning* that the way to Hel is to the North *and then leads below* (not South), "wodurch Hel dann beiden Ausrichtungen zugeordnet wird—der horizontalen und der vertikalen."[18] Schjødt takes this—as does everyone else—as confirmation that the information given in the sources simply conflicts. But note that Hel is to the north and then *leads below*—not South again. And "below," shamanistically, as we might say, releases us or disconnects us from the horizontal axis and attaches us to the vertical axis. Thus point *b* is *below* point *a* semantically—shamanistically—but not to the North of it—nor is it, indeed, to the South of it!

Yet it is the addition of the dimension of time that leads us into still further complications, for the temporal subsystems are as problematic as the spatial ones already outlined. The temporal modalities that are presumed to be analogous to the spatial are of course of a cosmogonical nature—dealing as they do with the world's beginning—and the eschatological, dealing with its end. Some authorities, Gurevich for example, take the latter as uniquely defining characteristics for Scandinavian mythology. Our problem, as before, is to interrelate and integrate the available spatial and temporal models. The vertical model is normally taken to be more sensitive to irreversible temporal processes, since Yggdrasill is a concentration of the world's fate, and hence possesses a vectorial quality supposedly lacking in the horizontal model. Thus it is the cosmic tree that is the most important element in eschatological pictures, even though it is itself "largely divorced from cosmogony."[19] Such an idea is presented as an alternative to the widespread mythical narrative in which a world is created from the parts of the body of some giant being. Meletinskij says that it is as if the world was created from Ymir, but that its morphology is modeled not on the form of a human body, but from the shape of a tree.[20]

Following Eliade's theory, the myth of a sacred center of Norse mythology would be that relating to the world of the Aesir. Both temporally and spatially, the world outside this center is considered both dangerous and profane.[21] This center, for many scholars, represents the intersection of the vertical and horizontal axes. And when worlds collide in such a fashion, there is within the mythological narrative "the permanent possibility of danger and uncertainty."[22] At such points of intersection and transition magic often plays a role, for magic can be a way of shifting from one axis to another, just as we have suggested occurs in the shamanistic journeys and rites of Oðin. It should occasion little surprise that magic can be seen as particularly effective at such points of intersection, whether these are taken to be within the world of cause and effect, or between such worlds.[23] Nonetheless, it is especially interesting that magical objects in Northern cultures were very often microcosmic versions of images of how the gods were seen in relation to fate—that is, they were bound in fetters or otherwise impeded in their actions. This will occupy us in some detail below, but for the moment we repeat the point made previously that in many languages the general conception of magic is expressed by the term or terms for "binding." Magic was considered as a way of releasing the "bonds of fate," if only in relatively minor ways: no one, for example, had access to magic that could avoid one's fated day of death. Yet so long as fate remained in the realm of the impersonal, its magicalization was impossible.[24] We might have expected more of such magicalization than is actually found, especially in relation to the world ash-tree, since sympathetic tree magic long predates the myth of Yggdrasill.

Of course, if we could rid ourselves of the notion that fate must imply irreversible time (putting to one side for the moment the much more radical claim that fate does not imply time at all), we might be able to superimpose the vertical onto the horizontal spatial system. But the point of intersection of two such time systems presents insuperable difficulties. The nodal point that is, for example, the Ragnarok, is something both in and beyond any such point of intersection only if one loops back and begins the process all over again, providing for Norse mythology an unambiguously cyclic view of time, as indicated by the final stanzas of *Voluspa*, which do indeed take us beyond the Ragnarok:

> I see green again   with growing things
> the earth arise   from out of the sea;
> . . . .
>
> Then in the grass   the golden figures,
> the far-famed ones,   will be found again,
> which they had owned   in olden days.[25]

But a cyclic view of time does not quite solve the problems raised in trying to make the vertical and horizontal systems cohere. If the pagan Germanic peoples had truly believed in a cyclic time (which can become terrifying, as events repeat themselves for ever), they would perhaps have embraced Christianity the more readily in all of Germania, offering as it did an eventual salvation that was a certain way of breaking free of any such cycle, by means of a permanent redemption.

One radical alternative way of confronting the most intransigent problems raised by any attempt to make the spatial and temporal systems of the eschatology and cosmogony of Norse mythology coalesce, is to deny that the tree system of Yggdrasill has anything to do with cosmogony and insist instead, with Rydberg, that this is first and foremost a *cosmology*. By removing time's arrow from the spatial coordinates of the world-tree, one is left with a straightforward mythical map of the cosmos that is essentially static, not dynamic. But before a judgment can be passed on such a reductive solution, we must examine more closely the nature of time itself in relation to the issues already raised.

The idea that Norse mythology offers a cyclic view of time takes its justification primarily, as we have seen, from the final stanzas of *Voluspa*, and from the lines from *Vafþruðnismal* referred to above: "at the world's last weird/he will wend again home to the wise Vanir."[26] In these poems the world is clearly said to renew itself after the catastrophe of the Ragnarok. It implies that the whole system will be reborn, but unlike various other myths of recurrence, there is no suggestion here that we are concerned with a cycle that will endlessly repeat, that it is, in effect, an example of the myth of *eternal* recurrence. There is the additional complication that many scholars see in the last lines of *Voluspa* in particular the clear influence of *Christian* eschatology, rather than anything with an unambiguous native Germanic cast, though nothing about such a suggestion implies that there could not have been some still more ancient pagan influence on the *Voluspa* narrative. Influences operate, after all, upon existing myths, as well as interpolating entirely new ones. We should always be open to the possibility that even where influence is clear, it occurs sometimes most readily where the preexisting mythology is prepared for modification, or even replacement, by virtue of deep conceptual similarities.[27]

Of course not all cyclic views of the fate of the cosmos conclude as equably as is the case with the optimism of *Voluspa*. In the case of ancient Egyptian beliefs, for instance, the answer to the question, "What will there be when the world has come to an end?" is that there will be the same chaos that prevailed before the world was created—a

3: COSMOGONY AND THE WORLD-TREE 71

chaotic world characterized by darkness and endlessness. What the Egyptians feared, however, was not the end of the world as such, but the disintegration of the dramatic context of the process of reality, with its effect on the cosmos. In this world of the imagination, ritual had the function of preserving its integrity.

In the following text—a magic or cultic dramatization—nature is represented as a wasteland:

> The earth is made waste,
> the sun does not rise,
> the moon does not appear, it no longer exists,
> The ocean sinks, the land spins round,
> the river is no longer navigable.
> The entire world moans and cries,
> gods and goddesses, humans, transfigured ones, and dead,
> small and large cattle cry out aloud . . .

These lines are concerned with the death of Osiris, bringing the cosmos to a standstill.[28] In the Hermetic text *Asclepius,* an apocalyptic prophecy describing the separation of mankind from the gods, we find the following chilling lines:

> The earth will shake, and the seas will be unnavigable,
> the sky will no longer be crossed by stars,
> the stars will forsake their courses,
> every divine voice will be silent, forced into silence.
> The fruits of the earth will be spoiled and the soil no longer
>   fruitful,
> and even the air will hang heavy and close.

This is not, says Assmann, "a description of the aftermath of a nuclear war, but rather of a 'disenchantment of the world' that seemed to loom on the horizon in the third and fourth centuries C.E., during the controversies between Gnostic, Jewish, and Christian movements."[29] The similarities with *Voluspa* here are striking. The death of Baldr is the mediate cause of the slide into catastrophe: the looming millennium (perhaps), and the threat to the old gods through the encroachment of Christianity, offer a distant echo of these ancient texts, where the coming conflagration is presented in similar doom-laden terms:

> Neath sea the land sinketh,   the sun dimmeth,
> from the heavens fall   the fair bright stars;

> gusheth forth steam   and gutting fire,
> to very heaven   soar the hurtling flames.[30]

This Egyptian comparison is highly instructive, not least because the ancient Egyptian view of the cosmos (and its end) was intimately related to their uniquely complex view of time and its relation to eternity. The graphic Egyptian concept of cosmos as drama implied that reality was *not* primarily spatial and material, but was instead temporal and performative. The cosmos was a living process, represented most impressively in the sun's daily journey across the sky. Assmann tells us that the ancient Egyptians possessed no concept of space qua category of cosmic totality. What they did have was a concept of time, whose fullness was expressed by means of a pair of words—*neheh (nhh)* and *djet (dt)*—for which no pair of words in Western languages offers an accurate translation.[31] They do not correspond with any real accuracy to our words "time" and "eternity"; as Assmann points out, this latter distinction has its roots in Greek ontology, which was "quite foreign to Egyptian thought . . . even contrary to it."[32] Either of these Egyptian words could be rendered as "time" or "eternity," since they each refer to the *totality* of cosmic time. Assmann goes on to say that we are so accustomed to the concept of infinity that we think of totality as finite and bounded, while the Egyptians saw it as the opposite of finite and bounded. For them, the boundaries of totality were not contrasted with the unbounded, but with the whole—with plenitude. *Neheh* and *djet* designate the comprehensive and absolute horizon of totality.[33] They refer to the *temporal totality* of the cosmos; it was in this way that the concept of being, or cosmos, was articulated. We should note that though *djet* was an abstract temporal concept, it was represented in the writing system by a spatial object—even though abstract concepts of all kinds were easily expressed in hieroglyphs. It is interesting also that *djet* should have been represented in just the way that it was, by the "bundle of reeds"—the *djet*-pillar—which within Middle Egyptian would seem to be conceptually much more significant than the tree ideogram itself. The latter seems to have carried no profound significance beyond its role as a determinative for, in particular, the sycamore, or for "tree" in general. So notwithstanding that the tree has sacred meaning—especially in the Pyramid Texts, where the sycamore "guards" both sides of the doors of the sky—it is the reed-pillar which possesses the most religious significance. This may also reflect the triumph of the Osirian over the Solar religion. We will see later in the discussion just how important and widespread the cosmic tree/pillar is in mythologies from many sources: the *djet*-pillar, we should note here, was also the determinative for "eternity."[34] This totalization of being on the temporal level is so foreign to our conceptions that some scholars, as Assmann notes, proposed that *djet* and *neheh* meant space *and* time, which he insists is not correct.[35] Both are unequivically temporal concepts, and in Egyptian thought they represented the *whole* of reality.

It has been noted that our dichotomy of time and eternity has its origins in Greek ontology. Assmann adds that our concept of time has its foundation in the system of tenses in Western languages. Instead of past, present, and future, the Hamito-Semitic language family (of which Middle Egyptian is a member) has two divisions, called aspects. And it is this that gives us the key to understanding the meaning of *djet* and *neheh*. The nearest linguistic analogy would probably be a pair of concepts such as "change" and "completion." In Egyptian, change was "*kheper,*" and completedness was "*tem*" (from which come the names for the gods Khepri and Atum). *Neheh* time "comes as a pulsating stream of days, months, years," while *djet* time "endures"—hence the *djet*-pillar as determinative for eternity—and this will be subject to no further change. *Djet* signifies the enduring continuation of that which, acting and changing, has been *completed in time*. Re and Osiris *together* yielded reality. Only their combined effect gave rise to the synthesis of *neheh* and *djet* that humankind experienced as time.

Just as the Egyptian language had no words for time and space as such, so it had no (single) word for cosmos. To express this therefore required a whole constellation of concepts, and, indeed, gods. The cosmos just was the sacred conceived as *acts,* as the combined work of many deities, as *drama* in which all the gods played roles—just as they do, invariably, in other polytheistic mythologies.[36] It is this that grounds the Egyptian *dramatic* conception of nature, wherein reality is seen as the collaborative effort of divine actions.

What this fascinating example offers us is, at the least, a caution that we do not too readily attribute simple conceptual errors to those who both framed and understood the cosmological systems with which we are concerned. We should not assume that our unified system of a space-time axis (which is historically Cartesian) is the sole way in which the world as imagined can be comprehended. The Egyptian distinction between *neheh* and *djet* is so complex—and so different from our own—that we cannot even express it with any facility. But it must not be assumed either that our system would have been of any use to them should they have known of it. We should remember that it is not only our ontology that is derived from the Greeks, but our *logic* also—a logic that relentlessly bifurcates the most intransigently complex features of the world into neat, *timeless* categories suitable for manipulation within the framework of abstract algorithmic systems.

Perhaps, after all, Rydberg's solution to the compatibility problem of the alternative Eddic subsystems is unnecessarily pessimistic; perhaps if we think of the two interacting systems as forming a totality, we can avoid the need to diminish the validity of one in favor of the other.

As we have noted, mythic space and time is clearly distinct from abstract space and time qua continuous quantities, infinitely divisible into successive parts that are homogeneous and isotropic. The ordering of symbolic events within a mythology need not conform in any way to the rigid logic that such an idealized system demands. In almost every culture, time was connected first to natural cycles. It should occasion no surprise that from this was generated the importance of cyclic time in religion and mythology. Yet some caution is demanded here. From the fact that all cultures must have observed and made use of the cycle of seasons—of planting, tending, harvesting; of birth, life, and death—it does not at all follow that they thereby *must* have conceived of time itself as cyclic. Although evidence from grave-goods suggests that many such cultures believed that the dead were embarking on a journey for which there were accompanying requisites, it does not follow that they believed that the dead were returning, no matter at what supposed distant point in the future. The putative anthropomorphic conception of time, where in Norse the word for "year" also meant "harvest," where there was always some specific *content* to time, may have confronted them with cycles, but the sagas themselves suggest, in addition, an acute awareness of what we can call narrative time. This could itself have been the foundation for a conviction that time—time *as such*—was linear.

That said, this idea of linear time for Norse cosmography is by no means orthodox, for their conception of abstract time is not so much chronological, as *genealogical*. What was of fundamental importance was a transparent consciousness of one's connection with the past, an organic bond with it. To this end a real, concrete chain of generations does service for the merely abstract lapse of time. Every individual lived within a genealogical framework, in which the count of generations assumed great significance.[37] This count reflected a way of understanding time: the genealogical list—found in legends but also, importantly, in the sagas—facilitated the locating of a man within a particular group that was a real bearer of relations linking—indeed, binding—the present with the past.

Though we must be careful not to see this as some kind of historical process—the suggestion being made here is that the former was constructed in preference to the latter, chronology having never actually taken hold as part of the cosmogonical belief-system—this idea that genealogy substituted for chronology was not unique to Germanic culture. Indeed, it may relate to a system of time-reckoning that is of great antiquity, for in both ancient Babylonia and Old Kingdom Egypt, every year was given an official title named for the chief event that occurred in it—a system that would eventually give way in each case to numbering in terms of regnal years. Closer to home, medieval French literature has been described as "deploying history as a series of biographies linked by the principle of hereditary succession, which *stands as much for the passing of time* as for the legal notion of transference."[38] So important was this idea that one of the signs of the coming catastrophe of the Ragnarok was the crime of *sifjaslit*—"breaking the bonds of affinity," as when "Brothers will battle to bloody end, and sisters' sons their sib betray."[39] Just as much as *Fimbulwinter* (the terrible winter that heralds the downfall of the world at the Ragnarok, an idea found also in Mazdaism) or the inundation of the earth, or the blacking out of the sun, the world's end is here signaled by the bonds of affinity being severed, as if time itself has been fractured, split asunder. Such an idea helps us to understand how it was that the present and the past form a meaningful continuum. The past endures *into the present* (like the concept of *neheh* for the Egyptians) and we will see how important this is for the concept of fate as we proceed. This focus on family relationships—names, localities, and functions—confirms that Norse mythical lore is, as Marlene Ciklamin puts it, "topical, not chronological," with the sequential narrative of *Voluspa* offering the primary exception, where the beginning and end of the world frame a *sequence* with little sense of chronological distance.[40]

This absence of any unambiguous unidirectional timeframe into which all events (past into the present) must fall does not mean that Norse mythology thereby lacked a sense of causality. Mythical thinking nowhere lacks the universal category of cause and effect (although many writings on comparative mythology proceed on the presupposition that they do), for this is precisely what cosmogonies—and theogonies—are concerned to describe. The difference between mythical concepts of causality and our own frequently reduces to the sense that in the former, the relationship between event *A* and event *B* (where *A* causes *B*) is often seen as logical necessity rather than temporal sequence. We must thereby take issue with S. Bhattacharji when he insists that fatalism conflicts with and contradicts "any just and logical system of causality." He says that the simple logical premise that a cause precedes and generates its effect "is so logically rounded up, neatly and completely, that it leaves no room for fate"—then concedes that "fatalism and causality have coexisted in most theologies."[41] The argument is that if causation is accepted as a cosmic and natural principle, it becomes immutable and irrevocable, leaving no room for fate. Bhattacharji says this on several occasions and seems to think that it is self-evidently true. But it is not. Indeed, universal causality is sometimes taken as a reason for *accepting* fate. After all, it depends entirely on what is taken to be a cause. The Norns might lay it down that a certain individual is to perish in battle at some stated time, but this does not mean that we (or the Norsemen) could not understand that the *cause* of his death is a thrust from a sword. Do the Norns *cause* his death in just the same way that the sword does? Of course not. The point, once again, is that causality is more plausibly seen as related to time, although it cannot unambiguously be seen as in itself a *temporal* notion, while fate certainly is not. Universal causation tells us nothing *one way or the other* about the nature of fate. If it is true that some individual will die on a particular day (a nontemporal statement about an event in time), his death will nonetheless be caused (at least a subtemporal concept) by some event or other. Paul Bauschatz writes that the concept of a preordained future, separate from the past, "seems quite foreign to early Germanic *Weltanschauung*. There is no feeling anywhere that all possible actions—all 'future' actions—are to be considered necessary, except in so far as they refer to general rules, required behaviour or statements of universal laws."[42] This is correct, but misleading. The conceptual essence of predestination is *the past*, where everything is laid out and written down—*not* the future. What happens *in the future* is preordained *in the past*.

Life and fate are represented in many mythologies through the image of a cosmic tree; Yggdrasill is therefore typical. But it is not only trees as the means of connecting different worlds that is found in so many cultures, but trees as such, for we can find many connections—and sometimes equivalences—between trees and men, as well as linguistic links between trees and the "book" of fate—the word "book"

3: COSMOGONY AND THE WORLD-TREE 77

itself having its Germanic roots in the word for "beech," pieces of which were used for the earliest writings. The term for "beech"—like that for "hornbeam"—is etymologically related to verbal forms meaning "to scratch" or "to make marks," showing clearly that the beech was used in ancient times for making graphic signs.[43] The oak was revered in particular in Indo-European cultures—an oak cult is attested throughout the Caucasus, where it is the great mythic tree, the Cosmic Tree—and we discover a possible linguistic comparison between Greek "cosmos" and Latin "*quercus,*" making the equation tree = world = man.[44] According to Mastrelli, careful consideration of the data concerning Germanic religion (Nordic in particular) can be used to illustrate the deep reason for that set of *kenningar* (poetic paraphrases) for the concept of man and woman that have their origin in common nouns for "tree," as well as for the names of specific trees. It had been maintained that the *kenningar* with the determinatum "tree" emerged as a way of emphasizing strength—attributed to the warrior. Mastrelli believes this to be a mistaken interpretation. He finds the explanation in the details of Norse cosmogony, where, following the creation of the world, the gods created man in the following way: Two tree trunks were discovered upon the shore, from which the first human couple were formed—Askr (male) and Embla (female), usually taken to indicate "ash" and "elm," respectively.

> To the coast then came, kind and mighty,
> from the gathered gods three great Æsir;
> on the land they found, of little strength,
> Ask and Embla, unfated yet.[45]

The ash in legend was the tree of sea-power, or power resident in water; and of course one of the names for Oðin was "Yggr"—from which comes the name for the Norse tree—and it has been further suggested that this name, Yggr, connects with *hygra*—Greek for "sea"—literally, "the wet element."[46] The watery association of the ash is also confirmed by the fact that in Greece the ash was sacred to Poseidon, who was also the patron saint of horses.[47] The significance of the ash has long been recognized. In Ireland, for example, the Tree of Tortu, the Tree of Dathi, and the branching tree of Usnech—three of the five Magic Trees whose fall in A.D. 665 symbolized the triumph of Christianity over paganism—were ash-trees; while in British folklore the ash was the tree of rebirth—naked children were once passed through the cleft of a pollard ash as a cure for rupture, the idea being that if the tree recovers from the cleft, then so will the child.[48] Also, the Druidical wand of the Celts was made of ash, while in Oðin's own Runic alphabet all the letters were formed from ash twigs; ash roots are said to strangle those of other forest trees, returning us once again to the idea that the wood from which man was made had special qualities of power and durability. Finally, we should note that Oswald Spengler considered the world ash-tree "typically Faustian."[49] The attribution that the ash was formed into the first man has deep mythological significance; Hesiod, for instance, has Zeus create the species from an ash-tree. Iranian myths employ a similar notion that trees were related to the first humans, an idea that we find also in Sioux Indian mythology and among the Carib and Antilles Indians, who each have legends relating that their ancestors were formed from trees. Strikingly, like Norse mythology, they also associate snakes with the roots of such trees. The essential difference is that for the Germanic example—and its most plausible direct ancestor, the Iranian—*dead* wood is brought to life as human, while these other myths represent the trees growing as humans in the first place.[50]

There is less widespread evidence as to why the elm—if that is how we translate "Embla"—should be chosen for woman, except perhaps that elm was always used for supporting young vines, with all the associated symbolism of growth and regeneration this implies; it became the *almer mater* of the wine god. (On the other hand, in ancient Greece the elm could also be a symbol of death.) Subsequently, the vine and the elm have invariably been seen as interdependent. There is also an Irish legend that tells of the first man being created from an alder tree, and the first woman from a mountain ash—the rowan tree. The rowan, in Anglo-Saxon was "*beam*" (tree) or "quicken-tree" (quickbeam) and was the tree of life; and the rowan (along with the oak) possessed magical and holy qualities for the Finnish *Kalevala*.[51]

Myths such as these help us to explain some, at least, of the ancient and persistent sense of a relationship between men and trees, manifested most vividly in Northern Europe through the concept of the "*Schutzbaum*"—that is, trees as protecting spirits. The most impressive and prominent example of this phenomenon is probably the Swedish "*Vårdträd,*" which seems almost to have been regarded as a personal being for those under its protection, a spirit not unlike that of the Norse *fylgja*. We need not follow Mannhardt's thesis that Yggdrasill and Vårdträd are "counterparts" in order to acknowedge the all-pervading influence of trees and their connection with man, life—and fate.

3: COSMOGONY AND THE WORLD-TREE

The use of a tree, or pillar, as a way of identifying man with life, or fate, is mostly secondary to the more pervasive idea of a tree as some mythic way of bonding gods to men. The tree/pillar image was seen often (and in a quite natural way) as a route, a pathway, between the heavens and the earth (to be traveled shamanistically, though by no means exclusively so), and as a fixed symbol of communication between the gods and humanity. Many Greek deities—Zeus, Dionysos, Hermes, Artemis—in their cults and legends possess the attributes of trees. In Norse mythology it is Heimdallr who is most closely identified with the world-tree, while Thor is the world-pillar to whose name are dedicated the high seat pillars that sustain the house, "for they are symbolic of the pillar that sustains the world—Thor is that pillar."[52]

We are now in a position to connect the significance of the world-pillar to the concept of time; the idea of the tree of fate (contrasted with the Norns, who *sustain* the world-tree) will come later. As we have already remarked, the Egyptian word for *enduring time* is *djet* (sometimes *djed*). The hieroglyph (determinative) for all abstract words in Middle Egyptian relating to the idea of enduring time is that of a "bundle of reeds" (as it is most often described) known as the *djet*-pillar: 𓊽. In the examples found where the *djet*-pillar retains its original colors, there is usually a green upper part above some differently colored lower part—suggesting that this is both a plant and/or a tree symbol.[53] The *djet*-pillar is occasionally given as "two-armed," these two outstretched arm-wings extending as a sign of protection. Sometimes this form is depicted with the addition of *ankh* signs suspended from each arm; the *ankh* is the sign for life, so this graphic juxtaposition may signify the dependence of life on eternity. This armed form may in turn be related to that of the winged axis—a form of the winged-oak of Zeus—that is, the cosmic-tree. Since the concept of fate as understood in Germanic paganism has a less dominant role to play in Egyptian religion—the god Fate and the goddess Fortune first assumed prominence in the Empire Dynasties, (1580–1150 B.C.), although an element of voluntarism also had a place in Egyptian ethical life—we would expect this pillar-cum-cosmic-tree to resonate with ideas rather of rebirth and regeneration in the religion of Osiris; and so, indeed, it does. Apart from the god Ptah being depicted sometimes as a pillar extending from the lowest to the highest heaven, the *djet*-pillar is constantly mentioned in the *Book of the Dead* in direct relationship with the cult of Osiris.[54]

The myth of the winged-oak of Zeus is most likely to have its origins in Phoenicia. Within the latter's mythology the universe was seen as an immense tree furnished with wings to indicate its possible motion; its roots plunge into the abyss, and its extended branches uphold the display of the "Veil of the Firmament." The Maruts—wind gods or *mill* gods—dwell in the tree *asvattha*. This, as we have noted, was the "horsed-tree," possibly yet another version of the winged-oak of Zeus. It seems clear that in all these examples the trunk is the axis—the beam—on which the cosmos turns.[55] We recall here, also, that in Norse mythology "beyond the heavens" there are nine giantesses who push a mill handle that turns both the mill and the heavens, beyond the world-mill or "maelstrom." The mysterious "Sampo" of the *Kalevala* is described as both the pillar of the world around which the sky rotates and as having the characteristics of a tree. It is also a mill with a decorated lid, though as Keith Bosley points out, its history is "hardly consonant" with such an image, which may even be a Scandinavian importation into the epic. As a tree/pillar, it is clearly comparable to Irminsul (the pillar of Irmin) erected at Eresburg and subsequently destroyed by Charlemagne. In some versions one of Sampo's roots is said to have pierced Mother Earth, while a second reaches into the sky, and a third into the water's edge, while in Canto 39 reference to its "bright-lid" manages to incorporate both the "mystical" number nine and the three roots:

> There the Sampo's been taken
> the bright-lid carried
> into Northland's rocky hill
> inside the slope of copper
> locked behind nine locks;
> in there roots have been rooted
> to a depth of nine fathoms
> with one root in mother earth
> and one in a riverbank
> and a third in the home-hill.[56]

And so we see a host of connections both linguistic and mythical relating trees, pillars, axes, the turning of the celestial sphere, life, regeneration—even the endless turning of mill wheels. Some of these connections will recur in what follows. John O'Neill saw Yggdrasill as the "doublet" of the winged-oak of Zeus, which he derives by means of a bewildering catalogue of etymological speculations linking Yggdrasill with force and circular motion, the energy of nature, the power of turning the cosmos, and so on. For example, "Drasill" from the Gothic *thracils*, Scythian *tracilus*, which provides us with words for race (as in mill race) wheel, waterwheel, etc., and then the Latin *"torque"* which means "turn," and the Sanskrit *"tarkus,"* meaning a spindle. Fanciful though such speculations may be in relation to the name Yggdrasill (and we may note in passing that the word "universe" itself means "the one that turns"), these concepts—universal fate, turning, spinning—are absolutely fundamental to an understanding of how it was that fate came to be seen and personified in many mythologies. We can certainly agree with O'Neill when he says that the name—the word *"Ygg"*—is incomplete without the word "ash," for we need both categories for a complete understanding of the Norse world ash-tree. This seems to be confirmed by Lotte Motz, who says that there are ten occurrences of the expression *askr Yggdrasills* in the *Voluspa, Grimnismal,* and *Gylfaginning;* eight occurrences of the noun *askr;* and only one instance of the form "Yggdrasill." Even this does not occur in all of the manuscripts, and is in any case used to describe *askr.* *"Askr"* appears by itself, while "Yggdrasill" occurs *only* in relation to *askr.* "Yggdrasill," therefore, does not function as the object or subject of a verb or a preposition, but only as a modifier of *askr.* Motz concludes that the evidence suggests that the cosmic-tree is not designated as "Yggdrasill" but rather as *askr* or as *askr Yggdrasill.*[57] Thus "Yggdrasils"—"the genitive form which appears in one manuscript"—should be translated as "Ash of Yggdrasill," confirming O'Neill's insight arrived at on completely different, and much more speculative, grounds.[58]

We saw earlier that in order to make graphic sense of the spatiotemporal mapping of Yggdrasill onto the remainder of Norse cosmography, Rydberg had proposed laying the tree on its side, so that the three roots would extend north-south and accommodate information on the known location of the three wells or fountains found elsewhere in the sources. Historically, such a maneuver would not have seemed in the least odd, since a much more radical reorientation of the cosmic-tree is attested in many cultures. This is the so-called inverted tree. This played an important role in a number of cultures, where the placing of the roots in heaven assumed symbolic significance, and also provides a further link with the notion of the cosmic pillar. In general terms, the roots represent the principles, while the branches are the manifestation of these principles. Some Hindu texts speak of two trees, one cosmic and the other supracosmic, one being the mirror image of the other and representing the two essences of Brahma. In the Avesta tradition there are also two trees, one white and one yellow; one of paradise, the other terrestrial.

(Yggdrasill, of course, is also white, although its whiteness may really refer to brightness rather than color in any literal sense.) In the Avesta tradition the terrestrial tree is a surrogate for the celestial version (at least so far as humankind can see things), like a Platonic shadow of an unreachable reality.[59] Zohar mythology speaks of two trees, one superior, one inferior; while in mythologies such as the Assyrian, it is possible to detect representations that indicate that one tree has been superimposed on another.

The properly inverted tree may symbolically represent both macrocosm and microcosm—the latter, of course, being mankind. Plato described man as a "celestial plant," like an inverted tree, where the roots reached skyward and the branches push toward earth.[60] This recalls the *vajra* symbol and the trident *trishula*. The latter forms the end point of a stem or trunk identified with the pillar (*skhamba*) that supports the heavens and the earth and with the "axle-tree" (*aksa*) of the Solar chariot—that is, the axis of the universe. One suggestion is that the *trisula* may be in effect a "single *vajra*": Siva is commonly represented holding in his hand a trishula or trident, called "Pinaka."[61]

And so we see mythologies employing the image of the tree in a kaleidoscopic variety of ways. It can be a means of connecting earth with the heavens or a picture of the relationship between microcosm and macrocosm. In addition to widespread tree cults, there are tree images used as symbols of regeneration and rebirth, of godhead, spirit, and of paradise—as in the case of the palm, which symbolized the "ascent"; it also assumed the role of guardian spirit, holy place, or as "*Opferbaum*"—a tree of sacrifice as in the famous Oseberg Tree. There was subsequently the tree's profound role in medieval alchemy, where it became the very symbol of the Hermetic philosophy. Given all of this, however, we would do well to caution ourselves that sometimes—to paraphrase Freud—a tree was just a tree. But sometimes it is the juxtaposition of images that is significant, and equally revealing of a deep connection of mythical meanings. One of the most pervasive of these is the link made between trees and snakes or serpents. Such relationships are found in many cultures across the ancient world and would seem to testify to profound symbolic significance. In Indian mythology the link with time is maintained—witness images showing Visnu resting upon the cosmic serpent Ananta—"Infinite"—who floats on the cosmic ocean. Very similar illustrations, from many different times and otherwise widely different cultures, link serpents and trees and differ only in that, for the tree of life (and knowledge, as in the Christian case), the snake winds *up-*

ward, while for the tree of death, it winds downward. In the case of Yggdrasill, the snake gnaws at the roots.

But for this discussion it is not the serpent on which we wish to focus attention; the serpent is important only insofar as it is the *tree* in which it chooses to live, the tree that the snake somehow attacks, or in whose roots it finds its nest. If the snake in Germanic mythology symbolizes the destructive possibilities for the tree of life and fate, it is the Norns who assume the contrasting task of nurturing it, of sustaining its well-being, of guarding it. Although cosmic-trees, such as Yggdrasill and other trees of fate, are clearly generated from a common mythological root stock, it is its being cared for by the fates themselves—the Norns—that sets this tree apart from others. It is to the nature of the Norns that we now turn our attention.

4
Spinning and Weaving Fate

> Like a knitter drowsed,
> Whose fingers play in skilled unmindfulness,
> The Will has woven with an absent heed
> Since life first was; and ever so will weave.
> —Thomas Hardy

It is the task of the Norns to sustain the World Ash-tree. In this respect the health of the tree and the lives of men and gods are intimately related. Although some aspects of their nature may well have been interpolated into Eddic poetry in Christian times—their precise names, for example—their functions are probably authentic expressions of pagan belief. It is unquestionable that many ancient cultures had similar goddesses of fate, and of death, as we shall see—these ideas being very often identified.

In Norse mythology the Norns are of the giants' race, a fact that makes them independent of both the gods and humankind. The connections with the Greek and Roman trinities of fate—the Moirai and the Parcae, respectively—are certainly of great interest, notwithstanding the uniquely Germanic cast provided for them in Eddic mythology.

In Roman mythology the Parcae were the offspring of Nox (Night) and Erebus (Hell). Erebus was the son of Chaos (and darkness); Nox (also a daughter of Chaos) was the mother not only of the Hesperides, Dreams, and Discord, but also of Death. We should note that that while Roman mythology more or less directly links Chaos with Darkness, Germanic mythology took a far more positive view of darkness, which was by no means always linked with negative or demonic aspects of life. The names of these Roman deities were Clotho, Lachesis, and Atropos; all three names are supposed to signify the roles played by each in allotting man's fate. The youngest, Clotho, was said to preside over the moment of a man's birth, and this function is attested in other mythologies, including the Germanic. It would seem that there are Norns—though not necessarily those goddesses of fate who sustain Yggdrasill—who assist in childbirth. Another example comes from the legends of the Saamis where there are said to be three such helpers—Sarakka, Juksakka, and Uksakka.[1] Indeed, the generic term "Parcae" is said to be etymologically related to *parta*—from whence comes the word "parturition," childbirth. While it is Clotho's task to preside over birth, it is for Lachesis (who was the Fortune-goddess) to spin out the events of a man's life; and finally, it is for Atropos to cut the thread of life with scissors. This function is disputed in some versions of the myth by Proserpine (just as in Greek legend Aphrodite usurps the role of spinning). Saxo translates Hel (or Death) as Proserpine in his version of the Germanic narrative. The Parcae's link with death is clear, just as is the case with the Norns. They are seen sometimes as ministers of the King of Hell—Erebus—and clothed in robes spangled with stars. This would suggest a direct connection between the Fates and cosmology, though more often their mode of dress is consonant with their precise functions. They were generally represented as three old women, with chaplets made of wool, interwoven with narcissus flowers, over which they would wear a white robe. Clotho sometimes appears in a variegated robe, wearing upon her head a crown of seven stars. Lachesis's robe also had a great number of stars, and near her were placed a variety of spindles. It is Clotho, however, who holds the distaff, shown sometimes as reaching from earth to heaven. Atropos would be clothed in black, holding scissors and threads of different sizes, according to the length of men's lives. The Parcae were also known as "secretaries of heaven," and "keepers of the archives of eternity."

The Alexandrian Hyginus, a librarian of the Palatine, produced a mythological history, wherein he attributes to the Greek Fates the invention of the first five letters of the alphabet. This is an interesting conceit in this context, since it introduces a link that will be affirmed throughout what follows, viz. that between fate and *words* (truth), rather than fate and time. The Latin forms *fatum, fata*—"that which is spoken" (from *fari* = speak)—appear to be etymologically related to the Greek Moirai.[2] Few doubt that the Parcae were modeled on the Moirai, and in this way we can see that at a fundamental mythical level, fate is associated with words both written and spoken, an idea that would seem to be very ancient indeed. In the Babylonian *Enuma Elish*—the "Epic of Creation"—for example, the very first lines link the period of prehistory with a time when things were not yet named—a time "When yet no gods were manifest,/Nor names pronounced, nor destinies decreed,/Then gods were born within them. Lahmu [and] Lahamu emerged, their names pronounced."And so just as it is in the mythically profound activity of naming that the world comes into being, so is it that fate, written as we have seen on the Tablet of Destinies, "is fetched and took and presented . . . for a first reading to Anu."[3] Related to this is the fact that within all mythologies there is an intimate connection between *speech* and *magic*. As noted above, as far back as ancient Egypt the hieroglyph for "spell" was a mouth—where the word for the former was "*rw.*" In Germanic culture *weaving fate* was always achieved with the assistance of runes, since weaving itself always seemed somehow magically associated with runes. The common juxtaposition of women, weaving, and fate is given further depth by M. J. Enright, who points out that some women may have been rune-masters: runes have been found inscribed on an early Germanic loom fragment from the sixth century.[4]

Why are there, or why did there become, just three Norns, three Parcae, three Moirai? The obvious answer is that three is a magic number for many ancient cultures, and, in any case, apart from its magical significance it could represent an indefinite "many," just as nine may have done for Germanic culture.[5] This is self-evidently true only for the "primary" Norns, but since there were other Norns in the cosmogony (the birth-helpers, for example), and since the number of Norns is not always given, it seems possible that every man had his own Norn (at birth, at least), making their number indefinitely large. However, it is clear that, according to de Vries, they clearly *became* just three.[6]

We have already given renderings of the names of the Norns as simply past, present, and future. Some offer Fate, Being, and Necessity.[7] What is striking about this from the point of view presented here is that *purely* temporal concepts have been replaced by two logical, *non-temporal* (or supratemporal) concepts—Fate and Necessity—and one temporal concept, Being. It would therefore be impossible to map two out of these three categories onto the past, present, and future of the former without either loss of meaning or confusion. In order to make better sense of the mythology and the etymology, philosophical coherence has been sacrificed. In this recasting of the names, the *past* has become fate—*not* the future. This is exactly where it belongs, though I fear that this has been too often overlooked—an exception being Bauschatz, who seems to find his way to the correct conclusion, only to more or less ignore it when he gets there.[8]

Bauschatz points out that the basic idea of *verda* contains an element that means "turning," which he thinks probably involves change of location in space. From thence its meaning develops logically from "turn"—from one position to another—into "turn into," and thence into "become." Leaving on one side for the moment how it was that turn qua change of *spatial* orientation had mysteriously become a *temporal* notion, Bauschatz says that in this way "Verthandi" and "Urth" are semantically related, and that Verthandi becomes that which is "in the process of becoming" (whatever that means) and Urth is that which has become.[9] He adds that "as Skuld is involved with necessity or obligatory action, she stands slightly apart from the other two. She seems to make reference to actions felt as obliged or known to occur, i.e., the necessity of their 'becoming' is strongly felt or clearly known that they present themselves as available to be incorporated into the realms of Verthandi or Urth."[10] But since necessity is a logical concept, that which is necessary is *already*—logically—"with Verthandi or Urth."[11] Bauschatz seems to understand this implicitly when he insists, quite correctly, that the essential difference between the classical tradition of the Moirai and the Parcae on the one hand, and the Germanic tradition on the other, is that the former stress predestination, while the latter does not. "Moira" emphasizes the working out of the present into the future; *wurd* stresses "primarily" the working out of the past into the present. Having reached the only acceptable philosophical conclusion—"neither the Moirai, nor the Parcae, nor the Norns, were basically concerned with the concept of a temporal separation of the past from the present, or the present from the future"—Bauschatz balks at stating the obvious conclusion, viz. that time ≠ fate. Instead, he concludes that the Germanic tradition emphasizes "the essential unity of past, present, and future," which is simply obscure. It seems quite clear that Bauschatz has implicity understood: a) that fate has nothing (logically) to do with the future; and b) that fate ≠ time, when he insists that *if* the Norns had to do with predestination, then it would be *Skuld,* not Urth, who would be the primary focus for talk of fate in all the Norse sources. But as he indicates, although she is named in *Voluspa* stanza 20, and again in 30, she is not mentioned again throughout Norse mythology. This would be utterly incomprehensible if the essence of fate were *future events*. What happens in the future is preordained *in the past*. This is why Urth is referred to again and again, why as *wyrd* she becomes central to subsequent—even post-Christian—mythologies and beliefs. It is from Urth's Well that the Norns draw the water nourishing Yggdrasill.[12] The well is named for Urth (Urðr)—her name represents the past, which embraces the actions of all beings who exist within the world ash-tree's branches. "Like the water, these actions find their way back into the collecting source; as this happens, all actions become known, fixed, accomplished. In one sense, it is these actions which form the strata which are daily laid in the well by the speaking of the *ørlog*." It is in this way that for Germanic mythology the power of destiny (*wurd*) appears as the "woof" of the Norns—the "weavers of fate"—and as primal law, *ørlog*—that which is laid down from the first upon men.[13]

It is possible to defend within Germanic mythology two views that seem at first sight to be so diametrically opposed that one wonders how both views could have been proposed using what is, after all, precisely the same evidence. On one side there is the affirmation, noted previously, that for the Germanic races there was no fatalism; on the other side there is a profound and persevering preoccupation with the all-encompassing power of fate as personified by the Norns. This universal power was both personal and impersonal, as well as being inescapable and having such hegemony as to embrace even the gods themselves. Sometimes attempts are made to reconcile these positions by insisting that an acceptance of fate, a resignation in the face of it, does not require the checking of human activity *inside* the limits that fate has decreed for a man. Within such limits, man can strive to bring about the greatest possible realization of his faculties. This consciousness of an all-embracing fate somehow leaves room for pride, dignity, and defiance, rather than an encouragement to supine submissiveness; a pride demanding that one not be oppressed even by the knowledge of what fate must already have decided—hubris, in fact. In Lithuanian mythology, a man's fate may be expressed through a verb as something he is to do or suffer, which would imply more than simply acceding to fate and, just like the Norse version, allows a man a certain freedom of will (or at least the illusion of it), making us somehow active participants *with* fate in the unfolding of our lives.[14] Living within such an apparent contradiction can be regarded as one of the achievements of the Germanic concept of the heroic consciousness, where a man's life was understood as being determined from first to last by an *unfolding lawfulness,* inside which an individual had his being. The commanding figure of Oðin would oversee and govern the lives of heroes at least, even though he was himself subject to fate and could not change it.[15]

There was of course one event that Oðin could foresee but not prevent—the destined threat to the order maintained by the gods that, like the destined death of each individual, was bound to come. Because the gods act only *within* time, and although they can foresee what will happen (that is, they know *that* such-and-such will occur) they are powerless to prevent it, since the truth cannot be changed. The nontemporal reality of the truths laid down by the Norns cannot be altered by the temporal (cause-and-effect) activities of the gods. They were thus partly deterministic, partly stoic in the face of disaster. If we live under an immutable fate, no supplication can change its decisions; it is useless to ask the oracles to reveal the secrets of a future that nothing can change, and prayers are thus, in the words of Seneca, "nothing but the solace of diseased minds."[16] However, this assumes a consistency between different layers of paganism that may never have existed. Certainly so far as *wurt*, *wyrd*, etc., were concerned, the Germanic pagans seem to have believed *both* in fate *and* in a certain degree of free choice—an ambiguity evident, still, after the conversion, at least in England, where *wyrd* was named in Alfred's translation of Boethius as the only force other than God whose power is acknowledged.[17] It is also fair to say that in most paganisms the acknowledgment of the role of fatalism was at its most prominent from the function given to astrology, which as a method of divination seems not to have existed to any noticeable extent within Germanic paganism. The extent to which the Germanic peoples tried to avoid or escape fate was nowhere near as developed as in other ancient cultures, even where fate was seen as just as powerful a force. In ancient Egypt, for example, where the goddess of fate was also the goddess of luck (thereby providing, in some respects, a much more modern reduction of fate to mere happenstance), there existed hundreds of magical rituals devised in order to try to escape fate; fate—and luck—were beings standing between gods and men, limiting the lives of the latter.

Given the absolute centrality of the concept of fate within Germanic mythology, it seems to be considered somewhat unfashionable to focus too much of one's attention upon it. In recent years, certainly, it is as if for mythologists and literary scholars alike, fate could be treated as though it could be reduced to descriptions of its various manifestations, with no residual philosophical or conceptual problems remaining to be dealt with. Perhaps just because these scholarly approaches are not primarily philosophical, the subject of fate is rarely tackled head-on as a complex conceptual issue of interest in its own right. For anyone only moderately familiar with the vast literature in Old Norse studies this might seem an unfair comment. At first sight, bibliographies would seem to contain a number of volumes dedicated to *Schicksalsglaube,* but we should note that by far the majority of these were published in German within a relatively narrow span of years. This in itself deserves comment. It certainly appears that a trend was established during the 1930s in which some (often implied) connection was made between the rising German consciousness and the ancient Teutonic conception of fate. This is not to say that any of these scholarly works were somehow designed to contribute to any such trend, but the statistics for such studies during that period do clearly suggest an interest in the subject that possibly reaches beyond any narrow scholarly domain of Old Norse and "Germanistik."

Ake Ström mentions the fact that during the 1930s there was, on average, one work a year on this precise subject—all with rather similar titles that included the word "*Schicksalsglaube,*" which with only two exceptions were in German, including titles from such scholars as von Hamel, Baetke, Naumann, Ninck, and Gehl. Strikingly, he points out that after that time, there was almost "complete silence" on the subject until 1955, when two treatises appeared (again in German) by Mittner, and Neumann.[18] It seems that either by design or more mysteriously, the ancient Germanic concept of fate assumed associations with German totalitarianism that were not easily shaken off. It is difficult to know for certain how such a connection was perceived or understood, since there is little or nothing in the mythical concept that would establish such a link with any definiteness. The banalization of the very idea of Destiny (cf. epithets of both Napoleon and Hitler, as Men of Destiny), tells us little or nothing of how men confronted fate in ancient times, and impinges not very much more securely on any natural connection than does the routine association of images of a fascist rally with the final bars of *Götterdämmerung*.[19]

In translating "*ørlog*" as "those things laid down," we may overlook an important element in the word's etymology, for the prefix "*or-*" signifies something that is beyond the commonplace. The prefix is found in all Germanic languages: there is Gothic *us-, ur-;* Old High German (and Modern German) *ur-;* Old Saxon *ur-;* and so on.[20] The primary meaning was the Gothic *urrunus*—("exit"), and Old Norse *orfar*—(departure, "outgoing"). Bauschatz says that the relationship of this prefix "outer" is exemplified by Grimm, who connects it with the Sanskrit *ud—hinauf, hinaus*. It suggests something of primary or originary significance, without, however, giving any indication of the scale on which this might be measured, giving to it an amorphous quality of something beyond. *Ørlog* is thus primal law, highest law—originary law from which all else is derived. It is those things "laid down" that are of the highest significance. Once again Bauschatz comes to what seems to be the correct solution, so often overlooked—namely, that since to speak of the *ørlog* meant to take account of everything that happens with respect to all that has happened already, the Norns—in speaking it—speak of *what has been,* of what is known. This is not predestination as it is normally understood and which is, as we noted, largely absent from Germanic mythology. Bauschatz goes on to say that it was in the Judeo-Christian tradition that predestination became irrevocably linked to fate, because fate "implies teleology."[21] This does not take into account sufficiently the fact that fate would come to be seen as in competition with the Christian theodicy, and therefore had to be absorbed into it. The "teleology" of God's purposes would contradict fate as that which was already laid down: either it could be overcome (and was thereby no longer the all-powerful force that Germanic paganism had taken it to be), or it was a direct competitor to God's own putative omniscience and omnipotence. We see now the significance of these lines from the *Voluspa:*

> To the coast then came,   kind and mighty,
> from the gathered gods   three great Æsir;
> on the land they found,   of little strength,
> Ask and Embla,   unfated yet.[22]

Normally translated "fate-less" (in Christian "teleological" terms "purposeless,"or "without a future"), *ørloglausa* really implies that, as found, the two trees, lacking sentience, breath, spirit, etc., *are not yet subject to law.* It is true that as yet they have no future, but only because, without *ørlog,* they really have no past. It is not so much that their future is open, but that it is empty, and would remain so without their becoming a part of the woof and weft of the world as created by the Norns.

In examining the meaning and significance of the Norn's *ørlog* as that which is laid down from the first, we naturally emphasize an abstract, quasilegalistic aspect of fate as having to do with laws—laws that cannot be breached, not even by the gods. But Norse mythology has more graphic and picturesque ways of describing the activity of the Norns, ways that are found in so many cultures as expressions for these same ideas that we are bound to ask once again whether such commonality is a manifestation of some universal impulse of human consciousness, or whether, indeed, linguistic and mythological diffusion from a shared ancestor might not be the most plausible account of such similarities. We are concerned, in other words, with a number of images of fate relating the activities of spinning, weaving, and also binding. The apparently unrelated but equally widespread metaphor for fate of "measuring" and "casting lots" will be considered later.

The Norns spin out man's fate, but in addition they also weave and bind. We shall require all three images for a full understanding of the Norse conception. The gods themselves are frequently referred to as "those who bind," but they too are subject to the fetters of the Norns; in this respect as in others, the parallels with earlier mythologies are striking. In Homer, several apparently different conceptions of fate coexist and usages frequently overlap. And since men become responsible for their actions leading to either their welfare or their undoing, fatalism in the full-blooded sense of predetermination cannot really be said to be a component part of the Homeric picture of the world. Nonetheless, the spinning metaphor occurs several times in Homer. In Hellenic mythology generally the gods—Zeus, especially—spin and bind fate; and once made, this allotment to man had to be respected. Indeed, it was almost taken as a moral sanction to do so. Allotting was like promising—once done, one must stand by its strictures, and not even Zeus could play fast and loose with it. Yet it is not that it is sanctioned by some still more powerful deity. In this respect it differs from the Norse example, where the gods are not moral, even in such a limited sense; any such sanction is removed, and located instead with the independent power of fate. In Homer the gods clearly clash with fate, just as in Norse mythology, although some classical scholars have attempted to reinterpret the various concepts of destiny found there in order to reconcile them.[23]

The "binding" process of the Greek gods upon men is their preferred mode of imposing fate upon mortals, and according to R. B. Onians was less of a metaphor than a true religious belief. It was, he thinks, almost a literal description, not some "trick of language." Fortune in its many forms was seen as a cord, or bond, or fetter, fastened upon a man by higher powers. The etymology of αναγκη, usually translated "necessity" is, says Onians, uncertain, but a connection with αγχειν, "to strangle," has been suggested, relating directly to the idea of a binding cord. We say that something is bound to happen, or that what one must do one is bound to do. Coming to this image from the other direction, we see that the Latin *expedit*—"it profits," "is advantageous"—had an original meaning of "it unfetters." And a man under an obligation for debt in Roman Law was described as bound—*nexus;* while property held subject to any such legal obligation was described as *"nexum."* When paid, such a debt was said to have been loosed—*luo, salvo.* A doomed man was *fatis debitus*— bound. In Hindu culture, also, a debt was a bond, just as we say in English "my word is my bond," where I bind myself, fetter myself— in other words, obligate myself.[24] This expression rather neatly offers the idea of someone taking it upon himself to connect *speaking* with *obligating* in a way that is a distant echo of the more doom-laden link between the speech of the Norns, and what *must* happen as a result of it.[25]

The Norse gods are referred to several times by a collective term meaning "bonds" or "fetters," viz. *bönd, höpt.* Such binding became a part of religious ritual. Tacitus says of the Semnones that their antiquity is confirmed by a religious observance involving reverence for a sacred grove, into which no man could enter "unless he is bound with a cord, by which he acknowledges his own inferiority and the power of the deity."[26] Oðin, as a sacrificial god, shamanistically hanging himself from the world ash-tree, is profoundly involved with the symbolism of fetters. "The solemn, religious bonds of the god upon his whole people, appear in Norse as a terrifying, capricious war-trick masterminded by a god infamous for his treachery, deceptions, and military favouritism. The bonds of *religio* have here become the bonds of pursuing fate, personified by the god of war."[27]

It seems probable that this binding, in the form of cords and fetters, was thought of as the *effect* of the spinning of fate (whether by the gods, as in Greek mythology, or the Norns) and was regarded as fate being fastened onto or ensnaring man. There was a positive, beneficial counterpart of the fetter in the cord-amulet, which magically brought *good* fortune—and, indeed, in popular thinking continues to do so. The belief that good fortune could be said to be "bound about one" has been offered as the explanation for the old proverbial saying, "Ungirt, unblest"; one can also be bound by love or good fortune, which Onians suggests as the origin for the bestowing of certain wreaths or crowns.[28]

Bauschatz was quoted above as saying that "fate implies teleology," and certainly τελος was not simply an abstract expression for "end" but connoted something quite concrete. And as such, it was the form under which some aspects of an individual's fortune might be visualized. Τελος may originally have meant "band," and relates to themes of turning, spinning, and so on. It was also the limit of ploughland—it was that place in which one could turn round. Thus with this root meaning of "turning around" τελος came to mean circle or circling. If τελος meant "circle," then when used of fortune, while visually conceived as a band around a man, it represented a portion of time and was experienced as a process or event by the individual upon whom it was placed: "It was the fate spun."[29]

This binding process can be seen as both literal and figurative. "The wrapping about the head of the death god with which he wraps or lends to others is related to that which enwraps a man at death much as the band of the love-goddess, which she also lends, is related to the band which she binds with love the ordinary mortal."[30] The custom found in many cultures of covering the head in burial or death has its counterpart in the Norse custom in which the eyes and nostrils were closed. A closely related image is the winding-sheet wrapped around a man. With this, a man is clothed with whatsoever quality he is seeking—energy, strength, courage, etc.[31]

The most widespread images for the activities of the goddesses of fate are those of spinning and weaving; these are the metaphors that we find employed again and again. The expression "the gods spun" is used by Homer on several occasions, as has already been noted. In those times spinning was mostly done while sitting, the tools required being a basket and a spindle. Since there was no distaff to support it, the unspun wool would apparently be retained in a basket situated to the spinner's left. Some of the wool would be taken up by the left hand and with the spindle attached would then be spun by the right hand, either over the knees or hanging down past the right knee. For this spinning of men's fate Homer uses επικλωθειν, (a property of the Fates who spun the thread of destiny), but also επινειν. From this is formed επινητρον, an instrument placed on the knee to help manipulate the wool. (I say that spinning was mostly done while sitting, yet there are sixth-century Attic vases showing women spinning while standing—and indeed using a distaff). Onians says that it is only with this precise image in mind that we are in a position to grasp Homer's famous expression for fate, in that "it lies on the knees of the gods." That the knees played a part in the spinning process is therefore quite clear. From the knees of Lachesis are taken "lots" and βιων παραδειγματα. Such lots merely determine the order in which the souls choose. The βιων παραδειγματα, on the other hand, are in effect the μοιραι, the portions that are spun, "the destinies which man must experience."[32] According to Onians, this is confirmed in a passage "hitherto neglected" by scholars in this description from Plato of the structure of the universe: "And from these ends hangs the spindle of Necessity, which causes all the orbits to revolve; its shaft and its hooks are of adamant, and its whorl a mixture of adamant and other substances."[33] The Μοιρα, the "portion" or fate of each soul about to be born is validated by the spinning of the Fates. For Plato the fate that "lay on the knees of the gods" was what was spun, from which expression presumably is derived also the more commonly used "in the lap of the gods," meaning as much mere chance as fate itself. There are fascinating connections between this classical imagery and a number of Northern European designs on bracteates from the sixth century. According to M. J. Enright, the associations in bracteate ornamentation between the activity of weaving and staff-bearing explain the peculiar names of some early Germanic women who were at the same time prophetesses, for example, *Ganna,* from Germanic *Gand-no, which may be compared to Old Norse *gandr,* meaning a magical staff. The author also mentions the figure of *Balouburg,* who was a prophetess of the Semnones; her name incorporates the word for staff from the Gothic, *walus,* and Old Norse *volr.* In all such cases, "the staff of the prophetess copied the weaver's beam of the goddess she represented."[34] This iconographical similarity in bracteates with such images of weaving women has sometimes been attributed to a Mediterranean influence on the Northern peoples. Enright disputes this, since he is convinced that the pictured objects are indeed weaving implements—weaver's "beams," handheld objects with crosslike bars on the top used to retain the yarn—and not crosses in a Christian sense. And since these bracteates were discovered in what are clearly cultic sites, he concludes that the most appropriate context for the weaving connection seems to lie "in a widespread Indo-European religious conception, and not in the field of Germanic alone." Thus the portrait of Mary the Weaver is not to be understood as the inspiration for the images in these objects, "nor were they 'Christian' or used as substitutes for pagan concepts."[35] It should also noted (referring to the discussion above) that there are quite clearly stars in these images, possibly linked with the activities of spinning and weaving as was the case in Homer, reiterated in Plato.

Several themes raised earlier seem to coalesce in such imagery. Certainly many scholars have noticed the persistence of the idea, from a wide range of mythologies, that life is somehow a thread that is cut upon death (modified into contemporary idioms such as life "hanging by a thread"), and we have seen one of the three Parcae, and one of the three Norns, provided with just such a precise function. It remains useful to maintain the distinction, as far as is possible, between the idea of fate as *spun*, and the idea of fate as *woven*. They will offer to us different images, different conceptions, of how the gods or the Norns prosecuted their role as allotters of man's fate. In the East the imagery is just as frequently of weaving as of spinning. In Egypt, for example, the same word—*msn*—could signify either activity. In Lithuanian myth, the spinning and weaving functions are, in effect, merged into the complex but unified idea of seven goddesses. Here, the first spins; the second draws out the yarn; the third weaves; the fourth casts a spell over the weave through her song, and thereby destroys it, causing ill-fortune for the men to whom it concerns; the fifth attempts to protect this "weft of life,"; the sixth cuts it through; while the task of the seventh is to purify it and deliver it up to god. And from this material a shroud or dress is made for the dead, which enables them to survey their past life from the other world.[36]

Does this spinning of the thread of life—of fate—have any connection to the movement of the stars and constellations? For Homer the stars had nothing to do with fate and were not brought into any relation with the gods. Yet the idea of being born under a "lucky" star is no doubt very ancient. And the spinning wheel as such can be a metaphor for the year. For Lithuanian myth, the spinning image binds one to a new star that, "under the force of necessity," is then to be observed in the sky on the birth of a new child. When the hour of death approaches, the thread is cut, and the star falls, extinguished in the sky—and the man dies. Such an ending of a man's life, its apparent arbitrariness, reflects the *span* of life (a word that itself maintains the connection between measurement and spinning, as in Old English *spann, spinnan*), that is, the length of material cut short at one point by fate. The span, or thread of life, is an image running through most mythologies, and usually maps onto the general conception of life as having been woven in the past, where it is then allotted, only to be cut at its end.[37]

Perhaps because it is such a pervasive image, and has therefore come to be seen as self-evidently appropriate, the question is rarely asked just why these activities of spinning and weaving seem to be so serviceable in expressing conceptions of the operation of fate on mankind. After all, it cannot be merely their artisanal function within a society that marks these tasks out as so singularly apposite. Making bread, making pots, making fire, even the act of birth itself, seem barely less critically foundational for a culture than these two—although the image of the divine potter, at least, may already have been used up, so to speak, in some mythologies: the Egyptian, for instance, where the god Khnum (or sometimes Ptah) is seated at the potter's wheel engaged in the act of creating mankind. Yet since so many mythologies employ such imagery, we might postulate here a true cultural universal, engaging some profound (and probably, by now, inexplicable) human impulse to associate just these tasks with the actions of fate. It is difficult to disagree with Onians when he writes that "the wealth of legend that seems to have grown up around the belief that fate was spun would seem to make mockery of any attempt to regard it as a mere figure of speech."[38] Of course the discovery of a mythography somewhere that employed the concept of fate in similar ways but did not have spinning and/or weaving—and had not simply dispensed with these qua metaphors in favor of something deemed still more appropriate—would provide an unequivocal Popperian refutation to such a conjecture. It is interesting to note in this regard that of all the most common implements in daily use employed within the Egyptian system of signs, whether as phonograms, ideograms, or determinatives, *none* is of a loom—although the spindle is found, and so, importantly is cloth.[39] It is fair to say that no such concept of fate *as spun* is found in Egyptian religion or mythology.

One answer to this question, at least in relation to spinning, has been offered in the fact that spinning yarn involves *turning*, and that it is the connection with turning that provides so many further resonances, not least in the perceived phenomenal relationship of spinning whorls attached to spindles and the revolution of the heavens. The etymological relationships that are involved are certainly highly suggestive. The word *"wurd"* is an abstraction from an Indo-Germanic root *"drehen,"* which itself means "to turn," and from the same root comes Middle High German *Wirtel,* and hence *Spinnwirtel*—images that survive in a Christian context in Alfred's translation of Boethius, where the dominant image that Alfred employs in the Old English text to describe the relation that man has to *wyrd* is the image of the wheel. The "wheel of Wyrd" circles the axle that is God.[40] While much of this would appear to account for the image of the Norns as spinning out a man's fate, some scholars argue that the original Germanic concept of fate was not that of spinning, but of weaving, and the bracteate images noted already connecting fate, prophetesses, and weaving seem to confirm this to some degree. But focusing on fate as woven rather than spun still cannot resolve any residual puzzlement as to the reasons this activity should seem so appropriate an image for fate. But there is something further. If it is indeed weaving, not spinning, that is the originary image, we no longer have the immediate, direct (and, it has to be said, natural) link between fate and turning, and hence fate and *time*. For spinning something out then demands an additional activity—for the whole purpose of spinning is to provide the raw material for weaving. Although the latter presupposes—both in fact and mythically—the former, the only reason to spin is to make it possible to weave. Weaving is therefore a much better metaphor for a man's life *as constructed as a totality by the Norns* than spinning would be. Of course the Norns spin, and bind, and also weave. *Njal's Saga* provides vivid images of both the first and last:

> A wide warp
> warns of slaughter;
> blood rains
> from the beam's cloud.
>
> A spear-grey fabric
> is being spun,
> which the friends
> of Randver's slayer
> will fill out
> with a red weft.
>
> The warp is woven
> with warriors' guts,
> and heavily weighted
> with the heads of men.
> Spears serve as heddle rods,
> spattered with blood;
> iron-bound is the shed rod,
> and arrows are the pin beaters;
> we will beat with swords
> our battle web.[41]

A net, a web, can entrap a man in obvious ways not open to the idea of fate as merely spun—though perhaps the totality of the concept requires both, just as did the Norns. Iranian mythology expresses it concisely: "[Even] the world-destroying lion and dragon cannot free themselves from the net of fate."[42] Nets entrap, but, analogously, cords *bind*—and fetters may be single strands (hence "spun") as well as woven webs. The Middle Egyptian word *sht,* meaning "to plait" or "to weave," contains the sign not for a loom, but for a snare or bird trap. The Greeks conceived of riddles—or word-traps—as woven rush baskets, and the beautifully crafted knots of Celtic (and Scandinavian) artifacts were likewise seen as traps for demons.

What all of this suggests is that whatever reason human consciousness has for using these activities in these contexts, somehow both of them are required for a comprehensive modeling of the ideas involved. Fate is spun, but *actualized* only in the weaving stage. We have already noted that weaving has invariably been seen within Germanic mythology as magically associated with runes; weaving fate is made possible with the help of runes.[43] Weaving is a widespread metaphor for creative work, more generally—unlike spinning, which tends to be employed more often for the lower end of creativity, reflected in such idioms as "spinning a yarn" for telling a story. All the names of the goddesses of fate in Lithuanian mythology have their linguistic roots in the verb *Lemti,* meaning "to declare" or "to pronounce" (as in the *ørlog*—to make a law by speaking it). This was knowledge that characterized Laima (the unified goddess of fate) *as* a goddess. The relationship between words, weaving, and creativity is made by many cultures that attribute cosmogonic powers to the word. The idea that "In the beginning was the Word" is certainly not limited to St. John's Gospel. Edward Casey tells us that "the Dogon of Mali . . . conceive of creation as a process of word weaving. . . . The word is the sound of the block and the shuttle. The name of the block means 'creaking of the word.' Everybody understands what is meant by 'the word' in that connection. It is interwoven with threads: it fills the interstices of the fabric."[44] The ancients also speak of the sounding or singing of the shuttle or warp threads. Loom and lyre were closely associated (being, among other things, almost a visual pun—the Greeks and Romans using vertical looms almost exclusively). And in one of the Anglo-Saxon "Loom Riddles" the word for fate—*gesceapo*—is given by the author as the "harmless ways" of the shuttle: "Its fate is ruled by one that stands by the way," which means that the ways, or "fate," of the shuttle are ruled by the web, or by the warp threads that "stand" by its way. We have here also a charming link with the tree qua fate, in that in another such loom riddle—"There was a tree close to where the bright creature stood/and it was covered with leaves" this does not denote a real tree, but according to Erika von Erhardt-Siebold, "may very well be the loom." This tree is the distaff with wool on it—"the plucking of the flax from the distaff suggests a leafy tree whose foliage goes into the making of the web."[45]

The most striking image of the Norns in action, so to speak, relates directly to the loom metaphor. It is that just referred to, where, in *Njal's Saga,* the web created was suspended with human heads as weights. Each warp thread represented a human life. But what of the woof, bound around each such thread: what did this represent? It was Onians's opinion that it would be quite natural to interpret these as the various phases of fortune that are any man's lot while he lives, and of which the last is death. This "woof of war" of the Norse gods represents one phase of a man's life as fraught with the supreme power of fate. "Upon it [the loom] has been stretched a warp of human-beings, a warp grey with spears, which the valkyries are filling with a weft of crimson . . . valkyries who are elsewhere said to 'bind' the doomed warriors."[46] The Valkyries—the Norns of the Battle—after deciding the fate of the armies, prepare fetters for the side they do not favor. One of these is named *Hlokk*—"chain"—and another *Herfjötur*—"war-fetters," a name that appears as the name of a Valkyrie in *Grimnismal.* These fetters paralyze and prevent escape. The Germanic death goddesses drag away the dead with a rope (just as does the Iranian death-demon and the Hindu god Yama), and are also provided with cord and net.[47]

There remains one further image describing the activity of the Norns (and other such figures) that is sufficiently widespread to demand our attention. This is yet another idea with both temporal and nontemporal characteristics, even though there would be sufficient reason in what follows to believe that this metaphor's rather abstract nature sits more conformably with the latter than the former. This is the idea of fate as an allotment, share, or portion, drawing attention to the quantity of life (if the expression can be allowed) somehow made over to the individual at birth, which can neither be gainsaid nor changed by any man during his lifetime, no matter what the nature of his actions.

Apart from the fate as spun image, Homer employed another expression for fate meaning "it is ordained," or "it has been apportioned." This idea of the goddess of fate allotting everyone their share is common to the personified Moirai of the Greeks, and the Lithuanian's Laima, among others. Even where fate has other names and functions, such as binding, spinning, or weaving, most mythologies also find room for this locution of a man's lot or portion, often simply as a way of differentiating men from the gods. We see this, for example, in Akkadian mythology, where the god's possession of the Tablet of Destinies means that they are able to assign finitude to man. It is this concept of fate that has retained its place within modern English, since the word "kismet" derives from the Arabic *"kismah,"* meaning share or portion—in this case that share attributed to man by God.

It should be clear that it is the Greek Moirai with which the most transparent connections can be made with Germanic mythology, since we have already noted the likelihood that, notwithstanding the probable existence of an indigenous concept of fate within Germanic heathenism, the subsequent influence of the Parcae (and hence the Moirai upon whom the former were clearly modeled) was sufficiently strong to give us reasons for attributing Moira's "allotting" significance to the Norns also. Yet if the concept of Moira qua fate was indeed developed from that of Moira qua share, what can we say that this share amounted to—what did it consist in? Usually, we see this most readily as man's share of *life,* his life span, but interestingly some inscriptions suggest, on the contrary, that this share was of death—in other words, that which is truly common to all men. It is at the moment of death that a man's Moira has been completed—better, that it has been fulfilled. And so we have the idea of Moira as both life *and* death. As death, Moira destroys everyone; yet she stands also for life, for the duration of life. Such expressions as these suggest the idea of Moira as somehow representing the span of life until she takes her subject in death.[48] As we have seen, some mythologies separate these functions in a psychologically satisfactory manner, and how far these two functions of Moira can plausibly coexist is not entirely clear, for one of them would seem to be redundant. If, like the Norns—who *lay down* (ørlog) or, in effect, plot (in the sense of a graph) a man's fate—the Moirai do this, then each man's death is already (implicitly) decided; "bringing death" is not so much a separate function, as a playing-out, a fulfilment, of the other function. The Greek Moira thus has more than a single task—as a deity, she is the agent who brings death; yet she also stands for death, and as an impersonal power decides it. Since human fate is, on such views, the work of the gods, the casting of lots cannot be seen as merely the acceptance of a decision that occurs in a literal sense as mere chance. More plausibly, the outcome of such an activity was accepted as being under the control of higher powers who simply reveal their will to men in such a fashion.

Whatever conclusions one might draw from the evidence adduced so far as to the nature of fate as accepted by the Germanic pagans, it would seem not a little curious to deny that they were, in broad terms, fatalistic in their outlook on the world. Such, however, is the complexity of this subject that it is in fact possible to find examples of quite contrary views founded upon the same source material. While most authorities would probably agree with, for example, Timmer's judgment that "there can hardly be any doubt that the outlook on life of the Germanic peoples was fatalistic," we can find another scholar, Van den Toorn, insisting that there is *no* fatalism in those races.[49] We have drawn attention already to that somewhat uncomfortable ambivalence that entered into discussions of Germanic *Schicksalsglaube,* particularly during the 1930s, such that destiny seemed to become (for a time and for some scholars) synonymous with war. This sense of discomfort is deepened when we read Hans Günther, who widens the issue still more in his insistence that it was "the spiritual strength of the Indo-Europeans to feel a deep joy in destiny," in a tension between the limitation of man and the boundedness of the gods, and it occasions no surprise that this is then related to what Nietzsche called *amor fati.* And yet Günther is one of those scholars who insist that this "joy in destiny" did *not* turn into an acceptance of fate. This particular view of destiny is, we should note, quite independent of fatalism as that is often understood, referring instead to "ultimate and hard reality," from an awareness of which Indo-European religiosity originates "to rise Godwards."[50] It is, however, plausible for less grandiose reasons to think of the heroic in much of Germanic literature as having been inspired by confrontations with destiny, and indeed that this confrontation is the *ver sacrum* of the hero's spiritual existence. It is plausible enough, in addition, to see any such hero—particularly as characterized in the Icelandic sagas—as one who "loftily understands the fate meeting him as his destiny, remains upright in the midst of it, and is thus true to himself," while Günther cites Erik Therman as finding "a mocking defiance in the face of destiny . . . despite recognition of its supreme power" as characteristic of the Edda.[51]

A. G. van Hamel was another scholar ready to repudiate the idea that the ancient Norsemen were fatalists. According to him, there was only one "absolute" fatality—and that was death itself.[52] In an everyday sense this was no doubt true—at least for most men most of the time—but probably not for the reasons that van Hamel gives. He insists that belief in gods *precludes* fatalism, which is a very odd position to take, especially in the Norse context, where even the gods themselves were subject to fate. The Norsemen were more likely to stop believing in gods than in fate, since fate was more powerful. And this is just what occurred. Belief in fate crosses over into Christianity, while the old gods were abandoned. And so it seems clear that belief in gods could not, per se, "preclude" fatalism, when the gods themselves must yield to it. Rydberg considered this naive: the relationship of the gods to fate—"a question which seemed to the Greeks and Romans dangerous to meddle with and well-nigh impossible to dispose of"—was "solved" by Germanic mythology by dividing the matter of life and death between divinity and fate.[53]

We must now meddle with fatalism; disposing of it will prove more difficult than even the Greeks and Romans imagined.

5
The Logic of Fatalism

> The readiness is all. Since no man of aught he
> leaves knows, what is't to leave betimes? Let be.
> —Hamlet

THROUGHOUT THIS DISCUSSION, NOTWITHSTANDING THE OCCASIONAL counterintuitive suggestion that the link between fate and time should be cut, we have considered fate and fatalism as if these concepts are not only unambiguous in themselves, but also philosophically unexceptional, for all their multifarious expressions and manifestations within Germanic and other mythologies to which attention has been drawn. This impression must now be corrected to a significant extent by looking more closely at just what may be meant philosophically, and logically, by the acceptance of fatalism. Some radical philosophical positions have often been seen—particularly by non-philosophers—as merely excuses for argument, as exemplars for the classroom, mere thought experiments rather than real views held by real people that somehow impinged upon their lives. The thesis of solipsism, for instance, sometimes appears in such a light: the belief that only oneself exists, or that at best one can never have sound, logical reasons for believing that anyone other than oneself exists, has that clear cast of the straw man, of an argument constructed exclusively for the purposes of philosophical debate. Fatalism is not such a doctrine. We have good reasons, as we have seen, to accept that fatalism has been accepted as true by many—if not most—ancient cultures at some time in their history. Of course, one would no doubt like to add that no one *now* is a fatalist. We all cherish the "indisputable" fact of our freedom of will, our freedom of action, and believe implicitly that the future is open and created each second, each day, by every one of us. We control our destiny; which, in effect, means that there is no such thing as destiny, at least so far as the ancients understood it. It is interesting that we have never managed to quite shake off this precise way of speaking. It seems, after all, that destiny is still real to us; it is just that it is now in our hands and is not controlled by some outside power. If fate were a completely fraudulent and psychologically vacuous idea, one wonders why we have not found other ways of expressing it by now (or *not* expressing it, since as a category it is supposed to be empty) apart from this shift of control of destiny away from something outside of us—through the Norns, or whatever personification happens to suit us—to ourselves. The explanation for this resilience of language is, one supposes, that it is now merely a metaphor, a pale one at that, and of course we do not believe a word of it any more.

Yet are we so certain that fatalism has indeed been either thoroughly discredited or is altogether absent from our contemporary attitudes? One twentieth-century survey (from Sweden) produced some rather surprising results. More than half of those questioned believed in chance, and 30 percent believed in fate; 35 percent believed that what is to happen, happens; 26 percent believed in the efficacy of mascots; and 26 percent in "nemesis."[1] Yet the fact that fate and fatalism continue to haunt the popular imagination cannot, we are sure, alter the fact that these concepts are redundant and discredited. What is interesting is that the impersonal concept of fate that seems in the Germanic case at least to have preceded its personification, has returned to our consciousness of ourselves in the form of the overwhelming belief in the hegemony of the workings of science, both in an abstract deterministic sense (based upon the invariability of physical law and, in particular, on universal causality); and in a more concrete sense through the astonishing redescription of human possibilities expressed through such as the human genome project. An intimate knowledge of the science involved may not support it, but it remains a fact that determinism (if not fatalism) has once again become a topic for intelligent debate and profound questioning. Other things being equal, we can once again ask whether individual human beings are programmed from the start to be certain things, to behave in certain ways—even to die at a certain time—all as a result of the functioning of a genetic code that is expressed and played out in the behaviors of us all. Of course, things are never equal in this fashion: and the indefinitely large number of variables involved in shaping the blueprint of a life will modify genetic expressiveness in a million ways. Yet in spite of the caveats, one can sensibly wonder how much of what one does is due in a fundamental sense to a completely open choice, rather than the effect of some rigid, laid-down, prior causal sequence over which we never did have any control. We are not talking of a scientific theory here, but of a human response to one—a response that has made many less certain of their sense of absolute freedom. The Newtonian universe had seemed to reduce everything to the ultimately predictable motion of particles, each one obeying the immutable laws of mechanics. The world of quantum physics on the other hand, seemed to have given us back randomness, probability, and unpredictability. And now it is as if genetics has thrown us backward again, onto the past—our past, as it was laid down at the moment of our conception, as a plan that must unfold.

What is more directly relevant to the themes of this book is the fact that the doctrine of fatalism has not received its logical coup de grâce, and that in terms of its philosophical merits, it retains a compelling interest. It has not been so discredited that it has quite disappeared as a focus of serious debate. Centrally significant to this discussion is that it can be prosecuted quite independently either of theology, or even of the science that seems to have fueled a resurgence in the terminology, at least, of fatalism. This is an issue in *logic,* and *of* logic; its importance is therefore directed to the core of what has gone before. Logic is timeless (notwithstanding that there are formal systems known as tense logics) and so if fatalism is found to have logical validity, we will have found supplementary corroboration for the view, arrived at here for quite other reasons, that insists that fate is not a function of time. However, since this book is not a logical treatise—nor, strictly, an essay in metaphysics—and since its purpose is to restore some sense of balance into an argument that has to a very great extent managed to pass by default, the following explanation will be restricted to putting the positive case for fatalism without any pretensions that full justice is being done to what are highly complex philosophical arguments. Such arguments would demand forays into various systems of formal logic of little interest to most readers of this book.[2]

Let us state the thesis as starkly as possible. Fatalism says that whatever occurs is unavoidable and always was unavoidable. That is the very simplest expression of the belief. It means that neither you nor I nor anyone else can change what is going to happen tomorrow, or in a fortnight, or in a hundred years. What happens is not up to you, and it is not up to me. What fatalism as a *logical* thesis does not claim is as important to this discussion as what it does. For fatalism is not a doctrine that pretends to *know* what is going to happen—which is the

5: THE LOGIC OF FATALISM

reason that divination (in spite of its invariable association with fatalism in cultures that cleave to the latter) does not impinge upon it. It is a doctrine that regards the future more or less as the rest of us regard the past—that is, *sub specie æternitatis*.[3] Indeed, it is in this difference between our attitude to the past as seeming to be in sharp contrast to our attitude to the future that leads us to think of some (at least) of the latter as possibilities, while no one would describe the former in such a way. It should not be assumed that this is reducible to a matter merely of language. It is in fact more than this: it is a matter of epistemology, and—in its implications—of psychology. For example, we happen to know more about what the past contains than about what is contained in the future, and also, our memory is as a matter of definition of things past: we cannot have a memory of something that has not yet occurred. And thus the question of fatalism, as the philosopher Richard Taylor sees it, is just this: of all the things that occur in the world, which ones, if any, are avoidable? For the logical fatalist, the answer is simple—*none of them*: "They never were. Some of them only seemed so."[4]

In order to proceed with his defense of fatalism, Taylor provides his own thought experiment in the form of a parable, which is so very much to the point here that I make no apologies for presenting it here as an extended summary. The story proceeds as follows. God (an omniscient, omnipotent kind of being) reveals to a scribe a collection of facts, which the scribe writes down in full, believing (correctly) that they have come from God. The facts described turn out to be episodes in the life of an ordinary man by the name of Osmo. These statements about the life of Osmo were chronologically ordered into a book, "The Life of Osmo."[5] The book finds its way into a modern library where, one day, it is discovered—by a man named Osmo. Upon initial perusal of the book (he was, of course, attracted to read it by the title), Osmo is thunderstruck to read in it that the birth date, place of birth, mother's name, early years, etc., coincided exactly with those events of his own life. On close (and by now, transfixed) reading, Osmo discovers that for every single event in his life there is an account in the book placed in precise, unerring, chronological sequence. His astonishment increases to stupefaction when he finds accounts of events in the life of the Osmo of the book that had occurred in his own life but a week before. Yet this book was clearly of great age, dust-covered, and had not been opened in years, if at all. He even reaches an account describing *that very day*—the day when Osmo finds a book in the library called "The Life of Osmo," etc. The narrative ends on a dismal note, in which Osmo's life comes to a ghastly conclusion in an airplane accident. There, of course, the book ends.[6]

A number of obvious avoidance strategies then quite naturally occur to Osmo—we pass over here the likely psychological consequences for a person of any such discovery—his doubts (quickly removed thanks to the absolute accuracy of the text), his terror, nervous amusement, etc. In his desire to ensure that one thing about the book at least turn out to be false—namely, his tragic end, he determines to simply refuse to board that particular airplane (the details of it, of course, being in the book). Then, under such circumstances, he reasons, even given that everything else about the book was chillingly and unerringly accurate, this most awful event, at least, could be sidestepped.

Notwithstanding this somewhat desperate but understandable ploy to change the course of events as a result of his experience reading the book, Osmo became a fatalist. He embraced the doctrine for the following completely logical reasons. He had discovered that there were in existence a set of true statements about his life, past, present, and future, and he had come to know what many of these statements were. He came to believe them—including many that concerned his future. It was not that he had come to believe that certain things would occur *no matter what*. As Taylor says, he did not come to believe that he would die in an airplane crash even in case he never again boarded an airplane. That would have been completely nonsensical. "The expression 'no matter what' by means of which some philosophers have sought an easy and even childish refutation of fatalism, is accordingly highly inappropriate in any description of the fatalist conviction."[7] Osmo became a fatalist with the acknowledgment that the events described in the book were unavoidable. The logical validity of fatalism is guaranteed by the fact that there existed a set of true statements about this man's life, past, present, and future. It was not the fact of their being written down that made them, as such, unavoidable, nor the fact that he had come to both read them and believe them. Their unavoidability was assured by the very fact that there *existed* such a set of statements, whether read by anyone or not, and whether or not known to be true. All that is needed for fatalism to be true, is that *these statements should be true*. It was precisely this that was held to be the case when the Norns were spinning and weaving a man's fate. The Norns did not expect that any one man would come to read these statements, let alone that he should somehow come to believe them. The fate that was spun for a man was the *truth* about that man, and this was all that mattered. Each of us has one and only one possible past, which is described by that totality of statements about us in the past tense, each one of which happens to be true. The sum of such statements is an individual's biography, a part of which has already been lived. "Osmo's biography was all expressed in the present tense because all that mattered was that the things referred to were real events: *it did not matter to what part of time they belonged.*" The fundamental presupposition of fatalism is simply that there is such a thing as truth, and that "*this has nothing at all to do with the passage of time.*" While it is absolutely true that a prediction must await fulfillment, it does not thereby for the first time acquire its truth.[8]

Taylor's parable concludes thus: "About three years later our hero, having boarded a flight for St. Paul, went berserk when the pilot announced that they were going to land at Fort Wayne instead [where the book indicated that Osmo had died]. According to one of the stewardesses, he tried to hijack the aircraft and divert it to another airfield. The Civil Aeronautics Board cited the resulting disruptions as contributing to the crash that followed as the plane tried to land."[9]

Taylor's argument rests, ultimately, not on theology, or science, or on the supposed truth of theories of divination. It rests instead on a fundamental law of logic, namely, the law of excluded middle. This law—the cornerstone of logic (and reason) since Aristotle—says that every meaningful proposition is either true, or if not true, then false. There is no middle category. As Taylor says, such a principle "leaves no handy peg between these two [truth and falsity] on which one may hang his beloved freedom of the will for safekeeping, *nor does it say anything about time.*"[10] Attempted refutations of fatalism are one and all predicated on the assumption that we are all of us completely free to realize alternative futures for ourselves, and yet *that* is the very point that is at issue. "Metaphysics and logic are weak indeed in the face of an opinion nourished by invincible pride, and most men would sooner lose their very souls than be divested of that dignity which they imagine rests upon their freedom of will."[11]

All of this is highly pertinent to our theme, for we have noted more than once that for our Germanic ancestors, it was the belief in the power of fate that generated just that dignity that we seem (today) to feel is available to us only through a fundamental and contrary belief in the freedom of the will. But belief in fate did not encourage resignation or passivity—indeed, almost the contrary is the case. Nor should we think that the thesis of fatalism is nothing but some logical or semantic piece of trickery. What is clear from Taylor's argument—and from those such as Steven Cahn who have also been prepared to confront it as a serious philosophical problem, rather than dismissing it without argument—is that a great deal of the confusion surrounding the fatalist thesis arises as a consequence of approaching it as if it were purely an epistemological problem when, as we have seen, it is at root a *logical* issue, with its related concerns about what it would make sense to say is really within a man's power. Fatalism says that the only actions which are within anyone's power to perform are those actions which he does, in fact, perform. Free will is an illusion. Steven Cahn agrees with Taylor in saying that the fatalist thesis implies that if a man thinks logically, then he must regard the future as most of us now regard the past. We *can* only do those things that we will, as a matter of fact, do—and what we will do is not up to us.[12] If it is fated that a certain man M will fight with another man, P at three o'clock, then it is fated that P will not leave town before three o'clock when the fight will take place. It is not of course *logically* impossible for P to leave town, for there must be many actions that are logically possible and yet not within anyone's power to actually perform. The fatalist does not—be it noted—say that our actions make no difference to anything: what the fatalist says is that they are *fated* to make a difference. What this means is that no one can prevent their making a difference—not that they make no difference.[13] None of this denies—indeed, it emphasizes—that there is a deep philosophical problem about so-called future facts, but what is philosophically perplexing is not their futurity, but their factuality. So-called three-valued logics have been constructed precisely in order to avoid fatalism, as in the system developed by the Polish logician Lukasiewicz, who says that unless one allows that statements about the future are regarded as not yet true or false, one will indeed be committed to the fatalist thesis.[14] The existence of tense-logic was noted above, and there are two quite different versions of such systems. There is that version put forward by the philosopher and logician W. V. Quine, in which he treats time as the fourth dimension of space for the purposes of formalization—temporal parts being treated on a par with spatial parts. A. N. Prior's alternative approach is, interestingly, Newtonian, where objects are described as occupying space and enduring through time.[15] But Susan Haack insists on a need to distinguish the importance of the expressive power of logic from the question of its doctrinal content. She writes that it is one thing to attempt to modify a logic's formalism in order that it can express arguments apposite to contemporary physics (Quine's strategy), but that it is quite another (as we have already noted) to give up a supposed law of logic *because of* developments in science. The aim of any formalization is to generalize, simplify, and increase rigor. But as Haack correctly indicates, this means that it is neither to be expected nor desired that any such formalization would be able to validly represent informal judgments of various kinds. Any such idealization disconnects that formalization from the material of experience that is its subject matter. "Rather, pre-systematic judgments of validity will supply data for the construction of a formal logic, but lead to discrepancies between informal arguments and their formal representation, and even in some cases perhaps to a reassessment of intuitive judgments."[16] It is worth remarking here that it is the intuitive judgments that Haack thinks would need to be reassessed, *not* the logic—confirming one of Taylor's points rather neatly.

What should be sufficiently clear from these considerations is that attempts to repudiate the kinds of arguments put forward by philosophers like Taylor (and also Cahn, who comes at the problem from a different direction, while conceding from the outset the compelling nature of Taylor's thesis) will have profound implications for our understanding of both logic and time. Cahn acknowledges that the only coherent way to undercut fatalism is indeed to deny the universal validity of the law of excluded middle: a solution that would be regarded by most philosophers as very much a Pyrrhic victory. In applying any of this to the picture we have painted of fate as understood centuries ago, we have to concede that it makes little sense to wonder how the "laws of logic" might have impacted on the religious and mythical beliefs of ancient cultures to which reference has been made throughout this discussion. We have seen that it can make sense to identify and isolate a logic of myth, whereby we concede that the law of noncontradiction might already have been breached through the acceptance of what (to us) are clearly mutually incompatible states of affairs within a cosmogony or cosmography. It would be completely implausible to claim that, in any conscious fashion, there was in addition the acknowledgment of the kinds of arguments for fatalism that Taylor, for one, provides. That would be extravagant, yet we can be just as sure that the logic of fatalism—its unavoidability—was accepted in a relatively sophisticated way. And it has been mentioned already that there were features of meaning that could be coherently expressed in, for example, Middle Egyptian that cannot be easily expressed in our languages—features that speak of complex ways of seeing the world very different from our own, such that even formal logic might struggle to accommodate them within the available symbolism.

I have incorporated these somewhat arcane philosophical considerations in order to identify a contemporary case for the plausibility (at least) of an ancient and widespread belief. Primarily, these logical considerations direct our attention to the idea that belief in fate is *coherent,* notwithstanding the obvious fact that none of these kinds of arguments could ever have entered the minds of anyone within those cultures for whom the concept of an all-embracing fate played such a significant role. This is not to say that there is any logical, or indeed psychological, impossibility in the idea that it could have been grasped in these ways, *mutatis mutandis.* But in the absence of anything that we would recognize as logical evidence, we must inevitably fall back on what we think we can say about the intuitions had by such people—intuitions expressed through the decidedly nonlogical vehicle of mythology. Yet giving attention to these contemporary discussions within philosophical logic does more than just lend plausibility to a thesis that has been so often discredited or contemptuously dismissed. More important still for the thesis of this book, it throws into sharp relief the admittedly counterintuitive idea that fate is most coherently to be regarded as a *supra*temporal concept and that, unlike the case of the purely logical analysis that supports this position, this aspect of the idea of fate is, as we have seen, by no means foreign to a number of ways in which the ancient cultures represented and expressed it.

By offering arguments that are primarily logical, Taylor was able to stand apart from any suggestion that fatalism must be linked to theories of divination. Indeed, one of the great merits of his argument is that this putative connection is transparently seen to be of psychological value only. It is undoubtedly true that a number of other (nonphilosophical) analyses of fate often have recourse to considerations concerning the internal validity of various means of divining the future, in order to support their case. The practice of divination within a culture would certainly seem to offer corroboration for a firm belief in fatalism for that culture. The future probably could not be thought to be divined if it had not already been planned. Yet we have seen above that, from a philosophical perspective, divination is quite beside the point, primarily because what can be known about the future (or even the past) does not touch the essence of the fatalist doctrine. For this is a doctrine about *truth,* not knowledge. It should be remembered that so far as divination is concerned (and this is equally true of astrology, which seems on all fours with other forms of divination in this respect at least), if something should fail to occur that has been divined, the strategy used to avoid embarrassment on the part of the diviner is invariably the same from one case to another, and that is, that one somehow lacks complete knowledge of the situation, or, in modern terminology, that the initial conditions were not fully known. We should remind ourselves also of Spengler's observation that the classical Oracle and also the Sibyl, like the Etruscan-Roman *haruspices* and *augurs,* did not foretell any distant future, but restricted their prophecies to a particular question having immediate bearing: indeed, the Oracle was always consulted for the individual case.[17] In any case, one could make perfectly good sense of the opposite idea, namely that both fate and predestination are actually incompatible with divination, insofar as the latter is seen as some kind of exercise in magic. From his Christian perspective, Augustine held that the use of oracles involved the use of demons— oracular cults thus being (simply) the worship of false gods. As Rosalie Wax has pointed out, magic can function "only in an environment where the gods or other powers [in this case, fate] are sensitive to sanctions, where they can be moved, impressed, bribed, or even threatened, by the prayers, repentance, good deeds, and sacrifices of men. . . . If the supreme power is conceived of as impersonal and immutable, magic of any variety becomes a futility."[18] The point is well taken and, given the widespread use of cultic acts (including sacrifices), the wearing of amulets, etc., it raises the issue of the relationship between magic and fate in Germania. It may have been just this kind of impotence in relation to an all-encompassing sense of fate that provided the impulse for fate's eventual personification—to its embodiment into a figure to whom such magic could be channeled and directed. Nonetheless, it seems to be as clear as anything can be in this context that the Germanic peoples continued to believe in the inescapability of fate. All cultures, at all times, have attempted to propitiate their gods, and yet it seems highly doubtful if, even on their own terms, such magical propitiation ever appeared to be wholly successful. There was a view that seems to have lodged in the minds of men that there existed a clear need to placate the gods, while simultaneously acknowledging its practical futility. Yet perhaps this is not, after all, really so very much worse, from a logical point of view, from that of contemporary man being confronted with a need to choose between either the truth of fatalism or the abandonment of a cherished belief in free will and—what is much more serious (at least for philosophers)—a resiling from the universal validity of the principle of excluded middle.

It is often argued that the possibility of divination simply presupposes predetermination. Jack Lawson, for example, suggests that while divination seems to imply that everything that happens is preordained, nothing is *necessarily unavoidable*. He thinks that fate—in this case, the Mesopotamian concept of *Simtu*—is, or was believed to be, somehow "conditional" upon whether one avails oneself of magic, through auguries, portents, and so on.[19] This curious idea of a "conditional fate" was a doctrine held by the Middle Platonists, who believed that if one decided on *A* as a course of action, then *X* must follow; while if one chose *B*, then *Y* must follow—the "must" here implying logical necessity. Such a strategy was considered to preserve the reality of fate, while still allowing for freedom of the will, thereby preserving moral responsibility.[20] We have seen from Taylor's analysis that in his opinion (and also that of Steven Cahn) what fate has decreed is indeed necessarily unavoidable. It is certainly true that for the popular imagination at least, the future may be, *per impossibile*, both fixed *and* avoidable, since it seems sometimes that a good two-thirds of contemporary science-fiction trades routinely on just such an idea. Interestingly, for just such fictional genres, the past would seem to be both fixed and *unavoidable*, an idea that has generated a sort of filmic mantra wherein some character or other must at all costs avoid changing the so-called time-line (or some such thing) for fear of changing the present. Taylor argues that logically we should treat the future just like the past: what is *true* is true (whether past or future) and is so whether we have knowledge of it or not.

We are now ready to examine more closely that idea of fate that is absolutely fundamental for any comprehensive understanding of Germanic paganism and the cosmogony associated with it, through the various cognate terms *Urðr* and *wurt/wyrd*. Its significance for this discussion, and what leads us to return to it again and again, is the fact that in an important sense it survived the transition from paganism into Christianity—not unchanged, certainly, but it is in those very changes that we can discover what was significant for the newly converted pagans, as well as for the early Christians. We are also in a position to doubt one view of *wyrd* that Bauschatz (who in several other respects, as we have noted, touches on the fundamental revisions we have been attempting) describes, in his insistence that, essentially, "man's time and *wyrd*'s time are . . . the same."[21] Clearly, we cannot ascribe to this, since we have suggested time and again that *wyrd* is not strictly a temporal concept at all; *a fortiori,* man's time cannot be identified with it. For Bauschatz, to say that man's time is *part of wyrd's* time is to say that it is not significantly different from cosmic time. It begins to seem unlikely that there is any plausibility in the idea that cosmic time played any important role within Germanic culture, if by that term is meant some abstraction, some absolute framework into which all events—mythical and nonmythical—are supposed to have unique temporal locations. What we see instead is a network of events with unique cross-referenced relationships; that event A is related (causally or otherwise) to event B is more important than that A occurs at some measurable temporal distance from B, and we have already insisted that Germanic time is more genealogical than it is strictly chronological.

We can be confident that *wyrd* and God—the Christian God—were seen as ethical opposites. This partly corroborates our view that *wurt/wyrd* was a *supratemporal* concept, for few would have argued at this time that God was temporal, or that God's time and man's time are fundamentally the same. And since *wyrd* had to be recast as providence in order no longer to threaten Christianity with any residual paganism, it must have been regarded as just such a supratemporal concept as was God's providence itself. Incidentally, for the limited purpose of understanding fate within Germanic paganism it does not matter, ultimately, whether God and *wyrd* had become ethical opposites, or whether (as has been argued) that they were, at root, identical. It is true that in the absence of unequivocally heathen poetry in the Anglo-Saxon period, the word *wyrd* might already have been Christianized, making it as plausible to adhere to the word's mythological meaning as to regard it as having been by that time fatally weakened, making the whole question "more a matter of conjecture than decision."[22] The reason that it does not matter, for this argument, whether God and *wyrd* are or became identified or were ethical opposites, is that either alternative makes the case that they were by implication equally nontemporal concepts. The Christian god was certainly regarded as nontemporal, from Augustine to Aquinas and beyond to the present, at least for Catholic if not Protestant theology. Thus "God" could not have been the ethical opposite of *wyrd* if the latter operated temporally and God was beyond time. And so if God and *wyrd* were even merely *conceived* as identical in this limited respect, they could not (logically) belong to commensurate temporal modalities.

However, this is to anticipate the discussion of the final chapter. We must at this point look at those very numerous and detailed attempts to grasp the meaning of "*Urðr*" for times less ambiguously pagan. We have frequently placed great emphasis on the past, rather than the future, for any fleshing-out of the Germanic idea of fate. But could this really make sense of "*Urðr*" in its most general, but often most powerful meaning, viz., as a foreboding of death? This impersonal notion—this *Todesschicksal*—which is often nothing more nor less than a synonym for death, is unlike the personal goddess of Norse mythology. Mittner says that the image of *Urðr* as found in the *Voluspa* is absent from West Germanic, where it is just a reference to something sacred—a word, which as such speaks only of something hardly to be spoken of at all, something "frightening and dangerous." Urd is the first and most important of the Norns. In Anglo-Saxon, *wyrd* was "ein unberechenbares, dem Menschen kalt gegenüberstehendes, *fast wesenloses Wesen* ist."[23]

Linguistically, *Wurd*—as "*wyrd*"—seems to have surfaced as a neutral term, meaning "event," or "state of affairs." This would subsequently become "*fateful* happening," and then simply "fate," before the term's personification was completed in the figure of the goddess of fate. In von Kienle's exhaustive survey of the word and its cognates, she says that the roots of "*Urðr*" are less clear than those of "*Wurd*." She points out that Grimm takes it to mean "the past," while Mogk says that Old Norse "*Urðr*" had nothing to do with the past, and instead meant "*Geschick*" in a quite general sense. Grimm goes on to place the word with Middle High German *wirt, wirtel,* meaning "*Spindelring.*" Although the roots *wurt* and *wirtel* come from the same original German **uerp,* von Kienle thinks that it is unlikely that *Wurt* meant "spinner"—and the Norns, she says, were always weavers, and not spinners—which was a view that she attributes to later folk mythology. In drawing attention to a number of such supposed derivations, von Kienle insists that none of these are plausible expressions for the past as such, "demnach muß man also für *wurt* eine Grundbedeutung 'das Werden, das Geschehen' annehmen, und *es als völlig zeitlos fassen.*"[24] *Wurt* is thus, in Old High German, the abstract, impersonal concept found in glosses translating Latin *fatum,* and sometimes *fortuna,* and *eventus.* The Anglo-Saxon *wyrd*—fate, doom, death—carries both abstract and personal connotations. In Anglo-Saxon poetry, the personification is quite common, where Fate is sometimes young, sometimes old.[25]

Yet is not the intimate connection between *wurt/Wyrd* and *werden*—"to become"—sufficient evidence in itself for a dynamic, and hence primarily temporal, concept of fate? Not really. We have not denied any sense that the Germanic concept might involve causal sequences, or that change was not accidental. Everything that "became" did so under "*werden*" as an unfolding necessity: what is, must be—"Muss so wird, muss so werden."

The idea that fate is actualized or realized is one thing; the idea that fate can in any way be altered is quite another, as we have remarked. It is certainly difficult to agree with the view sometimes expressed that *wurd* is some kind of ongoing force, changing the world as it goes along; logically, there is no separate "along" that is not already touched by fate. The world *is* the way it is—irrevocably and unavoidably so—and is not *changed* as Fate turns, but actualized. There is no world somehow set up and in motion, like some clockwork mechanism, with which fate can now and again tinker. The tinkering of fate is the world as it unfolds and is witnessed. Of course, human perceptions of this process, being inside time, see only this unfolding—indeed, see it *as* an unfolding.

It may very well be the case that it was *wurd*'s hostile, destructive power, which in the Germanic tradition held in it little that was truly life-enhancing, that contributed both to its perseverance into Christian times and its being refashioned as Providence. It was the ultimate certainty of destruction, the unavoidability of death, which contrasted so sharply with the Christian promise of renewal and everlasting life—notwithstanding the final stanzas of *Voluspa* which may, as we have remarked, have been shaped by Christianization. The idea of *wyrd* as a blindly ruling fate disappeared, eventually; the inevitability of the events of a man's fate remained but, as expressed through *wyrd,* was made subject to God. The all-consuming, unavoidable dictates of the goddess of death became almost domesticated; one could now enter into a relationship with one's fate through God's grace. *Wyrd* could mean "that which happens to a man," or the events of his life or his lot—just as Taylor says it should. No pagan associations need attach to such an idea. Even when the meaning is clearly negative and refers to a man's adverse lot, what this seems to express is that man should not struggle against his lot, because whether it is good or bad, it is ordained by God's providence. The domesticated version of *wyrd* thus equates to nothing much more threatening than life itself, "life" in general. Against this, it was no longer human heroism that was demanded for some kind of redemption, but submission to the will of God.[26]

All of this attests to the view that the authentically pagan mythical value and power of *wyrd* had been sloughed-off so far as the Anglo-

Saxons of the early Christian period were concerned. It was this that made it possible for *wyrd* to pass from paganism into Christianity, forming a bridge from one to the other. Curiously, therefore, it may be that belief in *wyrd*—belief, that is, in the unalterability of events and in the quintessential transitoriness of human life—was that which made the conversion easier: Christianity offered another chance, even beyond death.

This idea—that the remedy belongs not to this life, but to the next—can be found expressed in verses from the tenth to eleventh-century *Exeter Book*. A man must "abide" his *wyrd* in order to flourish. For example, examining three poems—"Judgment Day 1," "Resignation A," and "Resignation B"—Karma Lochrie identifies a common theme: these verses represent three different approaches to the concern with *wyrd* on mankind and—in very un-Germanic fashion—are "penitentially directed."[27] These three poems offer a theme on the inability of an individual to grasp the workings of *wyrd* in everyday life, and the human endeavor to live a meaningful existence when confronted by that very incomprehensibility. We are of course, in this context, talking of "God's *wyrd*," which cannot be frustrated or prevented. *Wyrd* frustrates all of our plans, and the individual must simply endure the "burning flame" that must, in the end, consume the whole of creation. And yet fate *can* be affected by thinking wisely in the present. "Resignation B" concludes with a pledge to maintain stoic resignation in the face of the inscrutable workings of *wyrd*. "Yet is it best when man cannot himself/change *wyrd*, that he then endure it well." Here, *wyrd* refers to the speaker's suffering and misery, which cannot be in any way avoided, while in "Judgment Day 1" *wyrd* denotes the final conflagration and Last Judgment. The lesson, however, is the same: one must not try to change, nor to appeal, one's fate. Instead, one must—in almost Buddhist fashion—"think well" so as to endure it. "Judgment Day 1" concerns *wyrd* only insofar as it affects the future judgment of mankind through the Word of God. For man, in the here-and-now, *wyrd* is simply a baffling force *which is bearing down on the present and turning it into the future.* Man's judgment will ultimately be determined by his capacity to recognize this movement of *wyrd*, and to anticipate the confrontation between present and future that *wyrd* constantly generates. The only appropriate response to *wyrd*'s workings is "prudence." This is expressed in the poem as a dislocation of man's thoughts from the present, to the future. "Like Job [in Job 14: 7–10] the speaker of "Resignation B" recognizes that *wyrd* means a process of regeneration for nature; it means punishment and death. If man is to receive his remedy, he must set his thoughts on God and develop prudence."[28]

We will see in the final chapter that accommodating fate and an omniscient Christian God raises further philosophical and linguistic questions that were regarded as crucial for the conversion of the pagan Germans to a new faith. One resolution of some at least of these difficulties was anticipated by Diogenes Lærtius, when he identified God—or Zeus, or Reason—with Fate. And for the Stoics, the active principle in the world could be taken variously as Fire, Breath, Nature, Reason, Law, God—and Fate. The cosmos is assumed to come into being by means of a process that is rational and that manifests the creative power of fire: this will eventually end in a cosmic conflagration that only Zeus will survive and, as in the Norse Ragnarok, from that point a new cycle of creation will begin.[29] And since the events in this process are all connected through causation in an endless chain, they must all occur through fate. Such a connection of every detail of the universe, past, present, and future, provides a "bond of sympathy" between all parts of the cosmos. Together with the providence of Zeus, this is sufficient foundation for the Stoic belief in the possibility of foretelling events through divination: "What must be, must be. But man, by his insight, may will to do what must be done, and so may act in harmony with nature." Alternatively—like the heroes of the sagas—he may resist. But it will make no difference, for it is not within man's power to overturn fate.[30]

Human acts in the face of fate are very much what the sagas focus upon, where an atmosphere of inevitable doom seems to cast a shadow over the main characters. The inescapability of fate, central to Norse theodicy, is that against which acts of bravery are set: the outcome of a battle, the moment of death, are fated to occur when they do occur. Yet the heart of the warrior remains independent of fate, and his bravery enables him to face death rejoicing in the fame that is certain to survive him.

> Well we have fought   and felled many Goths,
> stand on athelings slain   like eagles on tree;
> glorious we die,   whether today or tomorrow:
> lives till night no man   when the norns have spoken.[31]

6
From Pagan Fate to Christian Providence

> There's nothing serious in mortality: All is but toys.
> —Macbeth

IT WAS STATED IN THE FIRST CHAPTER THAT FOR SOME SCHOLARS PAGANism is capable of description only negatively, that is, as whatever someone believed before they became Christian (or Muslim, or Jew). Paganism, on such an interpretation, was regarded not so much as the name for a set of beliefs, but as a post-facto Christian designation for a vast range of cult practices followed by various cultures all over ancient Europe before the coming of Christianity.[1] To say with such confidence that there was no such thing as paganism per se is simply too strong, even though it might be seen to follow from the negative definition given. Although it has to be conceded that there was no unified system of beliefs *from* which pagans were converted, it does not follow from this that there could not have been beliefs held by some societies to which it would be convenient and appropriate (even if not historically accurate) to give the name paganism. A much more fruitful, though still broadly negative manner of approaching this problem is offered by Richard Fletcher, when he writes that if we were to ask ourselves the question, "What were the Germanic kings [for example] converted *from?*" we would be reduced to the admission that we know little about it, "and never will." Fletcher is quite correct in saying that this situation is due in no small part to the fact that Germanic paganism was "diligently obliterated" by its Christian successor. This obliteration was simple enough to achieve so far as any written records were concerned, given the virtual monopoly of the Christian church over literacy, with the result that what heathen literary memories remained did so almost by oversight.[2] There is thus an irony in the fact that so many of the most tantalizing glimpses of these beliefs should come down to us channeled through the conduit of Christian writers, who were to some extent (we can assume) reconstructing that pagan past. Yet if we do indeed know so little about these beliefs we cannot, a fortiori, know that they had none and observed only rituals, performed, so it is insisted, in the absence of beliefs. It seems to me that the primary justification for this frequently offered contrast between Christianity and paganism lies in the fact that we are able to interrogate the former but not the latter, which in turn justifes one way of describing that contrast (which is typical of all of them, insofar as this general idea is adhered to) as consisting in the fact that while "Christianity is not merely the performance of outward relgious observance, but [is] first and foremost the profession of belief," paganism, by contrast, consists primarily in "certain religious functions." In other words, it was a "*kultus.*" The real belief of the people (in Iceland, specifically, in this case) was a "*heimatru,*" or home belief, made up of all manner of folklore and superstition. That "merely" in the citation above is a small word, but a philosophically corrosive one, since it slyly begs all of the interesting questions vis-à-vis paganism qua belief-system.[3]

Before we turn to that sequence of events and undermining of beliefs that was to issue in the triumph of Christianity over Germanic paganism, it will be instructive to consider the process of conversion elsewhere, and even the psychological nature of conversion as such—for there are likely to be commonalities in any such process no matter where this has occurred, although particularly so when the conversion is from some variety of polytheism to monotheism. One such instructive example has already been alluded to briefly in the case of Roman paganism, where the conversion was to an alternative form of paganism. What is of special interest here is that it demonstrates that one set of *beliefs* was replaced by another. If paganism was always and everywhere merely the observance of cult rituals in the complete absence of belief, it is difficult to see how this could have been described as conversion or understood as such. The philosopher William James, in his classic work on religious experience, discusses conversion *only* as being a phenomenon relating one *Christian* experience to another, as if that were all that the idea of "conversion" can properly signify. Indeed, James insists that even that form of conversion is fundamentally a "normal adolescent phenomenon, incidental to the passage from the child's small universe to the wider intellectual and spiritual life of maturity."[4] One would not, I suppose, need to look far for examples of scholars willing to treat all ancient heathens as children, spiritually speaking; but all the same, such a view as this is too patronizing to be acceptable. It is better to see something more positive in James's view of conversion as involving the perception of truths not previously known or understood, and also in his useful distinction of two types of conversion—the volitional or gradual type, where piece by piece a new set of spiritual habits are constructed, and that other form of conversion regarded by James as "the vital turning-point of the religious life," viz. conversion by "self-surrender."[5] Yet whatever we think of the relevance of this analysis to the ancient Germanic case, it seems to me that by denying the category of belief to pagans, not only do we diminish their own religion, but we also narrow the process of conversion itself to the near-whimsical choice of one meaningless cult observance over another.

Rather than accept such dismissals of paganism as mere cult, it is more profitable to start from a different assumption, namely, that the spiritual experiences of men are the psychological roots of both paganism *and* Christianity, and that even so-called cult practices may in all likelihood have at their core what Otto Höfler calls "seelisch-geistig-numinosen Ursprungs."[6] And we can agree with Fletcher that we can be confident of this much at least, that the diversity of pre-Christian cults with which the early church was confronted "shared a core of what sociologists of religion like to call 'empirical religiosity'—the belief that proper cult brings tangible reward in this world and the next."[7] The cult was man's active relationship with his gods, and seems in principle to be not significantly different qua beliefs from the drinking of wine presumed to be blood, or the eating of bread as flesh, as in the Christian sacraments. We are not dealing with, on the one hand, *merely* childish superstition and, on the other hand, with a coherent and unambiguously rational belief system, antiseptically free of the cultic and the ritualistic. To start always from any such assumption is philosophically inept—and patronizing to boot. And as Fletcher says, "patronizing the past never helped anyone to understand it."[8]

In his book on Roman paganism, the classical scholar Franz Cumont states that "it is hardly necessary to state that a great religious conquest can be explained only on moral grounds." He goes much further, insisting that "whatever part must be ascribed to the instinct of imitation and the contagion of example, in the last analysis we are always face to face with a series of individual conversions."[9] Now this is really rather an extraordinary claim. If this were true, even if only in the context of Roman paganism, it would present to us the most striking possible contrast to everything we know or have speculated about in the Germanic example. It may at first seem that this is confirmation of what has been emphasized above in relation to belief within paganism, in that *if* beliefs are always (or often) involved in ritual practices as a presupposition, then given the logical and more particularly the psychological nature of such belief, every conversion must, as Cumont says, somehow involve a psychological "crisis"—"a transformation of the intimate personality of the individual." This view contrasts with the greatest sharpness with the view held much more generally, that behind every conversion one suspects, rather, political interests, and "la contrainte ou la vénalité."[10] It is of course possible that it is only in the case of Roman paganism that this psychological crisis is evidently the cause of an embracing of Oriental religions, but it seems unlikely that the Roman experience would have been so different from the Germanic as to demand explanation by means of some diametrically opposite considerations in the latter case. For example, consider the claim that "the Christian religion touched every chord of sensibility and satisfied the thirst for religious emotion that the austere Germanic creed had been unable to quench. But at the same time they satisfied the intellect more fully."[11] Would any such claim seem compelling from what we know of Germanic paganism? The reader has been misled, but for a purpose. That quotation is indeed taken from Cumont, except that "Oriental" has been replaced by "Christian," and "Roman" by "Germanic." The point is that it does *not* seem especially inappropriate, yet we certainly have little or no evidence in its favor. Would an early Christian have regarded Germanic paganism as "austere," with its apparent proliferation of gods, rituals, and cults? The idea of austerity in a religious context has a certain lability, and it may imply not the number of deified beings but a *spiritual* limitation, a narrowness of vision that would permit gods (plural), who were just as subject to the powers of fate as mankind itself. And it is perhaps the concept of fate as such that we can plausibly say was austere within Germanic religion, even though it was a manly duty to rail against it. There is a recognizable pattern here; the Stoic acceptance of fate, which in and of itself produced a strong religious impulse, produced a belief that the more powerful gods—Serapis and Isis, for example—might abrogate the decrees of destiny, and this may have been one of the primary reasons for the appeal of the Egyptian deities to Greece and Rome. In the Germanic example, it is as if the Christian God could relieve them of the relentless burden of confronting fate and, to this extent, it is witness to a certain power and dignity that seems to be absent from the classical example.[12]

It is certainly true that much of what Cumont says of the Roman case, when they were confronted with "Oriental" mysteries (Mithraism, for example, which as we have already seen accompanied the Roman army to as far distant a place as Hadrian's Wall), is valid for the Germanic case also, as in this: "they gave the intellect the illusion of learned depth and absolute certainty and finally . . . they satisfied conscience as well as passion and reason."[13] And it was perhaps in the pagan view of life after death—transformed by Mithraism and the cult of Isis in the one case, and Christian paradise in the other, into firm hope where there was once the uncertainty of a man's fate as laid down by the Norns—that any contrast in the two cases collapses into a single, pagan vision. The Christian God was superior to their own gods just insofar as he controlled fate and was not controlled by it. The Roman pagan saw in these religious structures not just truth of doctrine, not just greater beauty of ritual, but a superior morality. These things, taken together, attracted both the common man and the scholar: "The imposing ceremonial of their festivities and the alternating pomp and sensuality, gloom and exaltation of their services appealed especially to the simple and humble, while the progressive revelation of ancient wisdom, inherited from the old and distant Orient, captivated the cultured mind."[14] It seems that by offering both dogma and an ethical basis for conduct—"a basis for hope besides grounds for belief,"—the "Oriental" religions provided the required encouragement to Roman paganism to embrace the new.

Yet in spite of the insistence given here that paganism involved belief, and in spite of this precedent from Rome that conversion from paganism—even when this was to another such paganism—involved just that kind of belief and its replacement, it has to be conceded that, in the Germanic example, the situation would appear to be both more complex and a good deal stranger than this picture suggests. Most scholars seem to have accepted that, so far as conversion was concerned for the Germanic peoples, this was achieved primarily through demonstrations of power, both by the Christian church itself and, very significantly, by their own kings and chieftains. Yet this only relocates the philosophical question further back, so to speak, for we still wish to understand what it was that encouraged the kings and chieftains to give up the old gods and convert. Was this, in every case, a matter of the individual's belief? Or was it, too, political, and venal? Well it was clearly both of these, and no doubt was both of these for common men who would, in reality, have had little choice in the matter. Bede's account of the conversion of Ethelbert (whose wife was already a Christian when Bede reports that Augustine arrived in Kent) offers an interesting mélange of considerations apposite to much of this discussion, since Ethelbert's tolerance is as clear in this episode as is that of the Christian missionaries, in their attempts at conversion by exemplar, not force. Indeed, one could say that Ethelbert weighs the evidence of his pagan beliefs against the Christian alternative, finds the former wanting, and only then converts—subsequently taking his subjects with him. It would of course have been in Bede's interests to represent high-status conversions as in some sense rational, but nonetheless such accounts cannot disguise the sense that, in such cases at least, a pagan's beliefs were transformed through conviction.[15] Sometimes it seems that all that was at stake in conversion was the replacement of one religious ritual by another—what Fletcher describes as the "classic technique of rural evangelization," where "miracles, wonders, exorcisms, temple-torching and shrine-smashing *were in themselves* acts of evangelization . . . and where being converted partook of something of the nature of joining a club."[16] Of course it does not follow from the fact that conversion was sometimes like this that pagans did not believe things that were central to that pagan faith. It does not even follow from the fact that there were such beliefs—on a par, as we have insisted, with Christian beliefs—that they could not be abandoned in favor of others that they sincerely found to be superior in some sufficiently crucial respect to their lives, as the example of Ethelbert above seems to show, however we view the accuracy and objectivity of Bede's account. The bribing of pagans by certain Christian clerics surely tells us something about the nature of the individual responsible for this bribe, as well as those converted by means of it. The bishop of Bamberg, we are informed, "hastened" conversion by offering copious amounts of food (and drink) to those of modest means, while to the already rich and powerful "he gave rings and sword-belts, sandals, cloth of gold, and other precious gifts."[17] Thus "Become a Christian and get rich" no doubt tells us something of the venality of the wavering heathen; but it tells us at least as much about the supposed superior morality of the conquering Christians.

There seems no doubt, then, that conversion of the Germanic peoples involved an authentic engagement with them on three levels—cult, morality, and faith. It remains a matter of scholarly debate whether these represent separate—perhaps even mutually exclusive—categories, or whether what was happening was a complex process that presupposed that the first was somehow a more primitive stage than the second and third. Lyungberg, for one, reverses this order, insisting that "c'est la *foi* que les missionaires tentèrent d'apporter d'abord." It need occasion no great surprise—given the tolerance within paganism that we noted earlier—that this was not even the first time that the Germans had encountered a new religion, though it might be surprising to discover that a previous encounter of theirs may have been with Buddhism. In Sweden, a statuette of the Buddha has been found, which wore around its neck a ring clearly of Northern provenance.[18] Obviously we cannot be certain that the owner of the statuette truly knew anything of the Buddha beyond this image, or even that he worshipped some non-Germanic, "Oriental" god. But the point is that the Christian incision into the life of the Germanic peoples could never have been any sort of reflection of this tolerant attitude, being systematically intolerant as it was of all other gods: "Thou shalt" (after all) "have no other Gods before me." The pagan past had to be broken, not accommodated; and whether this was achieved by means of the presentation of a superior morality, a final victory over fate, or a simple bribe, did not really matter. They were all of them souls in peril—and they all counted. The Germanic gods were in some senses homelier—certainly less transcendent in nature—but the Germanic peoples may have been in a state of preparedness to accept change before it was Christianity that stood before them, and may have made just the tentative shift toward monotheism that we have seen had occurred in the example of ancient Egypt—that inevitable, psychological impulse that some scholars believe must have happened everywhere. Divinity begins to characterize their thinking about the gods as Oðin, for example, is transformed from Father of the Gods to Master of the Universe. It seems for some that Balðr had even dared to compete with the Christian God: Balðr as innocent—as sun-god—the god that one dared not name, assumes a role that is witness to a kind of crystallization of many gods into one—or at least into one or two.[19]

We have now identified four roads to conversion: cult, morality, faith, and conversion as a political act. For many there was yet a fifth—compulsion. The Friesians, for instance, seem to have converted as a result of the zeal of the Christian missionaries, who in this case achieved their purpose following almost a century of preaching and exemplary behavior—the kind of thing reported as commonplace by Bede. The Saxons, by contrast, were simply forced to convert under the iron fist of the Frankish kings and in spite of fierce resistance. Eligius gave his Saxon prisoners three options: go home;

remain in his service; or enter a monastery. In Saxony, in fact, any refusal to be baptized was punishable by death, "as was eating meat during Lent, attacks on churches, slaying of clergy, [and] participation in [pagan] rituals." Wholesale conversion followed not long after Widukind's baptism in A.D. 785.[20] This kind of persuasion was also exercized by the newly converted Norsemen:

> On hearing that the earl was there he sent for him on board his ship, and told him, without much parley, that he must allow himself to be baptized, and make all the people confess the Christian faith. The *Flateyjarbok* says that the king took hold of Sigurd's boy . . . and drawing his sword, gave the earl the chance of renouncing for ever the faith of his fathers, or of seeing the boy slain on the spot . . . Sigurd became a nominal convert, but there is every reason to believe that the Christianity which was thus forced upon the [Orkney] Islanders was for a long time more a name than a reality.[21]

It was noted above that in the classic text of William James, the concept of conversion was seen almost exclusively as having to do with the shift from one form of Christian belief to another, rather as if one was fast-tracked from the periphery to the core of the religion. While this inevitably speaks of a lack of interest in the idea of the transition from paganism to Christianity, it also reflects a much older limitation on the idea of conversion as expressed in that term. For the word "*conversio*" was not normally employed to designate that particular transformation, but was used in the main much more narrowly (and more precisely) to refer to the transition *within* Christianity, that is, from a less to a more intense form of Christian life. When referring to a king's adoption of Christianity, the verbs used were more often "accepting" or even "submitting to"—and certainly it would seem to have been the denoting of something essentially passive, usually involving the exercise of authority in which Christian ritual was compelled, or else a law involving Christian traditions and customs was enforced.[22] William Chaney has argued that a violent conversion to the new religion was, in any event, unnecessary, since the old beliefs offered so many parallelisms, that the tribal culture was able to absorb the new God without really disrupting too many of its basic presuppositions.[23] From the examples given above, such a reasonable idea would not seem to have always been given as much prominence as may have been possible though, to be sure, a good deal of paganism was to be absorbed and refashioned, rather than simply obliterated.[24]

The absorption that was taking place is clearly demonstrated in the example of the terms themselves that were used within Germanic paganism. These needed to be either eliminated from the everyday vocabulary or somehow cleansed of any heathen associations. And of the variety of words used by Germanic paganism to refer to their gods, only one would survive into the Christian era, and this by virtue of its evident adaptability to Christian purposes: that word was "*goþ.*" Maurice Cahen identifies nine different words for pagan divinity, including "*tyr,*" "*höpt,*" "*goþ,*" "*regin,*" and "*bönd.*" Cahen says that with the exception of *Tyr* (which is related to other Indo-European languages) and *regin,* the others are really poetic names. *Regin* comes from the Gothic *ragin,* meaning "a decision," as in a decision reached collectively by a council. Saxo has *regano giskapu,* meaning "destiny fixed by gods," or "decree of fate." D. H. Green suggests that this supports a semantic development of the order "decision, > divine decision, > the gods who decide."[25] The Scandinavian *regin* = gods is attested prior to the literary tradition, and is found on a runic inscription in Sweden of around A.D. 700; and Cahen believes that the poetic tradition utilized, and to a certain extent prolonged, the religious usages of the past. And it is from this root that comes *Ragn rok* = "the end of the gods," their ultimate fate. He says that clearly the alliterative force of the word would have been poetically attractive, yet the word retains clear religious connotations. However, it is not found in Christian poetic texts, from which Cahen concludes that it disappeared with the disappearance of paganism itself.[26]

But why did "*goþ*" survive the conversion? Partly, it seems, because it was the most general of the pagan terms for divinity. The very specificity of the other terms in the list above constrained the possibilities available for accommodation of new meanings. On the other hand, if Cahen is correct in his assertion that the most stable words of any religious vocabulary are those that designate the *essence* of that religion, we might have expected a greater reluctance on the part of the new religious authorities to tolerate it. The simplest explanation seems to be that the Christian church found what it was looking for in the word *goþ.* *Goþ* comes from **guda,* "a characteristic Germanic word, as *theos* is for Greek." The Indo-European origins of the word seem to make clear that what it denoted originally was an *abstract* power, referring to the impersonal force of destiny. As to its origin, Cahen prefers the Sanskrit *hu*—which signifies "to make an offering"; other dialects confirm that it is a religious word of great age. Cahen then relates *guda to Sanskrit *hutali,* meaning a divinity to whom one makes a libation. This word is represented in all Germanic dialects, and in every case with a religious function—such as Gothic *guþ;* Old

Saxon, Old English, and Old Friesian *god;* West Scandinavian *goþ;* East Scandinavian *guþ*. From this evidence, we can agree with Cahen that it is not credible to imagine that the Germans created their own religious vocabulary completely independent of one another, and the circumstances of the conversion contributed to the creation of a single religious vocabulary.[27] The choice of the word *goþ* was facilitated by the fact that all the other pagan words tended to be employed as plurals, making them rather starkly inappropriate for use within the new monotheism. *Regin,* for instance, was used only as a plural, and does not refer to any personal god, but instead denotes the *decisions* taken by the sky-gods variously. This paucity of terms to hand that might designate a single god would force the skaldic poets, according to Cahen, to give the plural forms *bönd,* and *höpt* a sense that was logically singular. Cahen gives the further example of "*Tyr*": the plural form "*tivar*" is actually the oldest, and its use as a singular name arose more or less from poetic necessity when a *kenning* was required as a synonym for *goþ*. From all of this we can see that such relatively dry matters of etymology and grammar take us to the heart of the Christian project of conversion, following which the word *goþ* as a neuter pagan term looked backward, while the new usage, *goþ* as a masculine singular, became the name for the god of the new religion. Indeed, the word for "pagan" was itself, in the Christian vocabulary, of masculine gender, enabling "True God" to be distinguishable from "false god." This is interesting not least because at that time there were no Latin texts available for which these were direct translations.[28] This seems to have been the practice in all Germanic languages: following the conversion this was the means for differentiating the old, impersonal pagan powers of fate, from the new, personal God of the Christians.[29]

It was suggested above that, prior to the extraordinary events of the Icelandic conversion, the psychological foundations for such a transformation had already been laid down. In the first place, as we noted in the first chapter, paganism was in itself so tolerant of other beliefs, other gods, other practices, that it was by its nature susceptible to outside influences. Cumont says that it was thus, in some sense, *bound* to yield to the ascendancy—some would say superiority—of Christianity.[30] We will see below that in purely doctrinal terms the most powerful attraction of Christianity to a pagan German may well have been the promise of escape from an all-encompassing fate. To evade the decrees of fate—to evade death, ultimately—through embracing a God who promised a kind of immortality must have been well-nigh irresistible, just as it was to the pagan Romans, who were seduced by such promises as were made by the priests of Isis and Serapis.[31] The idea was expressed somewhat grandly by Günther, who says that "the conversion of the Teutons to Christianity can only be explained by assuming that amongst them many men of softer heart could not withstand the gaze from the eyes of a merciless destiny and—against all reality—took their refuge in the dream image of a merciful God."[32]

The conversion of Iceland by the decision of the Allthing is certainly a very remarkable circumstance, and there has been much written on the subject. In summary, what happened was that, following a great deal of deliberation, the lawspeaker declared that there should henceforth be "one law and one faith," and that that faith should be Christian. Exceptions were made: the old law could stand in relation to the exposure of unwanted children, and the eating of horse-flesh was permitted. Sacrifice was also tolerated, but only if it took place in secret; somewhat paradoxically, it was still to be punishable by banishment if witnesses could be found who could prove it against someone. In the starkest of terms, that was all there was to it—a decision that Dag Strömbäck says leaves us "perplexed and mystified." He asks: "Was antique paganism so rotten at the core, so dilapidated a structure, that the first puff of opposition was enough to bring it down? Or was there such sovereign indifference to religion among Icelanders that they did not care whether the nation was pagan or Christian so long as they were left in peace?"[33] It is a fair point, and probably nourishes the idea, of wide currency, that paganism had no beliefs at all, only cults, and that perhaps it is psychologically—although perhaps not socially—easier to abandon cult practices than to give up deeply held beliefs. But we have already seen that, even in the case where paganism yields to *another* paganism (as in the Roman example, with the cults of Mithras and Isis), there are likely to exist profounder reasons than mere indifference that permit or encourage the transformation that is eventually wrought.

The easy case for thinking of Norse paganism as completely reducible to cults, and therefore having nothing whatever to do with belief, can be made through the simple expedient of pointing out that in Old Norse there existed no *original* expression for "belief" or "believe." Nor indeed was there, in any strict sense, a single word for "religion" itself. Gro Steinsland points out that instead, there was the word "*siðr*," which means "custom." Furthermore, there were no terms for "venerate" or "pray." All of which evidence leads Steinsland to conclude that this was indeed a paganism without dogmas.[34] But it also seems to leave it without content. The case being made here on this matter at least, is that this is not a religious matter, but a logical one. To affirm the distinction between paganism and Christianity in terms of the centrality of cults in the former, and beliefs in the latter, not only robs the cult of any authentic religiosity to which it might otherwise lay claim (which amounts simply to question-begging), but furthermore has the effect of stripping it of any meaning whatever; for cult practices performed—not just by anyone at any time, but also by priests at ritually significant times—in the complete absence of belief, are not cults at all, but repetitive actions that contingently occur within a context that just happens to be socially significant. This social significance must be independent of beliefs in its turn, else we could simply affirm that the meaning of the cult is in that very social significance, which itself is believed in by the culture—and so on, indefinitely. At some point, we must allow the meaning of the cult to be anchored in some beliefs located somewhere within the cultural context; in Wittgenstein's words, justification must have a stop. It is here that the social aspects become more prominent. In the absence of a true priesthood, Christian missionary work quite plausibly focused its attention on kings and chieftains, a pattern of approach seen almost everywhere in the Germanic world but particularly so in Iceland, since it was the kings and tribal leaders who were the guardians of both the sacral and judicial duties of the society at large.[35] What was in place was the so-called *"goðorð"* organization. The *goði* was the term for either a priest or a chieftain (often both), while the sagas refer to pagan priests as *hofgoði* (temple-priests). The primary sense of the term seems to have been "he who has to do with the divine."[36] Strömbäck believes that the *goðorð* system is "highly significant for the history of religion as such," being as it is the residue of a very ancient institution once found widely among the peoples of Scandinavia and the Continent, which gave the individual both priestly and legal responsibilities. Unsurprisingly, it was to be the former function of the *goði* that would disappear with the coming of Christianity.[37]

Perhaps another part of the answer as to why it seems to us that pagan Icelanders gave up their religion with such apparent ease, is that, in practice, many of them had not given it up at all—at least, in private. Since there are at least as many unanswered questions relating to the precise meaning carried by Christianity for the vast majority of ordinary people professing to be Christians in these very early years of the conversion, as there are in relation to the proper meaning of paganism itself for those undergoing conversion, we cannot say simply that at one time paganism was believed and that at another time (following the Allthing of A.D. 1000, or A.D. 999 as some authorities believe) it was abandoned, and Christianity was accepted. This may have been the official version, but such wholesale conversion makes sense only if we are indeed dealing with a system of beliefs *in each case*—something that, as we have seen, most authorities seem anxious to deny. If cult practices—independent of belief—are all that paganism involves, then Strömbäck's rhetorical question is answered: it *was* a dilapidated and rotten structure. But if such was truly the case, there would be no reason to expect any part of that rotten structure to be left standing following the conversion. Yet parts of it did survive, at least for a time. The subtle efforts of the church itself—through language-changes, etc.—and the not-so-subtle efforts when this failed or seemed less appropriate—through force, bribery, etc.,—are witness to a residual heathenism that yielded only with reluctance, rather than to a merely ramshackle collection of cultic practices affording little or no comfort or significance for those still indulging them. It is true that we can never answer the question: "What was a Germanic pagan?" with complete confidence. But it is also true that we delude ourselves in thinking that we know with much more precision what made anyone a Christian, either, at this time.[38]

The strategy of the church that involved the transformation of pagan deities into demons, first employed in the Mediterranean region, proved just as irresistible in the Germanic context. Martin of Braga, for example, has the pagan gods of the former characterized as "demonic ministers of the Devil when he was cast out of heaven." He goes on to say that "the rustics have angered God and do not believe with their whole heart in the faith of Christ, but are so inconstant that they apply the very names of demons to each day and speak of Mars, Mercury, Jove, Venus, and Saturn."[39] Martin concludes by asking: "why does no augury harm me or any other upright Christian?"—an empirical test that he would doubtless have been content to ignore in the case of many Christian rituals. It is impossible to disagree with Fletcher's comment on this that such sermonizing "makes plain the difficulty . . . for the modern historian of drawing hard-and-fast boundaries between the Christian and pagan, religion and superstition, piety and magic, the acceptable and forbidden . . . and is a salutary reminder of the penumbral ambiguities of our subject."[40] That ambiguity is sufficiently pronounced for us to doubt seriously both the idea that the Germanic pagans did not believe in the Christian

God—a proposition that we have already seen would be incompatible with the internal tolerance of heathenism, and the more surprising, but hardly impossible thought that, for some Christians, especially those newly converted through one of the less than religiously convincing ways outlined above, the pagan deities retained some reality.[41] It has been suggested that in its early years the Christian church in Iceland was not sufficiently strong to completely eliminate paganism, and certainly the unusual circumstances of that conversion will have contributed to the heathenism's resilience for those who had not voted away their faith at the Allthing. Such an arbitrary decision—for so it must have seemed to some—could not have so simply overturned their convictions. The decision had been taken that, in effect, determined which among the available gods was the more powerful and could do more to assist men in their daily lives. And so the church's teaching that the old gods were no better than devils may well have needed time to take root and propagate. The old gods were real, but converts were under an obligation to forget them. Belief on the popular level probably remained strong for the longest time following the official conversion, as witnessed by the large number of pagan charms that survived. According to Eric Sharpe, the peasant might well have given up his gods, "but he did not so readily give up his religion."[42] It cannot have been just in Iceland, with its peculiar religious transformation, where this residual paganism persevered. It is noted, for example, in the *Orkneyinga Saga* that "Christianity then was young, and newly planted in Sweden . . . [yet] . . . many men still dabbled in ancient lore."[43]

Such pagan survivals as there were, "beliefs and practises tolerated by a sagely easy-going church . . . [are often dismissed by historians] as being something that would subside harmlessly into the quaint and the folkloric," as Fletcher puts it. He goes on: "But this is to miss the point. The men of the 6th century . . . were engaged in an urgent and competitive enterprise. In a European countryside where over hundreds of years diverse rituals had evolved for coping with the forces of nature, Christian holy men had to show that they had access to more efficacious power." This was by no means an easy task. That "more efficacious power" could not prevent early Christians seeking help from pagan witch-doctors as a first resort, such that in A.D. 633 the bishops forbade clerics to consult such *"arioli"* or magicians, divines, or soothsayers.[44] There is no reason to think that this kind of thing was not widespread in those years in which paganism, while retreating, established redoubts into which they could lodge the diminishing reservoir of heathen faith. The myths—and magic—into which many of these beliefs were crystalized were likely to have been the most enduring in the popular imagination and educated class alike. As noted above in the context of Roman paganism, Cumont has suggested that it is indeed the magical texts which constitute "almost the only original literary documents of paganism that we possess."[45]

One could argue that all of this attests not so much to syncretism but to confusion; having signaled a rupture with the past, some retained elements of their former beliefs that could sometimes be accommodated within the new tradition. And if that pagan residue should seem to threaten the church, they were ready enough to take a stronger line. And it should be kept in mind that pagan reaction against Christendom in Sweden (and we should remember Mayr-Harting's observation that *resistance* to conversion has been very often ignored in favor of reasons *for* it) erupted every *nine* years—the mystical number—or in multiples of nine, that is, in 1021, 1039, 1057, 1066, 1075, 1084, and 1120. The implication is that pagan cult sacrifices at Uppsala were due every nine years, and that the Christians (obviously) refused to participate, "triggering a general hostility."[46]

It would seem that at least so far as Iceland was concerned, the traditional tolerance shown by paganism to other beliefs spilled over into the Christian attitude to the old faith, for there is little evidence for actual persecution after the conversion.[47] To this extent, Iceland at the conversion may have represented—whether or not one accepts the judgment that at this moment "the first European humanism had died"—the last throes of an authentically Indo-European belief system.[48] In his strange book, Günther, having suggested (uncontroversially) that "Indo-European belief without tolerance is inconceivable" (because any Indo-European religious form demanding "true believers" is inauthentic), adds that the "churchifying of a belief is an assertion of the spirit of the orient (desert lands). Churches, in this sense as a sacred and sanctifying device, can take root only where 'this' world is taken as 'unholy' and leading to 'sin'." Fletcher, on the other hand, argues that such churchifying was an important component of the process of Christianization. The impressive visual presence of all manner of treasure inside churches "should alert us to the impact... this might have made upon the sense of those who worshipped in them."[49]

We can be reasonably confident that ideas nourished by the Christian message of salvation took hold in Northern minds already to some extent attuned to this aspect of the new faith. Fletcher is quite correct in his insistence that the Germanic mind "was very far from being a *tabula rasa* on which the first words of salvation were to be written by the Christian church."[50] It is probably too strong to speak of syncretism between Germanic paganism and the early church, but there does seem to have been a strong impulse to accommodate one to the other—and coming not only from one side. What the church was unable to obliterate, it refashioned in its own image, and for its own purposes. Transition for the waverers was facilitated not least by leaving some familiar concepts to hand, if not quite intact, then still recognizable. And the most important of these was the concept of fate. Through the adaptation of this idea into a Christian framework, the remaining pagans drifted inexorably into the arms of a loving God who could satisfy their needs and rule for all time—and who could save them from the Ragnarok. As we have seen, the shift in the meaning of the word *goþ* had also made possible the participation of even nonconverted pagans, for they too "knew" Christ, and they knew that he was—at least—a god like Thor or Oðin. The final step would be taken when they were able to identify Christ *with* God. It was Christ's hegemony over all of creation that offered the greatest contrast with the pagan pantheon, wherein the gods would fail to overcome fate just like men. "At bottom, the conversion achieved its final victory through a process of decomposition—the old community of gods, piece by piece, and circumstance by circumstance, ceded to the new, all-powerful sky-gods."[51]

There are examples of resistance to this overwhelming power, and we should note the great sense of resolution and dignity that such examples manifest in the light of it. To continue to believe in the old gods when such power was on offer—as well as salvation—demands resolution and no small measure of courage. We read of Penda in England, who remained obstinately heathen, leaving Bede so little to say that the example was overlooked. We cannot ever be certain that the claims made on behalf of Christianity were wholly understood by converts, even royal ones. Some, inevitably, hedged their bets: Thorkell, described as "a most righteous heathen," asked to be taken into the open when he believed he was close to death, so that he could die in the light, "commending himself to whatever god had made the sun."[52]

There seem to have been two quite different—and contrary—strategies employed by the church to deal with the concept of fate. The most important, and the most orthodox method was to Christianize it; this will be discussed in a moment. But another nonstandard approach that was made—not directly in the Germanic case but an interesting example nonetheless—was offered by gnosticism, which itself was often seen as being sufficiently far away on the fringes of mainstream Christianity as to be a heresy. The gnostic view had its roots in a still more ancient teaching, viz., Platonism, from which the idea of a resolution to the problem of fate and its relation to both God and free will would be given in the form of what would much later in philosophical ethics come to be known as the doctrine of compatibilism. For the Platonist, it was acknowledged that fate (*heimarmene*), in its phenomenal sense of a nexus of cause and effect, was true of the physical world and in this sense effected everyone's life. However, as such it was still embraced by or subsumed under God's providence, and it left some room for freedom of action.[53] But gnosticism offered a more radical possibility, in the claim that fate was in complete control, but was nonetheless limited in its hegemony to a lower tier of heavenly powers, viz., gods, angels, demons, and humans. One could therefore avoid the inexorable demands of fate by placing oneself on a different spiritual plane from these—one could, in other words, become an initiate of the church. One famous gnostic passage affirms this; with reference to Valentinian teaching, Clement of Alexandria notes that: "They say, 'Prior to baptism, it is true (what is said) about fate. But after baptism, the astrologers are no longer correct.' Lord Himself, guide of humans, came down to earth to transfer those who believe in Christ *from fate into his providence.*"[54] One should note the contrast with the strategy in Germania. There, fate was to become providence; here, fate lives on, but can be overcome by providence. So instead of equating God with fate, or simply recasting fate as God's providence, the gnostic solution permitted a dichotomy of fate and God's power, where the one was not defeated by the other so much as protected from it through baptism. In fact Gro Steinsland makes a direct connection between Norse mythology and gnosticism. The latter, he says, remythologizes the myth of the Fall as we find it in Genesis, an idea that, he believes, is paralleled in *Skirnismal*. There are, he says, sources that may indeed support the possibility of gnostic influence on eleventh-century Scandinavia, for *Islendingabok* describes foreign bishops who stayed in Iceland at the time of bishop Isleifr. These foreign clerics were described much later as "Paulicians—a heretic group possibly from Armenia," who represented the gnostic doctrine that argued for a separation of the divine into two—the transcendent god and the lower god of creation, much like the Platonic position noted above, permitting also the dual concept of fate just referred to. Steinsland's main point is that medieval Scandinavia by no means represented a single, homogeneous, *Christian* dogma, but instead supported the hypothesis that the gnostic (heretical) tradition could have infiltrated the Nordic countries through the foreign clergy as early as the eleventh century. This seems highly plausible, given the resilience of pure pagan beliefs even after the formal conversion. Therefore, in the particular case of *Skirnismal,* the poet could have drawn on a number of different traditions—Nordic, mythological, and biblical (from Genesis), the latter quite possibly through the gnostic strand of Christianity. This leads Steinsland to his conclusion that the pagan tradition was, in effect, re-created at the time of the conversion, "for the biblical elements of *Skirnismal* are used within the frame of a lay which, in its deepest conception, is pre-Christian." And since the creation myth was a particular preoccupation of the gnostic tradition, any possible influence in this precise sense might account for the "gnostic tendency" that seems to exist in the *Voluspa* poem also.[55]

It should be obvious that insofar as a belief in fate proscribes—when it does not completely preclude—the reality of free will (and hence of moral responsibility), that the reasons for behaving well and ethically toward one's fellow man must have other grounds than such a belief. Since it was said that it was the ethical shortcomings of the pagan gods that contributed to the triumph of Christianity—which offered both rewards and punishments for [im]moral behavior—we should look briefly at just how morally acceptable conduct was encouraged and sanctioned within Germanic (here, specifically Norse) society. Reminding ourselves of Taylor's affirmation of the logical soundness of the doctrine of fatalism, and his view that *how* we respond (not least, ethically) to this challenge is revealing of us, it is of great interest that in Norse society their sense of what was judicially correct was never undercut by their belief in fate. It may be that they were extraordinarily successful in maintaining legal-cum-moral sanctions in the presence of a fate that governed their lives in such critically important areas, but it is a natural question whether the institution of feuding, for example, does not crucially count against the idea that this was in any way a morally coherent culture. Is not this unambiguously savage practice—seen as archetypically Norse—witness to a moral fault line that could never have withstood the contrast with the Christian doctrines of forgiveness and brotherly love? As we approach the conclusion of this discussion, we will see that the two central concepts of time and fate as we have described them here, come together with those of ethics, feuds, and the morality of a revenge culture and would be transformed and defeated *together* by the new religion, and that the church understood well enough the significance of all of them for the eventual triumph of their doctrines over the pagan tradition.

Although it is possible to start from the idea that somehow the heathen gods had failed the Norsemen ethically, that seems a rather loaded judgment. In the first place, where no such ethical demands were ever made, no failure can be attributed. While it may be true that the absence of ethical standards generated by their mythology was acknowledged by contrast with the Christian God, this does not mean that such a lack had been seen as a drawback before any such contrast was made possible. It is true that whatever moral code was in place before the conversion, it was not dictated to them by their gods; that code was in the latter's character as delineated through the mythology. It does not follow from this that this was seen as any kind of moral failure. Yet there was in this respect something like a doctrine of humanism in place here, since no man expected to be punished by the gods for wrongdoing or rewarded in heaven for doing the right thing. But given the highly developed judicial system at work, men did not simply do whatever they thought they might, with little or no thought toward the consequences. This humanism has been dismissed as merely rustic, although the truth of this depends somewhat on what one takes the literary source of the ethical code to be. If it is *Havamal*, where life is seen as the highest good, there is clearly no transcendent value on offer, and indeed no heroic contempt for death, no matter that fate is clearly accepted as universally powerful. Yet in *Sigrdifumal* (very different from *Havamal*), heroic values are emphasized, and revenge was a sacred, rather than a private satisfaction. Van den Toorn describes this—the "ultimate basis of valuation"—as "aesthetic" rather than moral.[56] The point is that this *aesthetic* valuation—curiously, and highly paradoxically, relating to such institutions as feuds and revenge—does indeed connect us quite directly to the Norse concept of time and temporality, through the preoccupation with genealogy that, as we have seen, does service in the Norse system for an abstract chronology.

In order to see how this admittedly rather bizarre-sounding idea might work, it is necessary to look in a little detail at the institution of the feud. The first thing to note is how well-ordered the practice of feuding was—it comes as something of a surprise to discover that there was little that was random or anarchic about it. In the first place, something could only be a feud if no kinsman were involved. In *Be-

owulf, for instance, if one kinsman were to slay another, it must be left to natural causes and fate to rectify the situation, however powerful the instinct for revenge. And accidental homicide, while not excused, does not seem to be followed by the normal punishment of exile. Murder *within* the kindred is deemed to break the tribal tie and is thence followed by outlawry.[57] The importance of outlawry was that the individual was no longer a *legal* entity, which would lead to him being edited out of any genealogical sequence of which he would otherwise have been a natural element. Since it was public opinion that set the standard for honorable conduct, the quintessence of past public opinion was located in history and legend. This history could not be tainted by dishonor, so in the lengthy genealogies in the sagas we will not find anyone named except those who are wholly honorable. This cannot mean that none of them ever engaged in feuding, but only that all of their killing was considered completely honorable.[58] Miller, however, asks whether we may even speak at all of feud when the Icelanders had no word for it. He says that feuds were "loosely designated in a descending order of frequency—disputes, suits, transactions, dealings, coldness, enmity." Feud was simply a part of the order of things, and what was perceived was not a reified institution, but *process itself*. Bloodfeud, specifically, was a framework for activity, the means by which that activity could be presented, and the ultimate sanction behind legal judgments.[59]

What then, is a feud in this quasi-judicial sense? First, it is a relationship of enmity between two groups—unlike revenge-killing, which could be a purely individual matter. Second, a feud is not open warfare, since only "occasional musterings" might be involved, rather than large forces. Third—and very important—violence is relatively controlled, and "casualties rarely reach double-figures." Fourth, the ethics of feuding implies *collective* liability, since the target of any particular violent act need not be the original miscreant. What confronts us here is a reasonably well-defined idea of reciprocity—action followed by reaction in a tit-for-tat sequence. As Miller says, disarmingly, "people keep score," and the entire process is governed by rules.[60] Such feuding cultures acknowledge some kind of (implicit) rules of appropriate, almost measured, response, such as *lex talionis*. And the point about *lex talionis*—not least in its most famous expression from the Bible in "eye for eye and tooth for tooth," where it is so often interpreted as vengeance *simpliciter*—is that it functions above all as a means of restoring equilibrium. This restoration of equilibrium, of the status quo antebellum, has about it something dynamic, spatiotemporal, as well as legal (static). The system is out of balance and can be restored only by the legal judgment backed up by feud, if necessary. "[It] starts with conflict, goes through Climax and Revenge, ends with reconciliation, followed by an Aftermath that brings the characters' genealogies down in time, just as the introduction brought them from origins. Something like this structure could easily be applied to the whole of Scandinavian mythology if it is systematised."[61] Most intriguingly, Lindow emphasizes that this systematization is possible especially if the Balðr myth is placed at the heart of the mythology, for his death "exposes a flaw in bloodfeud" that, through its link with the concept of honor was a device for "apportioning" social status. "The connection of the Baldr story to eschatology suggests that the flaw could be fatal."[62] Since no recompense is, in principle, available for such a deed, the balance cannot be restored, and the spatiotemporal system is thereby permanently fractured. Arbitration settlements—so-called "man-evening" (*mannjafnaðr*)—were the normal means to balance men one against another, even in death. The worth of a man was weighed and quantified, like a judicial version of the weighing of souls on the Day of Judgment (a fundamental Christian idea wonderfully illustrated, for example, on the tympanum of Notre Dame in Paris) or the ancient Greek practice of weighing souls.[63]

It may come as a further surprise to discover that, even for revenge-killing, there were rules of engagement. It was considered shameful to kill a man while he slept—reflected much later in the "most sacrilegious murder" of the sleeping Duncan in *Macbeth*—although one must add immediately that a victim might be prodded awake before being dispatched. There was a right to kill that had proscribed limits as to time, place, and person. "Blows that left no bruises had to be avenged at the time and place they occurred, but those which did or caused bleeding could be avenged up until the next Allthing." If vengeance was not taken before that, this right lapsed, and the dispute then became the subject of an outlawry action.[64]

In these ways vengeance became, for all its summary brutality, comprehensible and almost predictable—unlike fate, about which one knew nothing, except that it controled a man's life and death and was inexorable. We cannot say that there existed any logical relationship between the feuding and revenge culture on the one hand, and belief in fate on the other; contemporary examples of the former take place within a context of an almost mystical modern conviction that man is free to create his own destiny. Yet insofar as the quintessence of Norse feuding was the restoration of balance, we can see a mythographic connection between such a system and the quasichronology of the family history. And there is a very clear correlation between honor moralities and the existence of feuding as an institution. As Miller points out, societies that feud (routinely) will place honor at the center of their value-system. In Iceland, honor was "largely congruent with 'man-evening,' the comparing of men. Honour meant, above all, relations of reciprocity with other honourable people."[65]

Although we may have no exact way in which to translate "honor" in Old Norse, the various components of the concept can be expressed. Family prestige, for example, was expressed by terms usually translated as "honor": *virding*—"worth"; *metord*—"measurement"; *metnadr*—"esteem." Other common words are *somi, soemd,* which express what it is thought proper for a man to do—comparable to the English word "seemly." This sense of honor could produce some curious results. In the *Orkneyinga Saga,* Swein "asked his wife Ingrid where Earl Harald was, but she would not tell him. He then said: 'Say nothing then, but point to where he is.' She would not do that either."[66] This tells us something interesting about honor from both sides, for while Swein clearly thinks that merely gesturing would not somehow be a betrayal of the earl's whereabouts, Ingrid's response quite clearly shows that she does think of it as such.

We have noted on several occasions that one of the key reasons that made the new religion attractive to the Norsemen—a reason that links us quite directly to concepts of time and fate—was the possibility of avoiding the end of everything as described in the image of the Ragnarok. The eschatological drama played out there makes it clear that for Germanic, as for other pagan cultures, the notion of salvation (or its absence) was fully understood. It was not suddenly introduced to them by the Christian church, and by reshaping the symbolism of the Ragnarok they would be able to effect a transition to the particular contours of the Christian narrative, while still maintaining a certain degree of contact with their pagan past. The precise details of this continuity of mythic symbolism do not concern us here, but we should note that there must have been a sense of familiarity in the idea of celestial bliss for a people ready to believe in Valholl—notwithstanding that the latter was primarily reserved for battle heroes and (less comfortably) that such heroes would be wanted again in the final conflagration. And perhaps this was the hook onto which the nonheroic, ordinary Norse farmer would be caught by the new faith: suddenly, a version of Valholl was on offer that was more democratic, and—probably more important—was not a temporary feasting hall until one was required again when all hell broke loose.

Some commentators argue that, on the contrary, this Christian concept of salvation and its idea of a fixed, closed eternity, would have been rather difficult for Germanic paganism to accept. Bauschatz, for instance, says that the "temporal reorientation towards the future," which is characteristic of the Christian version, would have been a psychological obstruction to Germanic peoples who would have resisted the very idea that the past could somehow be obliterated as their sins were washed away and they were, through baptism, reborn. "No wonder that the Germanic version of Christianity should stress so heavily the Old Testament, with its genealogies and its emphasis on retribution rather than forgiveness"—or, as seems preferable now, its emphasis on the Old Testament idea of the restoration of equilibrium.[67] A similar idea is expressed by Cassirer (in terms that are both more general and more strictly philosophical) in his view that the emergence of pure monotheism represents "an important turning-point in the religious attitude towards time"—the point being that in the Prophets in particular there is expressed a turn away from nature "and from the temporal orders of the natural process."[68] However, it seems to me preferable to see this—for the Germanic case especially—as a consequence of the acceptance of the new religion, and in no sense part of its originating motive force. This interest in the Old Testament, "with its genealogies and its emphasis on retribution," is, as we have already noted, fundamental to an honor morality ready to stress vengeance as a social imperative. Retribution restores equilibrium: it restores the original dynamics to a social situation nudged out of balance.

As we have seen throughout this discussion, it is in the relationship of time to fate, and thereby to human choice, that paganism achieves its characteristic stamp, and that it would be this that would in part be carried over into the Christian model. Simultaneously, it would present the greatest challenges to the early church in its mission to overcome the heathen tradition. What is perhaps most striking—and surprising—about this, is the dilution of a powerful sense of human dignity in the face of the inevitable (as in the Norse case), in favor of a submission before an all-powerful God who promised something in the life to come, in exchange for the abandonment of defiance. What was happening philosophically can be guessed at from the linguistic and other evidence, as an all-embracing Urðr gave way to its domesticated version, as in the comparable Anglo-Saxon *wyrd*. This tension between the power of *wyrd* and the power of God is clear in the translation of Boethius's *Consolation of Philosophy* undertaken by Alfred, where the relation between predestination and freedom is discussed in detail, although the term "*wyrd*" itself appears only once in that translation. F. Anne Payne points out that of the seven occurrences of "*wyrd*" in the Old English version of Book I, six are related to the general question of whether *Wyrd* governs the world independently of God. Alfred gives most of fate's functions to God: rather than being that force in things that creates order, *wyrd* has the narrower function of being "God's work"—a deliberate and temporary action that must be performed each and every day. It is precisely because men are not part of God's order—the order that rules all creatures—that they can, indeed must, experience "the touch of *wyrd*."[69] What was happening *psychologically* ought to be no more difficult, nor more or less certain, than in this case. We know from the example of ancient Greece that there was a clear connection between belief in the plans of an omniscient God, and the individual's reaction to life as moral—and that human *will* was a decisive psychological component of this relationship. In the Greek case, it was thought that acting solely in accordance with one's own intellectual judgment could be considered as in itself a fatal failure, when only divine powers are supposed to be in a position to dispose of the future. This, too, is an Old Testament point of view, where praise can be offered to those who decide what to do by direct appeals to God *without* trying to perceive, through individual intellectual effort, the end of their action. "Their action . . . can be classified in the religious category of obedience. The philosophical equivalent could only be will." Dihle writes that both the concepts of choice, and that of will, must be understood not simply in terms of ethics and mythology, for there are corresponding ideas also in "cosmology."[70]

For some, any comparison between the highly abstract, intellectual, and authentically philosophical experience of ancient Greece and the cruder expressiveness of Germanic paganism is per se illegitimate. And even if the workings of the Germanic mind are not (as should by now be obvious) merely the robust expressions of a superstitious barbarism, it is surely clear that we are in this case trying to describe an altogether simpler mental topography.

According to Stephen Flowers, Christianization "simplified" Germanic concepts related to soul, mind, and spirit, while at the same time it created the dichotomy "body versus soul" and the trichotomy "body versus soul versus spirit."[71] He suggests that the best-attested

Germanic term for "soul"—*hog*—may be very ancient, and embrace several abstract, psychic functions, including some referring to the ideas of reflection and volition. There was a breath concept, an emotive concept relating to the idea of ecstatic inner power; and a cognitive aspect that included within it reflection, perception, and volition. In West Norse, terms for the soul fall into two groups, semiphysical and animistic or magical. The first group applies to those qualities with a divine origin (as in the mythological texts) that can be made visible, as in *Voluspa:*

> Sense they possessed not,　soul they had not,
> being nor bearing,　nor blooming hue;
> soul gave Othin,　sense gave Hœnir,
> being, Lothur,　and blooming hue.[72]

Flowers gives this "definite functional structure" as the underlying Germanic vocabulary of the psyche, and while the breath concept is less prominent than might have been expected, there is, he points out, evidence for its magical significance in images on bracteates from the Migration Age. These depict a figure—probably either Oðin or Balðr—with a rush of air issuing from his mouth.[73]

Baetke has written that "performances and actions" (*Vorstellungen* and *Handlungen*) are not some "outer garment" of religion, but its very body. But they are not its soul. *The soul of any religion is belief.*[74] Every religious act and expression *means* something, and is a sign for something inner—some belief. There seems no reason to deny this to Germanic paganism, for it is in this that we can come to understand it. It is true that in so far as we lack liturgical texts, we must always remain at a greater intellectual and psychological distance from these beliefs than is the case with living (and mostly monotheistic) religions. One way of approaching such an understanding is through knowledge of the relationship between these beliefs and language, for the history of a language is (for Baetke) a mirror in which we may see the history of religion. It is just so with other concepts, and when these concepts are such as time, space, and fate, which have a function both inside and outside religion—we can call them epistemological without undue strain—the task of understanding can yield results that must profoundly effect our way of seeing the people and their ideas.

By the time that the Christian poem *Heliand* was written, fate and time had become connected in ways not necessarily visible in the Norse sources—and this because the Christianization of the concepts

6: FROM PAGAN FATE TO CHRISTIAN PROVIDENCE   145

was more or less complete. As Green points out, the decisive step in that process was the attempt to equate fate with God, "a process culminating in Notker's decision to translate *fatum* on one occasion by *gotes uuillen*."[75] In *Heliand* fate comes to mean both birth and death, the two poles of human existence. We have seen how other pagan cultures connected these two ideas—sometimes identifying one with the other, most often through some personification within the mythology. In *Heliand*, fate becomes "*lebensfeindlichen Macht*," and in considering the poem, Hagenlocher remarks that as man came to place the problem of death more and more into the foreground, so his dependence on time became something of which he was increasingly conscious.[76] The final step was to reduce fate to being merely an attribute of providential omnipotence, when God was by now clearly superior to fate, and indeed disposes of it. "If Christianity criticised pagan fatalism for depriving man of freedom, but then equated fate with God . . . this still left open the problem of the relationship between providence and free will."[77] And that, it has to be said, is a problem with which Christianity has been confronted ever since.

And this brings us full circle. For only following the Christianization of fate does this problem of death and salvation in relation to God's power manifest itself with any clarity: only when fate has been pulled down from pagan inexorability, then linked with death *as a new beginning* through the Christian eschatology—only then does time truly fuse with fate in human consciousness. When fate had been temporalized, it could at last be avoided, through a baptism that promised eternal life. When fate was an atemporal *law,* the temporality of human consciousness meant that, while the laws could not be escaped, man could continue to act *as if* he exercized some control in the face of it. When fate had *become* time, then, suddenly, death *as a law* could be avoided—not in this life, but in the next.

Notes

INTRODUCTION

1. A comprehensive account of the many words used in the Germanic languages for fate can be found in D. H. Green, *Language and history in the early Germanic World,* (Cambridge: Cambridge University Press, 2000), 382–88. Cf. also Mathilde von Kienle, "Der Schicksalsbegriff im Altdeutschen," *Wörter und Sachen* 15 (1933): 81–112.

2. Anyone assuming that this is a serene corner of an academic grove would be mistaken. As an interloper, it was incumbent upon me sometimes to pursue ideas wherever they might lead. Occasionally, it seemed appropriate to read works long neglected (often for clear and very good reasons, it would seem—as in what might be described as the strange case of the "British" Edda). All the same, this approach would now and again lead to the discovery that some well-regarded authorities have been described by other well-regarded authorities as being "quite mad." It seems that Norse studies has few scholars content to sit on their hands.

3. See Margaret Clunies Ross, *The reception of Norse myths in medieval Iceland.* Volume 2 of *Prolonged Echoes: Old Norse Myths in Medieval Northern Society.* (Odense: Odense University Press, 1994–98), 12–13.

4. Ibid., 17.

5. See Oswald Spengler, *The Decline of the West,* vol. 1, trans. Charles Francis Atkinson (London: George Allen & Unwin, 1926), 117.

6. Ibid., 129.

7. See M. I. Steblin-Kamenskij, *The Saga Mind,* trans. Kenneth Ober (Odense: Odense University Press, 1973), 13.

8. This book proceeds on the assumption that etymology is an indispensable tool for understanding such continuity as is available to us. I am not sure how many scholars would agree with, for example, J. Simpson's comment that "extensive discussions of etymologies . . . are likely to seem irrelevant to modern readers . . . [and that nowadays] . . . it is archaelogy, not etymology, to which we turn for additional insight into early religion." See Jacqueline Simpson, Introduction to Benjamin Thorpe, *Northern Mythology* (Ware: Wordsworth Editions, 2001), viii–ix. I would have to respond to this by saying that such a dismissal of etymology in this context is shortsighted nonsense. While we should be alive to the danger of losing ourselves in "clouds of antiquity . . . [that are] really no more than the image of [our] own sensibility in a philological mirror," we can yet cleave to de Vries's attitude, when he says that though etymology is not to be used as a basis, it may be a "welcome confirmation" of results arrived at by other means. See Spengler, *Decline of the West,* 28—the citation above referring to

Bachofen, Burckhardt, and Nietzsche, and Jan de Vries, *The Problem of Loki* (Helsinki: Suomalainen Tiedeakatemia Societas Scientianum Fennica, 1933), 4. And such a work as D. H. Green's, far from being "irrelevant," strikes this reader as absolutely indispensable. See *Language and history in the early Germanic world.*

9. See Mary Beard, "Looking (harder) for Roman myth: Dumézil, declamation and the problems of definition," in *Mythos in mythenloser Gesellschaft: Das Paradigma Roms,* ed. Fritz Graf (Stuttgart and Leipzig: B.G.Teubner, 1993), 62–64.

10. See Cecil Wood, "The Viking Universe," in Evelyn Firchow et al., *Studies for Einar Haugen* (The Hague: Mouton, 1972), 573.

11. Rosalie Wax, *Magic, Fate and History* (Lawrence, Kans.: Coronado Press, 1969), 140.

12. Aeschylus, *Agamemnon,* trans. Philip Vellacott (London: Penguin Books, 1959), 51.

13. Spengler, *Decline of the West,* 117–18.

14. Paul Radin suggests that Kant could have saved himself the necessity of coining the term "*Ding-an-sich*" (Thing-in-itself) "had he written in Achomawi, an Indian language of northern California. . . . In that idiom every noun, pronoun and verb appears in two forms, an absolute-abstract form and a relative-concrete one." See Paul Radin, *Primitive Man as Philosopher* (New York: Dover Books, 1927), xxiii.

15. Sigurður Nordal, "Three Essays on *Voluspa,*" *Saga-Book* 18 (1970–71), 88. In the following text any citations from the *Poetic Edda* will be from the translation by Lee Hollander. See *The Poetic Edda,* trans. Lee M.Hollander, 2nd ed. (rev.) (Austin: University of Texas Press, 2001). This version offers both acceptable (though occasionally stilted) poetry, with comprehensive explanatory notes for anyone wanting historical and mythological contexts. For the latter reason also, Hermann Palsson's translation of the *Voluspa* is extremely valuable, even though no attempt is made there to render the poetic feeling of the original. See *Voluspa: The Sybil's Prophecy* (Edinburgh: Lockharton Press, 1996). It is unfortunate that the most widely available translation—*The Poetic Edda,* trans. Carolyne Larrington (Oxford: Oxford University Press, 1999))—in the Oxford World's Classics series, should be not only thin in terms of its mythological—let alone philosophical—contextualizing, but also too often poetically inept.

1. PAGANISM IN MYTH AND CULT

1. See Heinrich Zimmer, *Myths and Symbols in Indian Art and Civilization* (New York: Harper and Row, 1962), 218.

2. Ibid.

3. See G. Turville-Petre, *Origins of Icelandic Literature* (Oxford: Clarendon Press, 1953), 59.

4. See Viktor Rydberg, *Teutonic Mythology: Gods and Goddesses of the Northland,* 3 vols., trans. Rasmus Anderson (London: Norrœna Society, 1906), 412 and 488.

5. See Anders Hultgard, "Old Scandinavian and Christian Eschatology," in *Old Norse and Finnish Religions and Cultic Place-Names,* ed. Tore Ahlbäck (Åbo, Finland: Donner Institute for Research in Religious and Cultural History, 1990), 353.

6. See Jan Assmann, *The Search for God in Ancient Egypt,* trans. David Lorton (Ithaca: Cornell University Press, 2001), 152.

7. See Maurice Cahen, *Le Mot "Dieux" en Vieux-Scandinave* (Paris: Champion, 1921), 2.

8. The whole complex question of the relationship of Christianity to a putative *monotheistic* pagan past—a question it will be necessary to beg throughout most of this discussion—is taken up in Polymnia Athanassiadi and Michael Frede, eds., *Pagan Monotheism in Late Antiquity*, where it is argued that, far from arising as a reaction to Christianity, pagan monotheism "was a deeply rooted trend in ancient philosophy which developed under its own momentum." They go on, most intriguingly, to say that "we are inclined to believe that Christian monotheism is, historically speaking, part of this broader development." See Athanassiadi and Frede, *Pagan Monotheism in Late Antiquity*, (Oxford: Clarendon press, 1999), 20.

9. Ibid., 119.

10. "Die Psyche des germanischen Menschen ist in heidnischer Zeit durchaus religiös gefärbt." See Jan de Vries, *Altgermanische Religionsgeschichte*, vol. 1, (Berlin: Walter de Gruyter,1956–57), 325.

11. See Spengler, *The Decline of the West*, 187 and 403.

12. See Anthony Faulkes, "Pagan Sympathy: Attitudes to Heathendom in the Prologue to *Snorra Edda*." In *Edda: A Collection of Essays*, ed. H. Bessasson and R. J. Glendinning (Manitoba: University of Manitoba Press, 1983), 305.

13. See Richard North, *Pagan Words and Christian Meanings* (Amsterdam: Rodopi, 1991), 2.

14. See John D. Niles, "Pagan survivals and popular belief," in *The Cambridge Companion to Old English Literature*, ed. Malcolm Godden and Michael Lapidge (Cambridge: Cambridge University Press, 1991), 140.

15. A work like Hutton's, for instance, presents us with a treasurehouse of detail concerning the ways in which pre-Christians—hence, pagans—lived, worked, buried their dead, and worshipped. Hutton, however, insists from the outset that we can never know anything about paganism—and then proceeds to describe Anglo-Saxon paganism in great detail. A detailed description of an elephant *just is* an elephant description, even if we had no idea what the creature was called—or what it might call itself. See Ronald Hutton, *The Pagan Religions of the Ancient British Isles* (Oxford: Blackwell, 1993).

16. In this, I agree very much with Otto Höfler, who writes: "es gibt keine Kultakte ohne zugrunde liegende innerseelische numinose Erlebnisse, aber es gibt innerseelische numinose Erlebnisse, die nicht zu Kultakten und Kultinstitutionen führen." And in the same work: "Es ist psychologisch höchst unwahrscheinlich, daß in einer primitiveren ersten Kulturperiode die Menschen nur religiös gedacht, aber nicht religiös (im weitesten Sinn) gehandelt hätten . . . keine kultische Handlung ohne 'vorhergehenden' Gedanken möglich ist oder jemals war, und zwar ohne einen 'mythischen' oder 'religiösen' Gedanken." See Otto Höfler, *Verwandlungskulte, Volkssagen und Mythen* (Vienna: Der Österreichischen Akademie der Wissenschaften, 1973), 105 and 191.

17. Ibid., 178.

18. "to start with, there was no such thing as 'paganism' as a creed. The word can be used in a negative sense only, to indicate what a man did not believe, not what he did. In fact the word pagan means simply one who lives in a village, just as a heathen means one who dwells on a heath; that is, remote from civilisation, at a time when that had been assimilated to the Christian church." The quote is from Stuart Per-

owne, cited in Carole Cusack, *Conversion Among the Germanic Peoples* (London: Cassell, 1998), 177. See also Athanassiadi and Frede, eds., *Pagan Monotheism in Late Antiquity*, 4. The English word "heathen" is normally taken to have its roots in OE "*hæðen*": here, the authors give "heathen" as a translation of εθνικος, which had, next to a basic meaning of "outsider," the "pejorative connotations of 'rustic,' 'uneducated,' and 'ordinary,' and in that use it appears as an exact synonym of 'paganus.'" Ibid., 5. Cf. also Richard Fletcher, "Even in the country houses of the rich Christianity remained an urban religion." In *The Conversion of Europe: From Paganism to Christianity 371–1386 A.D.* (London: Fontana Press, 1998), 15. In any case "pagan"—as *paynim*—meant for most times the country in which such people were to be found; paynim being the opposite in such examples not of "Christian" but of "Christendom."

19. See Franz Cumont, *Oriental Religions in Roman Paganism* (New York: Dover Books, 1956), 63.

20. See Brian Branston, *The Lost Gods of England* (London: Book Club Associates, 1974), 49.

21. Cumont, *Oriental Religions*, 112–13.

22. Ibid., 132.

23. Ibid., 87–88.

24. Interestingly, Middle Egyptian also possesses two ways of expressing identity. This could be done either by using a nominal sentence—e.g., *ntk R'*, "You are Re," or by using an adverbial sentence—*m.k tw m mnjw*, "You are a herdsman." James Allen points out that logically these two constructions mean very different things. In the first case, the identity is considered natural or unchangeable, while in the second case it is merely temporary or acquired. "Thus *ntk R'* identifies who the subject is ("Re"), while *m.k tw m mnjw* identifies the subject's occupation (which is not necessarily permanent)." See James P. Allen, *Middle Egyptian: An Introduction to the Language and Culture of Hieroglyphs* (Cambridge: Cambridge University Press, 2000), 113. This is not the same as the distinction in predicate logic between the "is" of identity and the "is" of predication, although it superficially resembles it. In neither the former, as in "The Morning Star is the Evening Star," nor the latter, as in "The Morning Star is a celestial body being *x* number of miles from earth," do we have the equivalent of the Egyptian concept of a temporary or acquired characteristic. The key to this is the preposition *m*, meaning "in," giving us, in effect, a translation in the second case of something like "You are 'in' (that is, in the capacity, or identity, of) a herdsman." Middle Egyptian also has a way of distinguishing statements that are only temporarily true from those that are always valid. We will be using the results of linguistic research at all points throughout this discussion. While this invariably concerns etymology, this Middle Egyptian example serves as a reminder that we have much less research on the effect of syntax and grammar on mythological and philosophical themes.

25. See Cumont, *Oriental Religions*, 93–94.

26. See Assmann, *The Search for God*, 40.

27. Ibid.

28. Ibid., 7.

29. See William Chaney, "Paganism to Christianity in Anglo-Saxon England," *Harvard Theological Review* 53 (1960): 200.

30. See Ursula Dronke, "Eddic Poetry as source for the history of Germanic Religion," in *Germanische Religionsgeschichte: Quellen und Quellenprobleme*, ed. Heinrich Beck, Detlev Ellmers, and Kurt Schier (Berlin: Walter de Gruyter, 1992), 684.

NOTES TO CHAPTER 1

31. Turville-Petre offers this list of loan-words from Irish: *gealt*—"raving lunatic" (apparently common); *sust*—"a flail" (from Irish *suste); skjaðak*, "the sourness of stale beer" (from Irish *sceathach*, meaning "vomiting, emetic"); *slavak*—a kind of chickweed (from Irish *sleabhac*, laver, as in Welsh "laver-bread"); *tarfr*, "a bull," (from Irish *tarbh).* See G. Turville-Petre, *Origins of Icelandic Literature* (Oxford: Clarendon Press, 1953), 4.

32. Ibid., 6–7. He adds that "there is evidence that lays about Gothic heroes older than *Jormunrekkr* (died 375) were once current."

33. See Axel Olrik, *Ragnarok: Die Sagen vom Weltuntergang* (Berlin: Walter de Gruyter, 1922), 356.

34. See Turville-Petre, *Origins of Icelandic Literature,* 19. I doubt whether anyone would consider making such a claim in relation to a poem dealing with Greek legend, where poetry and meaning may sometimes comfortably coalesce.

35. Ibid., 56.

36. See Mary Niepokij, "Requests for a Hearing in Norse and Other Indo-European Languages," *Journal of Indo-European Studies* 25, 1 (1997): 50. The author provides a particularly interesting comparison of Norse and Vedic sources, where, for example, the equivalent of the Norse "law-speaking" function is the Vedic *vidatha,* or "assembly."

37. See Alexandre H. Krappe, *La Genèse des Mythes* (Paris: Payot, 1938), 259. For a fascinating analysis of the different explanations for the dissemination of both language and myth, see Colin Renfrew, *Archaeology and Language: The Puzzle of Indo-European Origins* (London: Penguin Books, 1989).

38. Ibid., 60.

39. See Dronke, "Eddic Poetry," 666–69; and Krappe, *La Genèse des Mythes,* 387.

40. See Margaret Schlauch, *Romance in Iceland* (London: Allen and Unwin, 1934), 24.

41. See Krappe, *La Genèse des Mythes,* 268; and Zimmer, *Myths and Sybmols,* 67. The Orphic conception of the Greeks connects serpents and fate more directly, since the serpent Χρονος was wound about the earth along with its mate, Αναγκη, ("necessity"), an image resembling the Norse idea of the serpent inhabiting the ocean surrounding the various worlds. For Homer, the earth was surrounded by a river, ωκεανος, with its serpent-god within it. For Pythagoras this strangely-named serpent Χρονος was indeed the mind, the ψυχη, of the universe. For early Greeks, both time and fate were seen as circles, and the passage of time was the movement of the circle around the earth. See R. B. Onians, *Origins of European Thought* (New York: Arno Press,1973), 251.

42. See Jan Assmann, *Monotheismus und Kosmotheismus: Ägyptische Formen eines "Denkens des Einen" und ihre europäische Rezeptionsgeschichte* (Heidelberg: Heidelberger Akademie der Wissenschaften, 1993), 5. Assmann points out that the term "monotheism" was not coined until the seventeenth century.

43. Ibid., 9.

44. Ibid., 10. According to Assmann, it was the Amarna religion of Akhnaton that was most typically "Kosmotheistisch," since it held to the belief in a *cosmic* power—Sun, and Light—and for Akhnaton only a *single* principle of creation was necessary. Amarna religion was also, incidentally, history's first *written* religion. See Assmann, *Monotheismus,* 27.

45. "Einer religion, die monotheistisch und polytheistisch zugleich denkt, muß sich die Wirklichkeit im Vordergrund und Hintergrund, Offenbarkeit und Geheimnis aufteilen." Ibid.,44.

46. According to Thomas Markey, there seem to have been five terms for "temple" in use within Germania: Old Saxon *nimid* (related to Greek *nemos*), meaning "sacred forested height," denoted a clearing where cult practices were performed; *hof* meant a farmstead, and originally carried no religious significance; *wih* denoted any hallowed place; Old High German *harg* was used to gloss all those Latin terms used as words for areas where rituals were acted out, and came to mean a small shrine; and then last there was *alh,* meaning "sacred grove." Markey concludes that of these, "only *harg* and *alh* are truly archaic and historically significant Germanic terms for cult places and/or temples, while the others are seen as subsequent borrowings." See Thomas Markey, "Germanic Terms for Temple and Cult," in *Studies for Einar Haugen,* ed. Evelyn Scherabon Firchow, Karen Grimstad, Nils Hasselmo, and Wayne O'Neil, (The Hague: Mouton: *Janua Linguarum,* 59 1972), 375.

47. Egypt would later revert, leaving open a subsequent evolution into true monotheism.

48. See Maurice Cahen, *Études sur le Vocabulaire Religieux du Vieux-Scandinave* (Paris: Champion, 1921), 5.

49. See Cumont, *Oriental Religions,* 119. The author makes a graphic point concerning the strange continuity between paganism and Christianity that could obtain, writing that "[all] efforts to maintain a barbarian religion stricken with moral decadence were in vain. On the very spot on which the last taurobolia [bull-sacrifice] took place at the end of the fourth century, in the Phrygianum, stands to-day the basilica of the Vatican." Ibid., 71.

50. See Peter Foote and David M. Wilson, *The Viking Achievement* (London: Sidgwick and Jackson, 1979), 401. It is from this usage that, presumably, comes the peculiarly British swear word "bloody." See also Henry Kratz, "The Vocabulary of Paganism in the *Heilaga manna Søgur,*" in *Sixth International Saga Conference* (Copenhagen: Kobenhavens Universitat, 1985), 640.

51. Ibid., 400.

52. See John Martin, "Some Comments on the Perception of heathen religious customs in the sagas," *Parergon* 6 (1973): 47.

53. Dronke goes on to say that such "ritual vomiting" is still practiced. "For one tribe it is an exercise aiming at total self-control, so that even fatal poisons can be swallowed and ejected without harm." See Dronke, "Eddic Poetry," 663.

54. See Edgar Polomé, "Approaches to Germanic Mythology," in *Myth in Indo-European Antiquity,* ed. Gerald Larson (Berkeley: University of California Press, 1974), 61–62. Nine is, of course, the mystical or magic number of Germanic mythology. The Finns seem to have possessed their own native names for the chief shamanistic phenomena. See Anna-Leena Siikala, "Singing of Incantations in Nordic Tradition," in Ahlbäck, *Old Norse and Finnish Religions,* 191–205. See also Elliott, who points out that runes were used on tombstones at a period when both Celtic and Roman lettering was available, suggesting a persevering belief in their magical efficacy. Indeed, so powerful was the "rune-master" that it is his name—not the dead person's—that occasionally appears on tombs. See R. W. Elliott, *Runes* (Manchester: Manchester University Press, 1959), 69. The word is found in many languages; Old Irish, for instance, has *run,* and Welsh *rhin.* Intriguingly, the Middle Egyptian word for "spells" is *rw,* as in the *Spells of coming forth by day* (better known by its modern name, the *Book of the Dead),* where the title is rendered as *rw nw prt m hrw.* The hieroglyph for "spell" is a human mouth, ⌒ (phonetic value *r*), the *rw* form being a plural.

55. See Régis Boyer, "L'Islandais des Sagas d'Après les 'Sagas de Contemporains'", (Paris: *Contributions du Centre d'Études Arctiques et Finno-Scandinaves* 6, 1967), 25. The sexual content of dreams would not be introduced into what might be called psychology until the Middle Ages. Although demons would visit sleepers in their dreams—the demon was an *Alp* or *Mahrt* (the latter comes from the Slavic, while the two words combine in English and German to give us *Alptraum*, "nightmare")—it was not until the Middle Ages that this demon took on the forms of the *incubus* and *succubus* figures well-known from Christian demonology.

56. See Stephen Flowers, "Toward an Archaic Germanic Psychology," in *Journal of Indo-European Studies* 11, 2 (1983): 121.

57. See Rudolf Simek, *Dictionary of Northern Mythology*, trans. Angela Hall, (Woodbridge: D. S. Brewer, 1996),129 and 96.

58. See Hilda Roderick Ellis, *The Road to Hel* (Cambridge: Cambridge University Press, 1943), 134.

59. From *Grimnismal*, stanza 20, in *The Poetic Edda*, trans. Lee M. Hollander, 2nd ed. (rev.) (Austin: University of Texas Press, 2001), 57.

60. See Richard North, *Pagan Words and Christian Meanings* (Amsterdam: Rodopi, 1991), 106 and 20. See also Simek, *Dictionary of Northern Mythology*, 164.

61. From Mircea Eliade, *Shamanism: archaic techniques of ecstasy*, trans. W. R. Trask (London: Arkana, 1964), 381.

62. See de Vries, *Altgermanische Religionsgeschichte*, vol. 2, 178, note 4.

2. MYTHICAL SPACE AND TIME

1. The Newtonian "container" theory of space and time—that is, space seen as an infinitely large empty box into which objects are placed, with "time's arrow" running through it (usually, and quite arbitrarily, from left to right—perhaps echoing the direction of writing, causing one to wonder whether cultures where writing runs in the reverse direction also saw time's direction in a similar way), is no more natural for us than space as heavenly ziggurat or time as a circle. Western European science has infiltrated everyday thinking such as to make it appear so, however. With that briefly stated, it seems to me doubtful whether readers of this book will wish to pursue the ideas of mathematical space and time—whether Newtonian, Einsteinian, or anything else—beyond this kind of basic definition of Newton's "absolutes," which is, in any case, hardly so transparent as to inspire confidence from the nonphilosopher or nonscientist that it has been understood. A summary of the Newtonian theory may be found in Max Jammer, *Concepts of Space* (Cambridge: Harvard University Press, 1954); and in Anthony Winterbourne, *The Ideal and the Real: An Outline of Kant's Theory of Space, Time and Mathematical Construction* (Dordrecht: Kluwer Academic Publishers, 1988), chapter 1.

2. See Kay Almere Read and Jason J.Gonzalez, *Handbook of Mesoamerican Mythology*, (Santa Barbara, Calif.: ABC-CLIO, 2000), 115.

3. See H. Hubert and Marcel Mauss, "La Representation du Temps dans la religion et la Magie," in *Mèlanges d'histoire des Religions* (Paris: Felix Alcan, 1909), 229. Cf. also: "Zeitordnung ist Festordnung, aber auch Stammesordnung," a theme taken up below. See W. Schultz, "Zeitrechnung und Weltordnung bei den Germanen," *Mannus,* 16 (1924), 124.

4. See Ernst Cassirer, *Mythical Thought*, vol. 2 of *The Philosophy of Symbolic Forms*, trans. Ralph Manheim (New Haven: Yale University Press, 1955), 84.
5. Ibid.
6. Ibid., 88.
7. Ibid., my italics.
8. See Mircea Eliade, *The Sacred and the Profane*, trans. W. R. Trask (San Diego: Harcourt Brace, 1959), 21–22.
9. Ibid., 57.
10. Ibid., 37.
11. Ibid., 63. It is interesting that Eliade has for the title of one section of this book "Temple, Basilica, Cathedral," where the distinctions, as well as the terminology, are very reminiscent of Spengler's division into "Appollinian," "Magian," and "Faustian" architecture, with their concomitant symbolic significance for ways of thinking. Spengler's work is not, however, mentioned by Eliade. See Oswald Spengler, *The Decline of the West*, vol. 1, trans. Charles Francis Atkinson (London: George Allen & Unwin,1926), chapter 6.
12. See Waldemar Bogoras, "Ideas of Space and Time in the Conception of Primitive Religion," in *American Anthropologist* 27, 2 (1925): 232.
13. See Cassirer, *Magical Thought*, 104–105.
14. Although this particular image (being c. 25,000 years old) falls well outside of her purview, Gimbutas's book contains a wealth of similar figures from across "Old Europe." See Marija Gimbutas, *The Goddesses and Gods of Old Europe 6500–3500 B.C. Myths and Cult Images*, new ed. (London: Thames & Hudson, 1982).
15. Cassirer, *Magical Thought*, 106. See also Spengler, *Decline of the West*, 424.
16. Cf. M. I. Steblin-Kamenskij, *Myth: The Icelandic Sagas and Eddas*, (Ann Arbor: University of Michigan Press, 1982), 58.
17. Ibid., 61.
18. "Le rajeunissement des mythes n'est pas un phénomène différent du phénomène général de leur localisation dans le passé, mais une forme parculière du même phénomène." In Hubert and Mauss, "La Representation du Temps," 194.
19. See Cassirer, *Mythical Thought*, 116, my italics. The Germanic gods were of course never administrators or guardians of destiny, and were certainly never so regarded by the people.
20. See Bogoras, "Ideas of Space and Time," 234.
21. See Heinrich Zimmer, *Myths and Symbols in Indian Art and Civilization*, ed. Joseph Campbell (New York: Harper and Row, 1962), 12.
22. "In a rock-stratum are embedded crystals of a mineral. Clefts and cracks occur, water filters in, and the crystals are gradually washed out so that in due course only their hollow mould remains. Then come volcanic outbursts which explode the mountain; molten masses pour in, stiffen, and crystallize out in their turn. But these are not free to do so in their own special forms. They must fill up the spaces that they find available. Thus there arise distorted forms, crystals whose inner structure contradicts their external shape, stones of one kind presenting the appearance of stones of another kind. The mineralogists call this phenomenon *Pseudomorphosis*." From Spengler, *Decline of the West*, vol. 2, 189.
23. To give just a single example for the present, scholars have noted just such a resonant detail connecting Norse and Indian mythology in the incident of Oðin whispering into Baldr's ear, and an Indian tradition whereby a father, on the birth

of a son, murmurs three times into his ear, "speak, speak," while offering the child curdled milk, honey, and butter. See Jan de Vries, *Altgermanische Religionsgeschichte* vol. 1 (Berlin: Walter de Gruyter, 1956–57), 300. The same tradition is echoed in the English expression of whispering "honeyed words" into someone's ear. While such similarities could, of course, be entirely accidental, and represent some human universal, it will be the global features of such narratives that will in the end convince.

24. Such a view is cited (not held) by Helmer Ruggren in "The Problem of Fatalism," in *Fatalistic Beliefs in Religion, Folklore, and Literature,* ed. Helmer Ruggren, (Stockholm: Almquist and Wiksell, 1964), 10.

25. Ibid., 12. See also Dalya Cohen-Mor, *A Matter of Fate: The Concept of Fate in the Arab World as Reflected in Modern Arabic Literature* (New York: Oxford University Press, 2001), 6.

26. Cohen-Mor, *A Matter of Fate,* 48–54.

27. See Paul Bauschatz, *The Well and the Tree* (Amherst: University of Massachusetts Press, 1982), 149.

28. It is false for rather abstract and counterintuitive reasons having to do with the strange logic of the mathematics of the "actual infinite." In all but mathematical (and sometimes philosophical) discussions, "infinite" seems interchangeable with "indefinitely large." For a mathematician this describes only the "potential infinite." No matter how large a number may be, *if* any finite number can be added to it (or subtracted from it) such that its magnitude has thereby changed, it can only have been an "indefinitely large" number—that is, "potentially infinite." The logic of the "actual infinite" tells us that one could "add" any number whatever to it (no matter how large), after which it is no "larger" than it was before—else it would not have been "actually infinite." Mathematicians operate with actually infinite numbers as easily as any other numbers, since they idealize these commonsense complexities to symbolic abstractions, even allowing for whole subclasses of such infinite numbers! When ordinary speech uses the term "infinite" it *never means* infinite in this true, mathematical sense, but only *very large indeed,* as in "there are an infinite number of stars in the universe." For if they could *in principle* be enumerated, their number is not infinite.

29. See Zimmer, *Myths and Symbols,* 13–19. Zimmer points out that this division of the world into four ages—or *yugas*—compares to the Greco-Roman tradition. It differs in that the Classical age borrowed names from metals—Gold, Silver, Brass, and Iron—"the Hindu from the four throws of the Indian dice game," a rather charming reminder of the intricate relationship between time, fate—and luck.

30. From *Vafþrúðnismal,* stanza 39: in Hollander, *The Poetic Edda,* 49.

31. See Jack N. Lawson, *The Concept of Fate in Ancient Mesopotamia of the First Millennium* (Wiesbaden: Harrassowitz, 1994), 20.

32. Cited in ibid., 50. The Dalley translation is rather different: "[The gods] appointed death and life./They did not mark out days for death,/But they did so for life." See *Gilgamesh,* in *Myths from Mesopotamia,* trans. Stephanie Dalley (Oxford: Oxford University Press, 1989), 109.

33. Cf. S. Bhattarcharji, *Fatalism in Ancient India* (Calcutta: Baulmon Prakashan, 1995), xix.

34. See Cohen-Mor, *A Matter of Fate,* 54.

35. See Algirdas J. Greimas, *Of Gods and Men: Studies in Lithuanian Mythology,* trans. Milda Newman (Bloomington: Indiana University Press, 1992), 116.

36. "The people ought to be taught that *Fortune* is the least blind of all goddesses; and that she is, like the Slavonic *Laima,* the wide-surveying and never-slumbering rewarder of Perseverance, Industry, Economy, Integrity, and Domestic Virtue." Charmingly, in Lithuanian legend the bird of "Mother Goodluck" (to be compared with grander versions such as the eagle as the bird of Jupiter, the dove of Venus, and the owl of Minerva) was the humble titmouse. See *Northern Antiquities: Illustrations from the Earlier Teutonic and Scandinavian Romances* (Edinburgh: James Ballantyne, 1814), 469–71.

37. Ibid. The Lithuanians (and Letts) called fate *likkinas, liktens*—from *lik-t,* "to lay down." See R. B. Onians, *The Origins of European Thought* (New York: Arno Press, 1973), 381, note. *Perkunas* was also the Proto-Baltic "thunder" god, and is related in Lithuanian mythology to the oak tree and oak groves—reminding us once again of the "tree/fate" nexus. See Thomas Gamkrelidze and Vjaceslav Ivanov, eds. *Indo-European and the Indo-Europeans* (Berlin: Mouton de Gruyter, 1995), 527.

38. Edgar Polomé, for example, writes that "it is striking to note that Hesiod, in his *Works and Days,* reports that Zeus 'created . . . a race of men . . . from the ash-trees.' But the parallelism goes no further." See Polomé, "Some Comments on *Voluspa,* Stanzas 17–18," in *Old Norse Literature and Mythology: A Symposium,* ed. Palomé (Austin: University of Texas, 1969), 266.

39. See B. C. Dietrich, *Death, Fate and the Gods* (London: Athlone Press, 1965), 327.

40. The quote is from Appius. See ibid., 334.

41. Cf. William Chase Green, *Fate, Good and Evil in Greek Thought* (Cambridge: Harvard University Press, 1944), 366.

42. This idea is suggested by Paul Schach, "Some Thoughts on *Voluspa,*" in *Edda: A Collection of Essays,* ed. Haraldr Bessasson and R. J. Glendinning (Manitoba: University of Manitoba Press, 1983), 98.

43. In Hollander, *The Poetic Edda,* 4. The square brackets are the translator's, of course, used to draw attention to his view (shared by most scholars) that the names "are now understood to be learned inventions of the twelfth century, on the pattern of the three Parcæ or Moirai of classical antiquity." Ibid., note 17.

44. See Bhattarcharji, *Fatalism in Ancient India,* 304.

3. Cosmogony and the World-Tree

1. See E. H. Meyer, *Die eddische Kosmogonie: Ein Beitrag zur Geschichte der Kosmogonie des Altertums und des Mittelalters* (Freiburg-im-Breslau: J. C. B. Mohr, 1891), 113.

2. "[Einer Kosmogonie] . . . setzt manche lange Denkarbeiten voraus. Darum ist ihrer Heimat nicht bei Hirten und Bauern, sondern in den Körperschaften gebildeter Priester, welterfahrener Sänger oder spekulativ angelegter Weiser zu suchen." Ibid.

3. Distinctions between what is inner and what is outer have always been of fundamental significance in both mythology and religion—here reflected also in legal terminology. Aside from the obvious pale within which the English had jurisdiction in the twelfth century in Ireland—anything outside being "beyond the pale"—there was the topographical inversion of the idea in Russia, where the pale marked the area within which the Jews were *allowed* to live. There is also the still more ancient

notion of profanity itself: to profane religious mysteries did not mean to reveal them illicitly, but to bring them "outside their fane," or temple, (Latin *pro-*, before, *fanum-*, a temple).

4. Gurevich gives the examples of *Medalhus, Medafell, Midgardr, Midhus, Midberg,* and points out that there were more than a hundred farms in Norway with similar appellations. See Aron Ya Gurevich, "Space and Time in the *Weltmodell* of the Old Scandinavian peoples," *Mediaeval Scandinavia* 2 (1969): 45.

5. Ernst Cassirer, *Mythical Thought,* Vol. 2, *The Philosophy of Symbolic Forms,* trans. Ralph Manheim (New Haven: Yale University Press, 1955), 98.

6. The quotes will be dropped from these terms from this point. There is so much discussion of them that, notwithstanding any reservations one might have, or indeed whether one might be begging a number of important questions about the distinction's validity, there is no need I think to detach ourselves still further from it. It will, however, be necessary to distinguish in almost every case between a cosmogony, a cosmography, and occasionally even a cosmology. These terms are precise, both for the way in which myths are delineated, and for the way in which we can now come to understand them. On this point, some cumbersome listing of the various terms will be unavoidable.

7. *Voluspa,* stanza 19, in Hollander, *The Poetic Edda,* 4.

8. See Margaret Clunies Ross, *Prolonged Echoes: Old Norse Myths in Medieval Northern Society.* Vol. 1, *The Myths* (Odense: Odense University Press, 1994–98), 229.

9. We will be examining later the idea that Norse myth incorporates a *genealogical,* rather than a *chronological* view of time.

10. The detailed argument, from which what follows here is an extended summary, comes from Ross, *Prolonged Echoes,* 235–38.

11. Ibid., 238.

12. See V. Rydberg, *Teutonic Mythology,* trans. Rasmus Anderson (London: Norrœna Society, 1906), 396–97.

13. Ibid.

14. See note 7, above.

15. Ibid., my italics.

16. See Stephen O. Glosecki, *Shamanism and Old-English Poetry,* (New York: Garland, 1989), 69 and 73. Margaret Clunies Ross, in referring to the significance of the nine days during which Oðin is hanging on the world ash-tree, says that the number within Germanic pagan tradition can be "somewhat formulaic," and suggests completeness, without any implication that an exact enumeration is intended. (See Ross, *Prolonged Echoes,* vol. 1, 51.) Here, it would seem more plausible that the number symbolism is more full-blooded, given the absolute centrality of this event for Oðin and for the cosmogony in general. That number is three, and its magical Germanic multiple, nine. The mystical number nine was founded on the perceived religious value of three—symbolizing the three cosmic regions. Thus nine becomes potent just because three is—witnessed in, for example, the nine-times repetition of the *Kyrie Eleison* in the Catholic liturgy or the nine choirs of the Holy Spirit. This number symbolism is well-known and widespread. One Greek source (Ion of Chios) wrote a treatise that begins with the words: "Everything is three and nothing more nor less than three: an object's completeness (*arete*) is in its threeness." And Aristotle had written that the "All and the Totality of Things is determined through the number three," while the Ennead—the group of nine—was central to the kinship genealogy of an-

cient Egypt. The number nine also threads through the shamanic systems of central Asia where there are nine-storied pagodas; Siberian myths mention nine worlds, nine heavens, nine gods, nine branches of the cosmic tree, and so on. This number symbolism based upon three would seem to be a far more widespread idea than that depending on seven, as is the case in Mesopotamian mythology. For details, see Mircea Eliade, *Shamanism: archaic techniques of ecstasy*, transl. W. R. Trask (London: Arkana, 1964), 274. See also Adolf Dyroff, "Zur griechischen und germanischen Kosmogonie," *Archiv für Religionswissenschaft*, 31 (1934): 110.

17. See Eleazar Meletinskij, "Scandinavian Mythology as a System of Oppositions," in *Patterns in Oral Literature*, ed. Hedi Jason and Dimitri Segal (The Hague: Mouton, 1977), 254.

18. See Jens Peter Schjødt, "Horizontale und Vertikale Achsen in der vorchristlichen skandinavischen Kosmologie," in Tore Ahlbäck, ed., *Old Norse and Finnish Religions and Cultic Place-names* [Åbo, Finland: Donner Institute for Research in Religions and Cultural History, 1990), 8.

19. See Meletinskij, "Scandinavian Mythology," 258.

20. Ibid.

21. See note 3, above.

22. John Lindow, *Murder and Vengeance among the gods: Baldr in Scandinavian Mythology* (Helsinki: FF Communications, 1997), 19.

23. R. B. Onians regards the *Kalevala* as just such a shamanistic epic, where great feats are achieved not by force of arms, but predominantly by magical means, by the power of words and incantations. See Onians, *The Origins of European Thought* (New York: Arno Press, 1973), 293.

24. Cf. Eduard Neumann, *Das Schicksal in der Edda* (Giessen: Wilhelm Schmitz, 1955), 127.

25. *Voluspa*, stanzas 58–60; in *The Poetic Edda*, 12.

26. From *Vafþruðnismal*, stanza 39; in Hollander, ibid., 49.

27. Cf. Spengler: "As to the meaning of a myth, its provenance proves *nothing*... What one people takes over from another—in 'conversion' or in admiring imitation—is a name, dress and mask for its own feeling, never the feeling of that other." In Oswald Spengler, *The Decline of the West*, 2 vols. Trans. Charles Francis Atkinson (London: George Allen & Unwin, 1926), 401.

28. Cited in Jan Assmann, *The Search for God in Ancient Egypt*, trans. David Lorton (Ithaca: Cornell University Press, 2001), 70.

29. Ibid., 73.

30. *Voluspa*, stanza 56, in Hollander, *The Poetic Edda*, 11.

31. Assmann, *The Search for God*, 74.

32. Ibid.

33. Ibid.

34. Egyptian signs are employed in three ways: as ideograms, representing the things actually depicted, such as the sign for "victory" (*nht*), 𓌂; as phonograms, representing sounds spelling out individual words; and as *determinatives*, which show that the preceding block of signs are to be taken as phonograms and, importantly, to indicate the generic category into which the word comes. In the above example, the man striking is the determinative for "force" or "effort."

35. Assmann, *The Search for God*.

36. It is for this reason that we should not neglect the roles played in such

mythologies by even minor deities, for their parts in such dramas may reveal something about the system as a whole that could be discovered in no other way. It is for this reason (among others) that old-fashioned accounts of the *entirety* of Norse mythology—such as Rydberg's—remain valuable sources.

37. See Gurevich, "Space and Time," 50.

38. See Ross, *Prolonged Echoes*, vol. 2, 87, my italics.

39. See *Voluspa*, stanza 44, in Hollander, *The Poetic Eddas*, 9.

40. Cf. Marlene Ciklamin, "The Chronological Conception in Norse Mythology," *Neophilologus* 47 (1963): 138.

41. See S. Bhattarcharji, *Fatalism in Ancient India*, (Calcutta: Baulmon Prakashan, 1995), 77.

42. See Paul Bauschatz, "Urth's Well," *Journal of Indo-European Studies* 3 (spring 1975): 68. This notion of a dual causality is thematic in the Homeric myths. We read in the *Iliad*, for example, after a description of the combat between them, that Sarpedon was "brought down" by Ares, yet with a spear wielded by Patroclus (*Iliad*, Book XVI). This, of course, is the will of the gods—not Fate as such—influencing the actions of men. Even so, the pattern seems quite un-Germanic.

43. See Thomas Gamkrelidze and Vjaceslav Ivanov, *Indo-European and the Indo-Europeans: A Reconstruction and Historical Analysis of a Proto-Language and a Proto-Culture* (Berlin: Mouton de Gruyter, 1995), 536.

44. See Carlo Alberto Mastrelli, "Reflections of Germanic Cosmogony in the *kenningar* for 'Man/Woman,'" in *7th International Saga Conference: Poetry in the Scandinavian Middle Ages* (Spoleto: Centro Italiano di Studi Sull'Alto Medioevo, 1988), 535. See also Gamkrelidze and Ivanov, *Indo-European and the Indo-Europeans*, 529.

45. *Voluspa*, stanza 17, in Hollander, *The Poetic Eddas*, 3.

46. The name of the Indian holy tree was "*asvattha*," which means "place of horses," hence the direct connection with Yggdrasill as "Oðin's steed."

47. See Robert Graves, *The White Goddess: A Historical Grammar of Poetic Myth* (London: Faber & Faber, 1999), 164.

48. Such "sympathetic magic" is echoed throughout ancient Europe. See E. A. Philippson, *Germanisches Heidentum bei den Angelsachsen* (Leipzig: Bernhard Tauchnitz, 1929), 51.

49. "Cypresses and pines, with their corporeal and Euclidean effect, could never have become symbols of unending space. But the oaks, beeches, and lindens with the fitful light-flecks playing in their shadow-filled volume are felt as bodiless, boundless, spiritual. . . . In the ash, the victory of the upstriving branches over the unity of the crown seems actually to be won. Its aspect is of something dissolving, something expanding into space, and it was for this probably that the World-Ash Yggdrasil became a symbol in the Northern mythology." See Spengler, *Decline of the West*, vol. 1, 396.

50. See Wilhelm Mannhardt, *Der Baumkultus der Germanen und ihrer Nachbarstämme* (Berlin: Borntraeger, 1875), 7–8.

51. "Be very wary of those/rowans in the yard: holy are the rowans in the yard/holy are the rowans' boughs/holy the boughs' foliage/the berries still holier." From *The Kalevala*, Canto 23, lines 11–16: trans. Keith Bosley (Oxford: Oxford University Press, 1989), 304. For anyone who, like myself, knew only the *Everyman* edition of this epic—a version that reads like a Finnish Hiawatha and strains the patience of the most dedicated reader—Keith Bosley's masterly translation comes as a complete revelation.

52. See Ursula Dronke, "Eddic Poetry as source for the history of Germanic Religion," in *Germanische Religionsgeschichte: Quellen und Quellenprobleme*, ed. Heinrich Beck, Detlev Ellmers, and Kurt Schier (Berlin: Walter de Gruyter, 1992), 666.

53. Cf. Klaus Koch, *Geschichte der ägyptische Religion* (Stuttgart: Kohlhammer, 1993), 411.

54. The coffin containing Osiris's body following his murder by Seth is found inside the trunk of the tree that had grown around it. And since the vine was sacred to Osiris, we can identify the Osiris-tree with the cosmic-tree itself. The "armed" version noted above is unusual (there is one in the Kunsthistorisches Museum in Vienna), but a composite form incorporating both the *ankh*, ♀, and the *djet*-pillar, 𓊽, almost certainly signifying life-everlasting, is found more commonly, as in the example of a faience in the British Museum (EA 54412) that shows the pillar in the loop of the *ankh* sign, with an overlaid *was*-scepter, and an image of *Heh*, the god of everlastingness.

55. In the Koran the hallowed tree is an olive, whose oil sustains the light of the lamp symbolizing Allah himself, who is "the Light of the heavens and the earth." See René Guenon, *Symboles fondamentaux de la Science sacrée* (Paris: Gallimard, 1962), 324.

56. *Kalevala*, Canto 39: 515. See also Bosley's Introduction to *The Kalevala*, xlii; and see also Felix J. Oinas, "The Balto-Finnic Epics," in *Heroic Epic and Saga*, ed. Felix J. Oinas (Bloomington: Indiana University Press, 1978), 291–92. On a purely historical note, in *Northern Antiquities* it is stated that "Leibnitz (*sic*) identifies the god Irmin [hence "Irminsul"] with Arimanius, an evil god of the Persians, and thence derives the national name *Herminiones*, or *Germani*." I have, unfortunately, been unable to locate the source of this in Leibniz. See *Northern Antiquities*, 218, note 7.

57. See Lotte Motz, "The Cosmic Ash and Other Trees of Germanic Mythology," in *ARV*, (Scandinavian Yearbook of Folklore), 47 (1992): 128.

58. The overwhelming weight of material employed in such texts as O'Neill's would require the work of several specialist scholars to unravel and properly assess. Such works as this—the scholarly equivalent of a Victorian cabinet of curiosities—must be read with ruthless selectivity, and no small measure of caution. But it is easy to be very modern and dismiss such work out of hand, which would also be unfortunate. It is possible to find in O'Neill small examples where one can confirm his conclusions, without having been fully awake during the meanderings of the argument. For instance, in his discussion of the reasons that the Egyptians used a rope cartouche inside which the names of gods were inscribed, he *speculates* that the circular form—which signified eternity—became elongated into the form we now see, so as to accommodate the names more easily. That is the same explanation for the shape given subsequently by one of the most respected authorities, Sir Alan Gardiner, in his classic (and indispensable) work on Egyptian grammar. Cf. John O'Neill, *The Night of the Gods: An Inquiry into Cosmic and Cosmogonic Mythology and Symbolism*, vol. 2, (London: Bernard Quaritch, 1893), 780: and Sir Alan Gardiner, *Egyptian Grammar*, 3rd ed. (Oxford: Griffith Institute, 1996), 74.

59. See Guenon, *Symboles fondamentaux*, 326.

60. Cf. Dante: "And as fir-tree tapers to the top/From branch to branch, so this one tapered down—/ Doubtless to hinder folk from climbing up." In *Purgatory:* Part 2 of *The Divine Comedy*, trans. Dorothy L. Sayers (London: Penguin Books, 1955), Canto 22, 244.

61. See Ananda K.Coomaraswamy, *Elements of Buddhist Iconography* (New Delhi: Munshiram Mansheirlal, 1935), 14.

4. Spinning and Weaving Fate

1. See Jan de Vries, *Altgermanische Reliogiongeschichte*, vol. 1, (Berlin: Walter de Gruyter, 1956–57), 272.
2. See Paul Bauschatz, "Urth's Well," *Journal of Indo-European Studies* 3, 11 (Spring 1975), 62.
3. See *The Epic of Creation*, in *Myths from Mesopotamia: Creation, The Flood, Gilgamesh, and Others*, ed. and trans. Stephanie Dalley (Oxford: Oxford University Press, 1989) [Tablet I], 233. The idea expressed here of a sequence—Language, Fate, Time, History—where each of these conditions the next, and where each is conceptually distinct, would seem to offer an interesting analogy to the thesis offered here in relation to Germanic ideas, and in particular, the idea that fate and time are not identical. (I am grateful to an anonymous reviewer for making this connection clearer to me.)
4. See M. J. Enright, "The Goddess who Weaves," in *Frühmittelaltlicher Studien* 24 (1990): 68.
5. "Keine andere erklärung zulassen, als die, dass auch diese dreiheit (die ursprüngliche endzahl der primitiven Menschheit) eine urtümliche ausdrucksform für unsere 'vielheit' gewesen sei." Cf. F. Kauffmann, "Über den Schicksalsglauben der Germanen," in *Zeitschrift für Deutsche Philologie* 50 (1923–26): 406.
6. See de Vries, *Altgermanische Religionsgeschichte*, vol. 2, 383.
7. Bauschatz, "Urth's Well," citing H.R. Ellis Davidson, *Gods and Myths of Northern Europe* (London: Harmondsworth, 1964), 67.
8. This most interesting part of Bauschatz's argument oddly—and disappointingly—disappears from the book's revised version of the original paper.
9. See Bauschatz, "Urth's Well," 67.
10. Ibid.
11. This concerns the logic of fatalism, which will be examined below.
12. Bauschatz, even in preferring to use the word "well" rather than "fountain" (as does Rydberg, for example) points out "the difficulty for speakers of modern Germanic languages, especially English, in grasping the exact nature of this *brunn*. Modern English lacks all etymological descendants of this word, except in such metathesized dialectical form as *bourne* or *burn*, 'stream,' 'rill'." He adds that the use of "bourne" to represent a small stream seems to be an extension of the active aspect of the word at the expense of the locational aspect—which were neatly and deliberately juxtaposed in Tennyson's "For tho' from out our bourne of Time and Place/The flood may bear me far," and I can confirm Bauschatz's remark from a very personal standpoint, since the remarkable concentration within a very small area of southern England (mainly Dorset) of hamlets and villages all prefixed "Winterbourne" (from which my own surname derives) or its variant "Winterborne," testifies to this "active" sense: a "winterbourne" (or, as in these cases, *the* "winterbourne") simply indicates a stream that runs only in the winter. See Bauschatz, "Urth's Well," 70.
13. Ibid., 75.
14. The Lithuanians and Letts, similarly, call fate *likkinnas, liktens*, from *lik-t*, "to lay down." See R. B. Onians, *The Origins of European Thought* (New York: Arno Press, 1973), 381, note.
15. See de Vries, *Altgermanische Religionsgeschichte*, 271–72.

16. See Franz Cumont, *Oriental Religions* in Roman Paganism (New York: Dover Books, 1956), 180, and Peter Foote and David M. Wilson, *The Viking Achievement*, (London: Sidgwick and Jackson, 1979), 391 and 431.

17. This ambiguity is partly the result of Alfred's problems translating Boethius's "*fortuna*," where two words were used: "wyrd" represented the force of "*fortuna*," and "woruldsælða" to represent the gifts associated with it. See F. Anne Payne, *King Alfred and Boethius: An Analysis of the Old English Version of the Consolation of Philosophy* (Madison: University of Wisconsin Press, 1968), 83.

18. See Ake Ström, "Scandinavian Belief in Fate: A Comparison between Pre-Christian and Post-Christian Times," in *Fatalistic Beliefs in Religion, Folklore, and Literature*, ed. Helmut Ruggren (Stockholm: Almquist and Wiksell, 1964), 67.

19. In Martin Ninck's book on Oðin and the belief in fate, he gives his interpretation of the notion of *ørlog*—the laws laid down by the Norns—"adapted for the Hitler period," and declares that "Krieg . . . ist *urlag* und damit zugleich 'Urgesetz' und 'Schicksal.'" This rendering of *Krieg* = *ørlog* was, according to von Kienle, precisely a product of the 1930s, where "the greatest and most prolonged Fate was, for the Germans, war itself." Cf. Ström, "Scandinavian Belief," 69, and Mathilde von Kienle, "Der Schicksalsbegriff im Altdeutschen," *Wörter und Sacher* 15 (1933): 103.

20. These details come from Bauschatz, "Urth's Well," 57.

21. Ibid., 59.

22. *Voluspa*, stanza 17: in Hollander, *The Poetic Eddas*, 3.

23. See B. C. Dietrich, *Death, Fate and the Gods* (London: Athlone Press, 1965), 329.

24. See Onians, *Origins of European Thought*, 331 and 439.

25. Onians cites Cynewulf, who had been "fettered by sins, but God unbound my body." See Onians, *Origins of European Thought*, 440, for these and many other examples.

26. Cf. Tacitus, *Germania*, in *The Agricola and the Germania*, translated by H. Mattingley, revised by S. A. Handford (London: Penguin Books, 1970), chapter 39, 134.

27. Ursula Dronke,"Eddic Poetry as source for the history of Germanic Religion," in *Germanische Religionsgeschicte*, ed. Heinrich Beck, Detler Ellmers, and Kurt Schier (Berlin: Walter de Gruyter, 1992), 661.

28. Onians, *Origins*, 409.

29. Ibid., 443. Onians adds: "If τελος meant circle or band we can explain its use to designate a body of men [in our use] of 'band,' 'circle,' 'knot,' and German '*Bund.*" These different bands or circles were different portions of life—hence also of time. The idea of a man's fate as a circle within which he is bound explains also the Wheel of Ixion.

30. Ibid., 409.

31. The *aegis*—goatskin—was Zeus's defensive covering, which Onians takes as originating in an interpretation of the idea of the storm-cloud. It is goats that the Norse storm-god Thor drives across the sky, and, in *Njal's Saga*, "Svan took a goatskin and waved it over his head and spoke: *Let there be fog,/And let there be monsters,/And fantastic sights to all/Who follow you.*" See *Njals'Saga*, §12, translated by Robert Cook (London: Penguin Books, 2001), 24.

32. See Onians, *Origins of European Thought*, 307. For Homer the stalk of the spindle was ηλακατη, to which is related meanings all connoting such a distaff shape, such as the windlass or, interestingly, that upper part of a ship's mast which was made to revolve; that connects us again with such as the turning of mill-wheels, as it is found in the context of fate in, for example, the *Kalevala*.

33. Plato, *The Republic,* Part Eleven [Book Ten], translated by Desmond Lee (London: Penguin Books, 1987), 450.

34. See M. J. Enright, "The Goddess who Weaves," *Frühmittelaltlicher Studien* 24 (1990), 68. And we have already noted that women may also have been rune masters—making a transparent logical/mythical connection between fate, goddesses, spinning, weaving—and *words.*

35. Ibid., 69.

36. See Uno Holmberg, *Der Baum des Lebens* (Helsinki: Annales Academiae Scientiarum Fennicae, 16, 1922–23), 104.

37. Some ancient religions and mythologies manage with a single deity for these different functions, e.g. the figure of Isis, in Egypt, who presides over past, present, and future.

38. Onians, *Origins of European Thought,* 352.

39. Linen, with bread, and beer, are the three commonest funerary offerings made in ritual texts.

40. See Ladislaus Mittner, *Wurd: Das Sakrale in der Altgermanische Epik* (Bern: Francke Verlag, 1955), 90. See also F.Anne Payne, *King Alfred and Boethius,* 97. Thus, for Alfred, men are caught in two positions at one and the same time: a moving position in the movement of the wheel, and a static position on the hub, spoke, or rim—making them further from or closer to, God—such that their freedom consists in their right to choose their static position. Ibid., 99.

41. *Njal's Saga,* §157, 303–4. A heddle was a series of vertical cords with loops in the middle to receive the warp thread: the shed rod was used to create the opening in the warp.

42. Onians, *Origins of European Thought,* 363.

43. Cf. Kauffmann, "Über den Schicksalsglauben der Germanen," 402, note. There existed "runic riddles," where the solutions were inserted into poems using rune names, "sometimes spelling backwards to enhance the puzzle." See Elliott, *Runes,* 74.

44. See Edward Casey, *The Fate of Place: A Philosophical History* (Berkeley: University of California Press, 1977), 7.

45. See Erika von Erhardt-Siebold, "The Old English Loom Riddles," in *Philologica: The Malone Anniversary Studies,* ed. Thomas A. Kirby and Henry B.Woolf (Baltimore: Johns Hopkins University Press, 1949), 11–15.

46. Onians, *The Origins of European Thought,* 352.

47. Ibid., 353, notes that this connection persisted into the Middle Ages, where Death carries a rope. He also points out how such an ancient—and almost mystical—connection is echoed in folk traditions and beyond, "where a piece of string was one of the most useful and precious possessions of uncivilized man no less than of the modern boy" (ibid., 371). Onians was writing (or publishing) in 1951. I can confim (with a certain sense of surprise) that in my own boyhood (rather around that time) I doubt that either myself or any of my friends were ever lacking such an item, secreted in one pocket or another. I cannot say why we all did this, but I rather doubt that small boys nowadays find the possession of such an item similarly indispensable.

48. See B. C. Dietrich, *Death, Fate and the Gods,* 75.

49. See B. Timmer, "*Wyrd* in Anglo-Saxon Prose and Poetry," *Neophilologus* 26 (1941): 24, and M. C. Van den Toorn, *Ethics and Moral in Icelandic Saga Literature* (Assen: Van Gorcum, n.d.), 145.

50. See Hans F. K. Günther, *The Religious Attitudes of the Indo-Europeans*, trans. Vivian Bird (London: Clair Press, 1966), 31–33.

51. Ibid., 35–36. Günther also quotes this from Geibel: "If there's anything more powerful than fate,/then it's courage, which bears fate unshaken." This human defiance—and dignity—in the face of the inevitable would be one positive characteristic that would give way after the conversion in favor of something with very different psychological contours, viz. Christian *humilitas*.

52. Cf. A. G. van Hamel, "The Concept of Fate in Early Teutonic and Celtic Religion," *Saga-Book* 11 (1928): 211.

53. Rydberg, *Teutonic Mythology*, 444.

5. THE LOGIC OF FATALISM

1. There was a slight gender difference also—men were more likely to believe in chance, women in fate. See Ake V. Ström, "Scandinavian Belief in Fate: A Comparison between Pre-Christian and Post-Christian Times," in Helmer Ruggren, ed. *Fatalistic Beliefs in Religion, Folklore, and Literature* Stockholm: Almquist & Wiksell, 1964), 83.

2. I am indebted to two philosophers, whose arguments I follow closely in what follows, the first of whom, Richard Taylor, is a main protagonist in the renewed interest in the debate within contemporary philosophy concerning the logical nature of fatalism, and the second, Steven Cahn, who, while framing his conclusions as a reason for denying the force of the claim that fatalism is indeed true, does full justice to the argument's complexity—and indeed to its compelling nature. For the primary source for what follows, see Richard Taylor, "Fatalism," *Philosophical Review* 71, (1962). And also *Metaphysics*, 2nd ed. (Englewoood Cliffs, N.J.: Prentice Hall, 1974). The former is much more difficult for the nonphilosopher. See also Steven Cahn, *Fate, Logic and Time* (New Haven: Yale University Press, 1967).

3. See Taylor, *Metaphysics*, 59.

4. Ibid., 65.

5. Taylor gives no reason for this somewhat eccentric choice of name within his parable. I am aware of only one Osmo—one of the shadowy ancestors of Väinomöinen in the *Kalevala*.

6. Ibid., 64.

7. Ibid., 65.

8. Ibid., 68–69, my italics.

9. Ibid., 64. This conclusion to Taylor's parable is precisely the kind of tale that appears in many more ancient stories depicting man's struggle with unavoidable destiny, and reminds us of Achilles's dilemma, where he must either win fame by dying at Troy, or return home to live out a long life. See *Iliad*, Book IX, 410–16, 154.

10. Taylor, *Metaphysics*, 70–71, my italics.

11. Ibid.

12. Cf. Cahn, *Fate, Logic and Time*, 21 and 9.

13. Ibid., 21.

14. See Susan Haack, *Philosophy of Logics* (Cambridge: Cambridge University Press, 1978), 162 and 208. In so far as the laws of logic are sacrosanct, it is small wonder

that those such as Lukasiewicz search nervously for ways around the principle of bivalence. We should note, finally, that logicians find themselves in a state of permanent dispute over the success of Lukasiewicz's project. Taylor's thesis has a particular clarity here: the laws of logic *are* sacrosanct—therefore fatalism is true.

15. Ibid., 158–60.
16. Ibid., 33.
17. See Oswald Spengler, *Decline of the West*, trans. Charles Francis Atkinson (London: George Allen & Unwin, 1926), 132. Following Spengler, we should prefer Hollander's translation of the *Voluspa* as "The Prophecy of the Seeress," to Palsson's "The Sybil's Prophecy," though not much hangs on the choice.
18. See Rosalie Wax, *Magic, Fate and History*, 152.
19. See Jack N. Lawson, *The Concept of Fate in Ancient Mesopotaia of the First Millenium* (Wiesbaden: Harrassowitz, 1994), 79.
20. See Michael Alan Williams, *Rethinking "Gnosticism": An Argument for Dismantling a Dubious Category* (Princeton, N.J: Princeton University Press, 1996), 202–3. This notion of conditional fate goes back to Homer, at least, where it can be considered typical, in that the oracles presuppose the existence of an order in what happens, which still leaves open the possibility of limited human choice. See William Chase Green, *Fate, Good and Evil in Greek Thought* (Cambridge: Harvard University Press, 1944), 23–24, and Appendix 6, 402.
21. See Paul Bauschatz, *The Well and the Tree*, 150.
22. See B. Timmer, "*Wyrd* in Anglo-Saxon Prose and Poetry," *Neophilologus* 26 (1941): 6.
23. See Mittner, *Wurd*, 87.
24. See von Kienle, "Der Shicksalsbegriff," 83, my italics.
25. Ibid. See also note 69, chapter 6, below.
26. Cf. Timmer, "*Wyrd* in Anglo-Saxon Prose and Poetry," 27. Only one of the major monotheistic religions makes this fully explicit—"Islam" meaning, of course, "submission." Timmer sees this Christian resignation to the inevitability of the course of events as ordained by God's Providence, that idea that throughout the *Beowulf* poem replaces the old Germanic belief in fate. While Hagenlocher, in analyzing *Heliand*, tells us that of the seven occurrences of *wurd* in that poem, four relate to the story of the Passion: the other occurrences concern births (of John and Christ), which seems to dovetail with the idea that fate had come to be associated by then almost entirely with the terminal events of birth and death. See Albrecht Hagenlocher, *Schicksal im Heliand: Verwendung und Bedeutung der nominalen Bezeichnungen* (Cologne: Böhlau, 1975), 63.
27. This differs in emphasis (though not much) from Alfred's notion that wisdom was a virtue gained in spite of *wyrd*, and not something gained in the confrontation with it. See F. Anne Payne, *King Alfred and Boethius: an Analysis of the Old English Version of the Consolation of Philosophy* (Madison: University of Wisconsin Press, 1968), 104. See also Karma Lochrie, "*Wyrd* and the Limits of Human Understanding: A Thematic Sequence in the *Exeter Book*," *Journal of English and Germanic Philology* 85 (1986): 324. Lochrie's views concerning the nuances of meaning in regard to *wyrd* are certainly not atypical and are widely held by scholars. The lines from Job noted by Lochrie read as follows: "For there is hope of a tree, if it be cut down, that it will sprout again, and that the tender branch thereof will not cease./Though the root thereof wax old in the earth, and the stock thereof die in the ground;/ *Yet* through

the scent of water it will bud, and bring forth boughs like a plant./But man dieth, and wasteth away: yea, man giveth up the ghost, and where *is* he?"
28. Lockrie, "*Wyrd* and the Limits of Human Understanding," 327, my italics.
29. See Green, *Fate, Good and Evil*, 340.
30. Ibid.
31. From *Hamðismal*, stanza 30; in Hollander, *The Poetic Edda*, 321. This notion of the importance of a man's reputation surviving his death—crystalized in the famous *Havamal* lines: "Your cattle shall die; your kindred shall die; you yourself shall die; one thing I know which never dies: the judgment on each one dead"—was trenchantly criticized by Rydberg, who says (or at least his translator does) that these supposed words of Oðin, far from being words of wisdom, are "the most stupid twaddle ever heard declaimed in a solemn manner." See V. Rydberg, *Teutonic Mythology*, vol. 2, trans. Rasmus Anderson (London: Norrœna Society, 1906), 497.

6. FROM PAGAN FATE TO CHRISTIAN PROVIDENCE

1. See note 18, chapter one.
2. See Richard Fletcher, *The Conversion of Europe: From Paganism to Christianity 371–1386 A.D.* (Lodon: Fontana Press, 1998), 4.
3. See Jonas Gislason, "Acceptance of Christianity in Iceland," in Tore Ahlbäck, ed., *Old Norse and Finnish Religions and Cultic Place-Names*, (Åbo, Finland: Donner Institute for Research in Religions and Cultural History, 1990), 229 and 246. Cf. also Spengler: "It was, indeed, one essential character of [paganisms] that they were numerous, and another that they were religions of pure performance; for them, therefore, the question of toleration, as the word is usually understood, did not arise." See Oswald Spengler, *Decline of the West*, vol. 2, trans. Charles Francis Atkinson (London: George Allen & Unwin, 1926), 203. I am not sure if that word "toleration" is any longer understood. It seems to be used most often by those either already agreeing with such-and-such a belief, or those indifferent to it—but in neither case is "tolerance" being exercised. Toleration presupposes disapproval; otherwise there would be nothing to tolerate.
4. Cf. William James, *The Varieties of Religious Experience*, (1901–2), (London: Collins, 1960), 203.
5. Ibid., 209 and 213.
6. "Jedes Menschliche Erzeugnis ist letztlich geistigen Ursprungs, und wenn es ein religiöser Gegenstand ist—eine Kultwagen, eine Opferschale, eine Kultmaske, ein Kultgewand—dann ist er 'seelisch-geistig-numinosen Ursprungs.'" In Otto Höfler, *Verwandlungskulte Volkssagen und Mythen*, (Vienna: Österreichischen Akademic der Wissenschaften, 1973), 180.
7. Fletcher, *The Conversion of Europe*, 6.
8. Ibid., 7.
9. See Franz Cumont, *Oriental Religions in Roman Paganism*, (New York: Dover Books, 1956), 27.
10. Ibid. and cf. R. L. M. Derolez, *Les dieux et la religion des Germains* (Paris: Payot, 1962) 240.
11. See Cumont, *Oriental Religions*, 30–31.

12. See Garth Fowden, *The Egyptian Hermes: A Historical Approach to the Late Pagan Mind* (Cambridge: Cambridge University Press, 1986), 94.
13. Cumont, *Oriental Religions,* 35.
14. Ibid., 44.
15. Similar considerations apply to that account in which the priest Coifi converts and then agrees to undertake the profanation of pagan altars and shrines himself. Coifi, however, seems to come over rather less well than did Ethelbert, for he somewhat churlishly complains that he might have expected greater favor from the gods in return for his more zealous service to them than others. He does, however, insist that he had been searching after truth and confessed that the new teaching seemed likely to afford "the blessings of life, salvation, and eternal happiness." Whatever else this demonstrates, it does not seem to be merely the throwing over of a meaningless cult in favor of true belief, and Bede in no way presents it as such. See Bede, *Ecclesiastical History of the English People,* trans. Leo Sherley-Price (London: Penguin Books, 1965). [Book I.25–26], 75–76; and [Book II.13], 129–30.
16. See Fletcher, *The Conversion of Europe,* 45 and 51.
17. Ibid., 444.
18. See Derolez, *Les Dieux et la religion,* 241–42.
19. Ibid.
20. See Fletcher, *The Conversion of Europe,* 146; for other examples, see Derolez, *Les Dieux et la religion,* 245.
21. See *The Orkneyinga Saga,* trans. Jon A.Hjaltalin and Gilbert Goudie, ed. Joseph Anderson (Edinburgh: Mercat Press, 1999), xxvii. Also: "King Olaf offered the Earl to ransom his life on condition that he should embrace the true faith and be baptized; that he should become his man, and proclaim Christianity over all the Orkneys." Ibid., 3.
22. See Fletcher, *The Conversion of Europe,* 515.
23. Such parallelisms would include "Heaven" and "Valholl," "Hell" and "Niflhel," and "*wyrd/wurd*" and its Christianized version. See William Chaney, "Paganism to Christianity in Anglo-Saxon England," *Harvard Theological Review* 53 (1960): 209.
24. We can pursue parallelisms with ancient Egyptian religion in this matter as well. Assmann points out that the "new" religion of Akhnaton "proceeded with unprecedented brutality. The new religion was not promoted, it was imposed. Tradition was not questioned, it was persecuted and forbidden . . . [The] common man had little share in the official cult of the new god. Instead, he had an even greater share in the coercion of the state, which was vigilant lest he secretly practice some forbidden cult." What we see here is a pattern that has become depressingly familiar across cultures, and across millennia. See Assmann, *The Search for God in Ancient Egypt,* trans. David Lorton (Ithaca: Cornell University Press, 2001), 199 and 222.
25. See Maurice Cahen, *Le Mot "Dieux" en Vieux-Scandinave* (Paris: Champion, 1921), 18–20, and D. H. Green, *Language and History in the Early Gemanic World,* (Cambridge: Cambridge University Press, 1998), 13–14.
26. See Cahen, *Le Mot "Dieux,"* 21.
27. Ibid., 25.
28. Ibid., 28 and 41. Cahen insists that such change of gender was no grammatical accident, corresponding as it did to a new sense introduced by Christianity. In the pagan vocabulary, *goþ* was a general notion applicable to divinities of both sexes. With the coming of Christianity, it became a proper name (ibid., 35). Cahen goes

on to say that even within modern Icelandic separate vocalizations are retained for *goð*—neuter, signifying "heathen god" and *guð*—masculine, signifying "God"—a distinction maintained in compound words such as "falsgoð"—"false god." See ibid., 47.

29. See Green, *Language and history*, 14.
30. Cumont insists on this, but nowhere says why this should be so. See Cumont, *Oriental Religions*, 70.
31. Ibid., 93.
32. He continues: "Indo-European men of strongest heart have always been, like Frederick the Great, born stoics who, standing upright like the devout Vergil have recognised a merciless fate." See Hans F. K. Günther, *Religious Attitudes of the Indo-Europeans*, trans. Vivian bird (London: Clair Press, 1966), 30. Notwithstanding the florid language, this does express the point made above, that this dignity in the face of fate seems to have been a heroic characteristic of the ideal Norseman.
33. See Dag Strömbäck, *The Conversion of Iceland*, trans. Peter Foote (London: The Viking Society, 1975), 26.
34. See Gro Steinsland, "Pagan Myth in Confrontation with Christianity," in *Old-Norse and Finnish Religions and Cultic Place-names*, ed. Ahlbäck, 23.
35. See Strömbäck, *The Conversion of Iceland*, 39.
36. Ibid. Strömbäck says that the origin of the term is found in an ancient Germanic word that is found in the Gothic biblical translation of Ulfilas, as well as in Viking runic inscriptions.
37. Ibid., 44.
38. As Fletcher asks: "And anyway—what makes a Christian." See Fletcher, *The Conversion of Europe*, 9.
39. Cited in ibid., 53.
40. Ibid., 54.
41. "Die Heiden haben nicht am Dasein des christlichen Gottes gezweifelt und die Christen nicht am Dasein der heidnischen Götter." See Hans Kuhn, "Das nordgermanisches Heidentum in den ersten christlichen Jahrhunderten," *Zeitschrift für deutsches Altertum* 79 (1942): 151.
42. "The White Christ might have ultimate power of life and death, but was it so sure that he knew about everyday concerns of the farmer in the field and forest and stable.?" See Eric Sharpe, "Salvation, Germanic and Christian," in J. R. Hinnels and E. J. Sharpe, *Man and his salvation* (Manchester: University of Manchester Press. 1973), 256. As Sharpe points out, most people were farmers, not warriors or kings, and they still looked for divine protection through their ritual practices.
43. See Hjaltalin and Goudie, ed., *Orkneyinga Saga*, 50.
44. See Fletcher, *The Conversion of Europe*, 64 and 55. Also: "We have heard that some of you make vows to trees, pray to fountains, and practice diabolical augury. What is worse, there are some unfortunate and miserable people who not only are unwilling to destroy the shrines of the pagans but even are not afraid or ashamed to build up those which have been destroyed. Why did they receive the sacrament of baptism—if afterwards they intended to return to the profanation of idols?" Ibid., 52.
45. See Cumont, *Oriental Religions*, 63.
46. See H. Mayr-Harting, *Two Conversions to Christianity: the Bulgarians and the Anglo-Saxons* (Reading: Reading University Press, 1994),13. See also Derolez, *Les Dieux et la Religion*, 247.

47. There is a salutary reminder that paganism was also capable of protecting itself from attack, in the reference to Hialti Skeggjason, who was banished for composing a poem disparaging the pagan gods, and which contained the lines: "In barking at gods I am rich:/Freyja strikes me as a bitch;/one or the other must be:/Odin's a dog—or else she." See *Njal's Saga*, §102, 177. I cannot resist including the more vigorous version of this, given in *Northern Antiquities*, 501, which runs as follows:"I will not serve an idol log/For one, I care not which,/But either Oðin is a dog,/Or Freya is a bitch."

48. See Cecil Wood, "The Viking Universe," 573.

49. See Günther, *Religious Attitudes*, 65, and Fletcher, *The Conversion of Europe*, 62.

50. See Fletcher, *The Conversion of Europe*, 261.

51. See Cahen, *Le Mot "Dieux,"* 65.

52. See Strömbäck, *The Conversion of Iceland*, 44.

53. See Michael Allen Williams, *Rethinking "Gnosticism": An Argument for Dismantling a Dubious Category*, (Princeton, N.J.: Princeton University Press, 1996), 202–3. Gnosticism would seem to be a theme running through centuries of Germanic thought, surfacing from time to time in public expressions of religiosity, but more often present as an occult influence, a shadow, providing a mysterious contour to other forms of belief, both religious and political. For a fascinating, and slightly disturbing, account of its influence up to and including the Third Reich's private obsession with the religious occult, see Jean-Michel Angebert, *Hitler et la Tradition Cathare* (Paris: Robert Laffont, 1971), esp. chapter 2.

54. Williams, *Rethinking "Gnosticism,"* 207, my italics.

55. See Steinsland, Pagan Myth, 326.

56. See M. C. Van den Toorn, *Ethics and Moral in Icelandic Saga Literature* (Assen: Van Gorcum, n.d.), 35. Some caution is required in judging the moral tone of *Havamal:* some scholars consider it as the product of the late twelfth or early thirteenth century, making it more closely allied to the moral world of the Christian Middle Ages than to ancient Germanic heathendom. On this idea of the "aesthetic" in morality, Green points out that Greek ethics is sometimes said to be largely "intellectual or aesthetic," relating this to the reestablishment of "right proportion" in a manner reminiscent of what I think is the essence of *lex talionis*. See Green, *Fate, Good and Evil*, 22.

57. See F. Seebohm, *Tribal Custom in Anglo-Saxon Law* (London: Longmans, Green & Co., 1902), 71–72.

58. See Peter Foote and David M. Wilson, *The Viking Achievement,* (London: Sidgwick & Jackson, 1979), 432.

59. My remarks here closely follow Miller's excellent survey. See W. Miller, *Bloodtaking and Peacemaking: Feud, Law, and Society in Saga Iceland* (Chicago: University of Chicago Press, 1990), 179–81. "Vengeance," on the other hand, did have a word—"*hefnd.*"

60. See ibid., 181.

61. See John Lindow, *Murder and Vengeance Among the Gods: Baldr in Scandinavian Mythology,* (Helsinki: Svomalainen tiedeakattemia, 1997), 75. Green remarks that during the classical period Greek equivalents for the word "sin" are all but absent: "We find instead expressions that imply 'going too far,' 'overshooting the mark,' 'disturbing the right proportion' or 'mean.'" And even the characteristic idea of *hubris* "is probably founded on the notion of excess." See Green, *Fate, Good and Evil*, 22.

62. Green, *Fate, Good and Evil*, 175.

63. The Greeks had the concept of "κηρ," literally the "heart," but also the soul of a departed person; when Zeus consults the scales, he weighs the κηρ of a hero. This is superficially comparable to the Egyptian idea of weighing the heart of a dead person—weighed in a scale against a feather. Should the two balance, the person was deemed to have lived a just and proper life. He would then be declared "justified," literally "true of voice" (a common epithet found on funerary stelae), and permitted to join the society of the dead. It should be pointed out, however, that any connection between the Greek and Egyptian conceptions in this matter is dismissed as unlikely by Onians. See Onians, *Origins of European Thought*, 398.

64. See Miller, *Bloodtaking and Peacemaking*, 192–96.

65. Ibid., 302. Miller points out that the plural of Old Norse "honor" meant "compensation."

66. See Hjaltalin and Goudie, ed., *Orkneyinga Saga*, 173.

67. See Bauschatz, *The Well and the Tree*, 154. The church's difficulties are made clear, as D. H. Green points out, in that the word *"humilitas"* was for the Christian the *virtue* of humility, whereas in the eyes of the Germanic people, such "humiliation" or "shame" was quite a different matter, especially as done to one's kin. "Such forgiveness and willingness to abandon the duty of feuding dealt a shocking blow to the kindred as a central support for Germanic society." See Green, *Language and history*, 51.

68. See Cassirer, *Mythical Thought*, 119.

69. See Payne, *King Alfred and Boethius*, 78 and 86–88. An example of the temporalization of fate is seen in that Boethius's term *"fatum"* is inseparably linked in meaning to the term *"prouidentia"*—God's "eternal plan." Payne points out that fate is here the temporal manifestation of this plan. *"Wyrd"* becomes confined to an "incident" in time, and thus has fewer functions than Fate. Yet, for Alfred, *wyrd* still binds all men together to a greater or lesser degree, and thus becomes "a kind of corporate retribution." Ibid., 87 and 101.

70. See Albrecht Dihle, *The Theory of Will in Classical Antiquity* (Berkeley: University of California Press, 1982), 71.

71. Flowers's discussion of "archaic psychology" is, philosophically, rather weakened by his reliance from the outset on a simple dictionary definition of the fundamental concept of "soul"—I doubt that a philosopher writing about the meaning of *wyrd* would be permitted any such luxury. For all that, his subsequent analysis manages to yield some interesting results. See Stephen Flowers, "Toward an Archaic Germanic Psychology," *Journal of Indo-European Studies* 11, 2 (1983): 119.

72. *Voluspa*, stanza 18, in Hollander, *The Poetic Edda*, 3.

73. Flowers, "Toward an Archaic Germanic Psychology," 134, note.

74. W. Baetke, *Das Heilige im Germanischen* (Tübingen, 1942), 50.

75. Green, *Language and history*, 386.

76. See Albrecht Hagenlocher, *Schicksal im Heliand: Verwendung und Bedeutung der nominalen Bezeichnungen*, (Köln: Böhlau, 1975) 64.

77. See Green, *Language and history*, 389.

Bibliography

Adams, William Y. *The Philosophical Roots of Anthropology.* Stanford: CSLI Publications, 1998.
Aeschylus. *The Oresteian Trilogy.* Translated by Philip Vellacott. London: Penguin Books, 1959.
Ahlbäck, Tore, ed. *Old Norse and Finnish Religions and Cultic Place-Names.* Åbo, Finland: Donner Institute for Research in Religious and Cultural History, 1990.
Allen, James P. *Middle Egyptian: An Introduction to the Language and Culture of Hieroglyphs.* Cambridge: Cambridge University Press, 2000.
Anderson, R. B. *Teutonic Mythology.* London, 1889.
Anderson, Stig, ed. *Die Aktualität der Saga: Festschrift für Hans Schottmann.* Berlin: Walter de Gruyter, 1999.
Angebert, Jean-Michel. *Hitler et la tradition cathare.* Paris: Robert Laffont, 1971.
The Anglo-Saxon Chronicles. Translated and edited by Michael Swanton. London: Phoenix Press, 2000.
Assmann, Jan. *Ägypten: Eine Sinnesgeschichte.* Munich: Carl Hanser, 1996.
———. *Monotheismus und Kosmotheismus: Ägyptische Formen eines "Denkens des Einen" und ihre europäische Rezeptionsgeschichte.* Heidelberg: Heidelberger Akademie der Wissenschaften, 1993.
———. *The Search for God in Ancient Egypt.* Translated by David Lorton. Ithaca: Cornell University Press, 2001.
———. *Zeit und Ewigkeit im Alten Ägypten: Ein Beitrag zur Geschichte der Ewigkeit.* Heidelberg: Abhandlungen der Heidelberger Akademie der Wissenschaften, 1975.
Athanassiadi, Polymnia, and Michael Frede, eds. *Pagan Monotheism in Late Antiquity.* Oxford: Clarendon Press, 1999.
Auld, Richard. "The Psychological and Mythic Unity of the God Odinn." *Numen* 23 (1976): 145–60.
Ausenda, Giorgio, ed. *After Empire: towards an ethnology of Europe's barbarians.* Woodbridge, England: Boydell Press, 1995.
Baetke, W. *Das Heilige im Germanischen.* Tübingen, 1942.
Balslev, Anindita Niyogi. "Time and the Hindu Experience." In *Religion and Time.* Edited by Anindita Niyogi Balslev and J. N. Mohanty. New York: E. J. Brill, 1993. 163–81.
Bauschatz, Paul. "Urth's Well." *Journal of Indo-European Studies* 3, 1 (spring 1975): 53–86.

———. *The Well and the Tree*. Amherst: University of Massachusetts Press, 1982.

Beard, Mary. "Looking (harder) for Roman myth: Dumézil, declamation, and the problems of definition." In *Mythos in mythenloser Gesellschaft: Das Paradigma Roms*. Fritz Graf, ed. Stuttgart and Leipzig: B. G. Teubner, 1993, 44–64.

Beck, H., D. Ellmers, and K. Schier, eds. *Germanische Religionsgeschichte: Quellen und Quellensprobleme*. Berlin: Walter de Gruyter, 1992.

Becker, Udo. *Lexikon der Symbole*. Freiburg: Herder, 2002.

Bede. *Ecclesiastical History of the English People*. Translated by Leo Sherley-Price. London: Penguin Books, 1965.

Beowulf. Translated with an introduction and commentary by Howell D. Chickering. New York: Anchor Books, 1977.

Bernheimer, Richard. *Wild Men in the Middle Ages*. Cambridge; Harvard University Press, 1952.

Bessason, Haraldur, and R. J. Glendinning, eds. *Edda: A Collection of Essays. University of Manitoba Icelandic Studies 4*. Manitoba: University of Manitoba Press, 1983.

Bhattacharji, S. *Fatalism in Ancient India*. Calcutta: Baulmon Prakashan, 1995.

Bogoras, Waldemar. "Ideas of Space and Time in the Conception of Primitive Religion." *American Anthropologist* 27, 2 (1925): 205–66.

Boyer, Régis. "*Herfjötur(r)*." In *Visages du Destin dans les Mythologies Mélanges*. Jacqueline Duchemin, ed. Paris: Sociéte d'Edition "les Belles Lettres" (1983): 153–68.

———. *L'Islandais des Sagas d'Après les "Sagas de Contemporains."* Paris: Contributions du Centre d'Études Arctiques et Finno-Scandinaves, 1967.

———. *Yggdrasill: La Religion des Anciens Scandinaves*. Paris: Payot, 1981.

Brandl, Alois. "Zur Vorgeschichte der Weird Sisters in *Macbeth*." *Forschungen und Charakteristiken von Alois Brandl*. Berlin: Walter de Gruyter, 1936. 82–97.

Branston, Brian. *The Lost Gods of England*. London: Book Club Associates, 1974.

Bremner, Rolf. "Hermes-Mercury and Woden-Odin as Inventors of Alphabets." *Old English Runes and Their Continental Background*. Alfred Bannesberger, ed. *Anglistischer Forschung* (winter 1991): 409–19.

Brunner, Helmut. "Die Grenzen von Zeit und Raum bei den Ägypten." *Archiv für Orientforschung* 17 (1954–55): 141–45.

Buchholz, Peter. "Geschichte, Mythos, Märchen—drei Wurzeln germanischer Heldensage?" *Seventh International Saga Conference: Poetry in the Scandinavian Middle Ages*. Spoleta: Centro Italiano di Studi Sull'Alto Medioevo, 1988. 391–404.

Byock, Jesse. *Feud in the Icelandic Saga*. Berkeley: University of California Press, 1982.

Cahen, Maurice. *Études sur le Vocabulaire Religieux du Vieux-Scandinave*. Paris: Champion, 1921.

———. *Le Mot "Dieux" en Vieux-Scandinave*. Paris: Champion, 1921.

Cahn, Steven. *Fate, Logic, and Time*. New Haven: Yale University Press, 1967.

Campbell, Joseph. *Occidental Mythology*. Volume 3 of *The Masks of God*. London: Souvenir Press, 2001.

———. *Oriental Mythology*. Volume 2 of *The Masks of God*. London: Souvenir Press, 2000.

———. *Primitive Mythology*. Volume 1 of *The Masks of God*. London: Souvenir Press, 2001.

Cardona, George, Henry Hoenigswald, and Alfred Senn, eds. *Indo-European and Indo-Europeans*. Philadelphia: University of Pennsylvania Press, 1970.

Carver, Martin, ed. *The Age of Sutton Hoo: The Seventh Century in North-Western Europe.* Woodbridge, England: Boydell Press, 1999.

Casey, Edward. *The Fate of Place: A Philosophical History.* Berkeley: University of California Press, 1977.

Cassirer, Ernst. *Mythical Thought.* Volume 2 of *The Philosophy of Symbolic Forms.* Translated by Ralph Manheim. New Haven: Yale University Press, 1955.

Chadwick, Hector Munro. *The Cult of Othin.* London: Cambridge University Press, 1899.

Chaney, William. "Paganism to Christianity in Anglo-Saxon England." *Harvard Theological Review* 53 (1960): 197–217.

Ciklamin, Marlene. "The Chronological Conception in Norse Mythology." *Neophilologus* 47 (1963): 138–50.

Clark, R. T. Rundle. *Myth and Symbol in Ancient Egypt.* London: Thames & Hudson, 1959.

Clover, Carol J., and John Lindow. *Old Norse–Icelandic Literature: a critical guide.* Ithaca: Cornell University Press, 1985.

Cohen-Mor, Dalya. *A Matter of Fate: The Concept of Fate in the Arab World as Reflected in Modern Arabic Literature.* Oxford and New York: Oxford University Press, 2001.

Coomaraswamy, Ananda K. *Elements of Buddhist Iconography.* 2nd edition. New Delhi: Munshiram Mansharlal, 1972.

Cox, G. W. *Mythology of the Aryan Nation.* 2 vols. (London, 1870), Port Washington, N. Y., 1969.

Craigie, W. A. *The Religion of Ancient Scandinavia.* London: 1906.

Cross, Tom Peete. "Celtic Mythology and Arthurian Romance." In Kirby and Woolf, *Philologica: The Malone Anniversary Studies,* 110–14.

Crossley-Holland, Kevin. *The Penguin Book of Norse Myths.* London: Penguin Books, 1993.

Cumont, Franz. *Oriental Religions in Roman Paganism.* New York: Dover Books, 1956.

Cusack, Carole. *Conversion Among the Germanic Peoples.* London: Cassell, 1998.

Davidson, H. R. Ellis. *Gods and Myths of Northern Europe.* London: Harmondsworth, 1964.

Derolez, R. L. M. *Les dieux et la religion des Germains.* Paris: 1962.

Dietrich, B. C. *Death, Fate and the Gods.* London: Athlone Press, 1965.

Dihle, Albrecht. *The Theory of Will in Classical Antiquity.* Berkeley: University of California Press, 1982.

Dronke, Ursula. "Eddic Poetry as source for the history of Germanic Religion." In *Germanische Religionsgeschichte: Quellen und Quellenprobleme.* Heinrich Beck, Detlev Ellmers, and Kurt Schier, eds. Berlin: Walter de Gruyter, 1992. 655–84.

Dumezil, Georges, *Mythes et dieux des Germains.* Paris: 1939.

Dyroff, Adolf. "Zur griechischen und germanischen Kosmogonie." *Archiv für Religionswissenschaft* 31 (1934): 105–23.

The Poetic Edda. Translated with an Introduction and Notes by Carolyne Larrington. Oxford: Oxford University Press, 1999.

The Poetic Edda. Translated by Lee M. Hollander. 2nd ed., rev. Austin: University of Texas Press, 2001.

Eliade, Mircea. *Images and Symbols*. Translated by P. Mairet. London, 1961.

———. *Myths, Dreams and Mysteries*. Translated by Philip Mairet. London: Collins, 1960.

———. *Patterns in Comparative Religion*. Translated by R. Sheed. London, 1958.

———. *The Sacred and the Profane: The Nature of Religion*. Translated by Willard R. Trask. San Diego: Harcourt Brace Jovanovich, 1959.

———. *Shamanism: archaic techniques of ecstasy*. Translated by W. R. Trask. London: Arkana, 1964.

Elliott, R. W. *Runes: An Introduction*. Manchester: Manchester University Press, 1989.

Ellis, Hilda Roderick. *The Road to Hel*. Cambridge: Cambridge University Press, 1943.

Ellwood, Robert. *The Politics of Myth*. Albany: State University of New York Press, 1999.

Enright, M. J. "The Goddess Who Weaves." *Frühmittelaltlicher Studien* 24 (1990): 54–70.

Erhardt-Siebold, Erika von. "The Old-English Loom Riddles." In Kirby and Woolf, *Philologica: The Malone Anniversary Studies*. Baltimore: Johns Hopkins University Press, 1949. 9–17.

———. "Old-English Riddle No. 57." *Modern Language Association of America* 62 (1947): 1–8.

Erman, Adolf. *Die Religion der Ägypter*. Berlin: Walter de Gruyter, 1934.

Faulkes, Anthony. "Pagan Sympathy: Attitudes to Heathendom in the Prologue to *Snorra Edda*." In Bessasson and Glendinning, eds., *Edda: A Collection of Essays*. Manitoba: University of Manitoba Press, 1983, 283–314.

Fell, Christine, and Wilson, David, eds. *The Northern World: The History and Heritage of Northern Europe A.D. 400–1100*. London: Thames & Hudson, 1980.

Firchow, Evelyn Scherabon, Kaaren Grimstad, Nils Hasselmo, and Wayne O'Neil, eds. *Studies for Einar Haugen. Janua Linguarum 59*. The Hague: Mouton, 1972.

Fleck, J. "The knowledge-criterion in the *Grimnismal*." *Arkiv for nordisk Filologi* 86 (1971): 49–65.

Fletcher, Richard. *The Conversion of Europe: From Paganism to Christianity 371–1386 A.D.* London: Fontana Press, 1998.

Flowers, Stephen. "Toward an Archaic Germanic Psychology." *Journal of Indo-European Studies* 11, 2 (1983): 117–38.

Foote, Peter, and David M. Wilson. "Conversion." In Phillip Pulsiano, ed. *Medieval Scandinavia: An Encyclopedia*. New York: Garland Publishing Inc., 1993. 106–8.

———. *The Viking Achievement*. London: Sidgwick & Jackson, 1979.

Fowden, Garth. *The Egyptian Hermes*. Cambridge: Cambridge University Press, 1986.

Fox, Robin Lane. *Pagans and Christians*. London: Viking Press, 1986.

Frazer, J. G. *The Golden Bough: A Study in Magic and Religion*. Abridged edition. London: Macmillan. 1995.

Gardiner, Sir Alan. *Egyptian Grammar: Being an Introduction to the Study of Hieroglyphs.* 3rd ed., revised. Oxford: Griffith Institute, Ashmolean Museum, 1996.

Gerritsen, Willem P., and Anthony G. van Melle. *A Dictionary of Medieval Heroes.* Translated by Tanis Guest. Woodbridge, England: Boydell Press, 1998.

Gillespie, G. T. *A Catalogue of Persons Named in German Heroic Literature.* Oxford: Oxford University Press, 1973.

Gimbutas, Marija. *The Goddesses and Gods of Old Europe 6500–3500 B.C.: Myths and Cult Images.* New edition. London: Thames & Hudson, 1982.

Gislason, Jonas. "Acceptance of Christianity in Iceland in the Year 1000 (999)." In Ahlbäck, ed., *Old Norse and Finnish Religion and Cultic Place-Names.* Åbo: Donner Institute for Research in Religious and Cultural History, 1990. 223–55.

Glosecki, Stephen O. *Shamanism and Old-English Poetry.* New York: Garland Publishing Co., 1989.

Goblet, d'Alviella, Eugène. Count. *The Migration of Symbols* (1892). First English edition 1894, with an Introduction by Sir George Birdwood. Wellingborough: The Aquarian Press 1979.

Godden, Malcolm, and Michael Lapidge, eds. *The Cambridge Companion to Old English Literature.* Cambridge: Cambridge University Press, 1991.

Gordon, E. V. *An Introduction to Old Norse.* 2nd ed., revised. A. R. Taylor, eds. Oxford: Clarendon Press, 1956.

Graves, Robert. *The White Goddess: A Historical Grammar of Poetic Myth.* Edited by Grevel Lindop. London: Faber and Faber, 1999.

Green, D. H. *Language and history in the early Germanic world.* Cambridge: Cambridge University Press, 1998.

Green, William Chase. *Fate, Good, and Evil in Greek Thought.* Cambridge: Harvard University Press, 1944.

Greimas, Algirdas J. *Of Gods and Men: Studies in Lithuanian Mythology.* Translated by Milda Newman. Bloomington: Indiana University Press, 1992.

Grettir's Saga. Translated by Denton Fox and Hermann Palsson. Toronto: University of Toronto Press, 1974.

Griffiths, J. Gwyn. "Wisdom About Tomorrow." *Harvard Theological Review* 53 (1960): 219–21.

Grønbech, Vilhelm. *Culture of the Teutons.* Translated by W. Worster. London: 1931.

Guenon, René. *Symboles fondamentaux de la Science sacrée.* Paris: Gallimard, 1962.

Günther, Hans F. K. *The Religious Attitudes of the Indo-Europeans.* Translated by Vivian Bird, in collaboration with Royce Pearson. London: Clair Press, 1966.

Gurevich, Aron Ya. "Space and Time in the *Weltmodell* of the Old Scandinavian Peoples." *Mediaeval Scandinavia* 2 (1969): 42–53.

Haack, Susan. *Philosophy of Logics.* Cambridge: Cambridge University Press, 1978.

Hagenlocher, Albrecht. *Schicksal in Heliand: Verwendung und Bedeutung der nominalen Bezeichnungen.* Köln: Böhlau, 1975.

Hamel, A. G. Van. "The Concept of Fate in Early Teutonic and Celtic Religion." *Saga-Book* 11 (1928): 202–14.

Harms, Ernest. "Five Basic Types of Theistic Worlds in the Religions of Man." *Numen* 13 (1966): 205–40.

Harrison, Robert. *Forests: The Shadow of Civilization*. Chicago: University of Chicago Press, 1992.

Hastrup, Kirsten. *Culture and History in Medieval Iceland: an anthropological analysis of structure and change*. Oxford: Clarendon Press, 1985.

———. *Island and Anthropology: Studies in past and present Iceland*. Odense: Odense University Press, 1990.

Hatab, Lawrence J. *Myth and Philosophy: A Contest of Truths*. La Salle, Ill.: Open Court Publishing, 1990.

Haugen, Einer. "The Edda as Ritual: Odin and His Masks." In Bessason and Glendinning, *Edda: A Collection of Essays*. University of Manitoba Icelandic Studies 4. Manitoba: University of Manitoba Press, 1983. 3–24.

———. "On Translating from the Scandinavian." In Polomé, ed. *Old Norse Literature and Mythology: A Symposium*. Austin: University of Texas, 1969. 3–18.

Havamal: The Words of Odin. Translated and introduced by Paul Edwards and Hermann Palsson. Edinburgh: Lockharton Press, 1998.

Helm, Karl. *Altgermanische Religionsgeschichte*. 2 vols. Heidelberg: Carl Winter, 1913–53.

———. "Weltwerden und Weltvergehen in altgermanischer Sage, Dichtung und Religion." *Hessische Blätter für Volkskunde* 38 (1940): 1–35.

Herrmann, Paul. *Nordische Mythologie* (1903). Berlin: Aufbau Bibliothek, 1992.

Höfler, Otto. *Verwandlungskulte, Volkssagen und Mythen*. Vienna: Österreichischen Akademie der Wissenschaften, 1973.

Holmberg, Uno. *Der Baum des Lebens*. Toimituksia Annales Academiae Scientiarum Fennicae, Series B, Vol. XVI, Helsinki, 1922–23.

Homer. *The Iliad*. Translated by Robert Fitzgerald. Oxford: Oxford University Press, 1974.

Hornung, Erik. *Das geheime Wissen der Ägypter und sein Einfluß auf das Abendland*. Munich: Deutscher Taschenbuch, 2003.

Hubert, H., and Marcel Mauss. "La Representation du Temps dans la religion et la Magie." In *Mélanges d'histoire des Religions*. Paris: Felix Alcan, 1909. 189–229.

Hultgård, Anders. "Old Scandinavian and Christian Eschatology." In Ahlbäck, ed. *Old Norse and Finnish Religions and Cultic Place-Names*. Åbo: Donner Institute, 1990. 344–57.

Hutton, Ronald. *The Pagan Religions of the Ancient British Isles: Their Nature and Legacy*. Oxford: Blackwell, 1993.

James, William. *The Varieties of Religious Experience* (1901). London: Collins, 1960.

Jammer, Max. *Concepts of Space*. Cambridge: Harvard University Press, 1954.

Jente, Richard. *Die mythologische Ausdrücke im altenglische Wortschatz*. Heidelberg, 1921.

Kalevala. Translated by Keith Bosley. Oxford: Oxford University Press, 1989.

Kaufmann, F. "Über den Schicksalsglauben der Germanen." *Zeitschrift für Deutsche Philologie* 50 (1926): 361–407.

Kemp, Anthony. *The Estrangement of the Past: A Study in the Origins of Modern Historical Consciousness.* New York: Oxford University Press, 1991.

Kienle, Mathilde von. "Der Schicksalsbegriff im Altdeutschen." *Wörter und Sachen* 15, (1933): 81–112.

Kirby, Thomas A., and Henry B. Woolf, eds. *Philologica: The Malone Anniversary Studies.* Baltimore: Johns Hopkins University Press, 1949.

Krappe, Alexander H. *La Genèse des Mythes.* Paris: Payot, 1938.

Kratz, Henry. "The Vocabulary of Paganism in the *Heilagra manna Sögur*." In *Sixth International Saga Conference.* Copenhagen: Det arnamagnæanske Institut, Kobenhavens Universitat, 1985. 629–43.

Krohn, K. "Das schiff Naglfar." *Finnisch-ugrische Forschungen* 12 (1912): 154–55.

Kuhn, Hans. "Das nordgermanische Heidentum in den ersten christlichen Jahrhunderten." *Zeitschrift für deutsches Altertum* 79 (1942): 133–66.

Kummer, B. *Midgards Untergang: Germanischer Kult und Glaube in den letzten heidnischen Jahrhunderten.* Leipzig: Pfeiffer, 1927.

Lapidge, Michael, and Helmut Gneuss. *Learning and Literature in Anglo-Saxon England.* Cambridge: Cambridge University Press, 1985.

Larson, Gerald, ed. *Myth in Indo-European Antiquity.* Berkeley: University of California Press, 1974.

Lawson, Jack N. *The Concept of Fate in Ancient Mesopotamia of the First Millennium: Toward an Understanding of Simtu.* Wiesbaden: Harrassowitz, 1994.

Lindow, John. "Bloodfeud and Scandinavian Mythology." *Alvíssmal* 4 (1995): 51–68.

———. *Murder and Vengeance among the gods: Baldr in Scandinavian Mythology.* FF Communications. Helsinki: Suomalainen tiedeakattemia, 1997.

Littleton, C. Scott. *The New Comparative Mythology.* Berkeley: University of California Press, 1973.

Lochrie, Karma. "*Wyrd* and the Limits of Human Understanding: A Thematic Sequence in the *Exeter Book*." *Journal of English and Germanic Philology* 85 (1986): 323–31.

Lönnroth, Lars. "Saga and *Jartegn:* The Appeal of Mystery in the Saga Texts." In Anderson, ed., *Die Aktualität der Saga.* Berlin: Walter de Gruyter, 1999. 11–24.

MacCulloch, J. A. *The Celtic and Scandinavian Religions.* London: Hutchinson's University Library, 1948.

Mackenson, Lutz. "Baumseele." *Zeitschrift für Deutschkunde* (1924): 1–21.

Magoun, Francis B. "On some survivals of pagan belief in Anglo-Saxon." *Harvard Theological Review* 40 (1947): 33–46.

Mannhardt, Wilhelm. *Der Baumkultus der Germanen und ihrer Nachbarstämme.* Berlin: Borntraeger, 1875.

Markey, Thomas L. "Germanic Terms for Temple and Cult." In Firchow et al. ed., *Studies for Einar Haugen.* The Hague: Mouton, 1972. 365–78.

Martin, John. "Some Comments on the Perception of heathen religious customs in the sagas." *Parergon* 6 (1973): 45–50.

Martin, John Stanley. *Ragnarok: An Investigation into Old Norse Concepts of the Fate of the Gods.* Assen: Melbourne Monographs in Germanic Studies, 1972.

Mastrelli, Carlo Alberto. "Reflections of Germanic Cosmogony in the *'kenningar'* for 'Man/Woman.'" *Seventh International Saga Conference: Poetry in the Scandinavian Middle Ages.* Spoleto: Centro Italiano di Studi Sull'Alto Medioevo, 1988. 535–44.

Mayr-Harting, H. *The Coming of Christianity to Anglo-Saxon England.* London: Batsford, 1991.

———. *Two Conversions to Christianity: The Bulgarians and the Anglo-Saxons.* Reading: Reading University Press, 1993.

McCreesh, Bernadine. "Contrasting Christian and Pagan Motifs in Certain Family Sagas." Workshop Papers II, *Sixth International Saga Conference.* Bibliotheca Arnamagnæana 30, Munksgaard, Copenhagen, 1985. 304–38.

McKinnell, John. *Both One and Many: Essays on Change and Variety in Late Norse Heathenism.* Rome: Il Calamo, 1994.

Meletinskij, Eleazar. "Scandinavian Mythology as a System of Oppositions." In *Patterns in Oral Literature.* Heda Jason and Dimitri Segal, eds. The Hague: Mouton, 1977. 251–60.

Meyer, E. H. *Die eddische Kosmogonie.* Freiburg: J. C. B. Mohr, 1891.

———. *Voluspa: Eine Untersuchung.* Berlin: Mayer & Miller, 1889.

Miller, W. *Bloodtaking and Peacemaking: Feud, Law, and Society in Saga Iceland.* Chicago: University of Chicago Press, 1990.

Mittner, Ladislaus. *Wurd: Das Sakrale in der Altgermanische Epik.* Bern: Francke Verlag, 1955.

Moisl, H. "Anglo-Saxon Royal Genealogies and Germanic Oral Tradition." *Journal of Medieval History* 7 (1981): 215–48.

Momigliano, Arnaldo. "Time in Ancient Historiography." In *Essays in Ancient and Modern Historiography.* Oxford: Blackwell, 1977. 179–204.

Motz, Lotte. "The Cosmic Ash and Other Trees of Germanic Myth." *ARV* 47 (1992): 127–41.

———. "The Northern Heritage of Germanic Religion." *The Mankind Quarterly* 23 (1983): 365–82.

Myths from Mesopotamia: Creation, The Flood, Gilgamesh, and Others. Edited and translated by Stephanie Dalley. Revised edition. Oxford: Oxford University Press, 1989.

Neumann, Eduard. *Das Schicksal in der Edda.* Giessen: Wilhelm Schmitz, 1955.

Niepokij, Mary. "Requests for a Hearing in Norse and Other Indo-European Languages." *Journal of Indo-European Studies* 25, 1 (1997): 49–78.

Njal's Saga. Translated with introduction and notes by Robert Cook. London: Penguin Books, 2001.

Nordal, Sigurður. "Three Essays on *Voluspa.*" *Saga-Book* 18 (1970–71): 79–135.

North, Richard. "The Pagan Inheritance of Egill's *Sonatorrek.*" *Seventh International Saga Conference: Poetry in the Scandinavian Middle Ages.* Spoleta: Centro Italiano di Studi Sull'Alto Medioevo, 1988, 147–67.

———. *Pagan Words and Christian Meanings.* Amsterdam: Costerus, Rodopi, 1991.

Northern Antiquities. Illustrations from the Earlier Teutonic and Scandinavian Romances. Edinburgh: James Ballantyne and Co., 1814.

Oinas, Felix J., ed. *Heroic Epic and Saga: An Introduction to the World's Great Folk Epics.* Bloomington: Indiana University Press, 1978.

Olrik, Axel. *Nordisches Geistesleben in Heidnischer und Frühchristlicher Zeit.* Heidelberg, 1908.

———. *Ragnarok: Die Sagen vom Weltuntergang.* Berlin: Walter de Gruyter, 1922.

O'Neill, John. *The Night of the Gods: An Inquiry into Cosmic and Cosmogonic Mythology and Symbolism.* 2 volumes. London: Bernard Quaritch, 1893.

Onians, R. B. "On the Knees of the Gods." *Classical Review* (1924): 2–6.

———. *The Origins of European Thought.* New York: Arno Press, 1973.

Oosten, Jarich. *The War of the Gods: The Social Code in Indo-European Mythology.* London: Routledge & Kegan Paul, 1985.

Orkneyinga Saga. Translated by Jon A. Hjaltalin and Gilbert Goudie. Edited by Joseph Anderson. Edinburgh: Mercat Press, 1999.

Östwold, Torbjörg. "The War of the Aesir and the Vanir: A Myth of the Fall in Nordic Religion." *Temenos* 5 (1969): 169–202.

Ovid. *Metamorphoses.* Translated by Mary Innes. London. Penguin Books, 1955.

Owen, G. R. *Rites and Religions of the Anglo-Saxons.* Newton Abbot: David & Charles, 1981.

Page, R. I. *An Introduction to English Runes.* 2nd ed. Woodbridge, England: Boydell Press, 2003.

Payne, F. Anne. *King Alfred and Boethius: An Analysis of the Old English Version of the Consolation of Philosophy.* Madison: University of Wisconsin Press, 1968.

Peuckert, Will-Erich. "Germanische Eschatologien." *Archiv für Religionswissenschaft* 32 (1935): 1–37.

Philippson, E. A. *Germanisches Heidentum bei den Angelsachsen.* Leipzig: Bernhard Tauchnitz, 1929.

Phillpotts, Bertha. *Edda and Saga.* London, 1931.

Plato. *The Republic.* Translated with an introduction by Desmond Lee. 2nd ed. revised. London: Penguin Books, 1987.

Polomé, Edgar. "Approaches to Germanic Mythology." In Larson, ed., *Myth in Indo-European Antiquity.* Berkeley: University of California Press, 1974. 61–62.

———. "The Indo-European Component in Germanic Religion." In *Myth and Law Among the Indo-Europeans: Studies in Indo-European Comparative Mythology.* Jaan Puhvel, ed. Berkeley: University of California Press, 1970. 55–82.

———. "Some Comments on Voluspa, stanzas 17–18." in Polomé, ed. *Old Norse Literature and Mythology: A Symposium.* Austin: University of Texas, 1969. 265–90.

Pulsiano, Phillip, ed. *Medieval Scandinavia: An Encyclopedia.* New York: Garland Publishing Inc., 1993.

Radin, Paul. *Primitive Man as Philosopher.* 2nd ed. New York: Dover Books, 1957.

Read, Kay Almere, and Jason Gonzalez. *Handbook of Mesoamerican Mythology.* Santa Barbara, Calif.: ABC-CLIO, 2000.

Renauld-Krantz. *Structures de la Mythologie nordique.* Paris: Maisonneuve et Larose, 1972.

Renfrew, Colin. *Archaeology and Language: The Puzzle of Indo-European Origins*. London: Penguin Books, 1989.

Ross, Margaret Clunies. *Prolonged Echoes: Old Norse Myths in Medieval Northern Society*. 2 volumes: *(i) The Myths, (ii) The reception of Norse myths in medieval Iceland*. The Viking Collection. Odense: Odense University Press, 1994–98.

———. "Quellen zur germanischen Religionsgeschichte." In *Germanische Religionsgeschichte: Quellen und Quellen-probleme*. Heinrich Beck, Detlev Ellmers, and Kurt Schier, eds. Berlin: Walter de Gruyter, 1992. 633–55.

Ruggren, Helmer, ed. *Fatalistic Beliefs in Religion, Folklore, and Literature*. Stockholm: Almquist & Wiksell, 1964.

Rydberg, V. *Teutonic Mythology*. 3 volumes. Translated by Rasmus Anderson. London: Norrœna Society, 1906.

Sagas of Icelanders: A Selection. Preface by Jane Smiley. Introduction by Robert Kellogg. London: Allen Lane, Penguin Press, 2000.

Salo, Unto. "Agricola's Ukko in the Light of Archaelogy. A Chronological and Interpretative Study of Ancient Finnish Religion." In Ahlbäck, ed., *Old Norse and Finnish Religions and Cultic Place-Names*. Åbo: Donner Institute, 1990. 92–190.

Sawyer, Birgit, and Peter Sawyer. *Medieval Scandinavia: From Conversion to Reformation 800–1500*. Minneapolis and London: University of Minnesota Press, 1993.

Schach, Paul. "Some Thoughts on Voluspa." In Bessasson and Glendinning, *Edda: A Collection of Essays*. Manitoba: University of Manitoba Press, 1983. 86–116.

Schjødt, Jens Peter. "Horizontale und Vertikale Achsen in der vorchristlichen skandinavischen Kosmologie." In Ahlbäck, ed., *Old Norse and Finnish Religions*. Åbo: Donner Institute, 1990. 35–57.

Schlauch, Margaret. *Romance in Iceland*. London: Allen & Unwin, 1934.

Schultz, W. "Zeitrechnung und Weltordnung bei den Germanen." *Mannus* 16 (1924): 119–26.

Schütte, Gudmund. *Dänisches Heidentum*. Heidelberg: Kultur und Sprache 2, 1923.

Seebohm, F. *Tribal Custom in Anglo-Saxon Law*. London: Longmans, Green and Co., 1902.

Sharpe, E. "Salvation, Germanic and Christian." In E. J. Sharpe and J. R. Hinnels, *Man and his salvation*. Manchester: University of Manchester Press, 1973. 243–62.

Siikala, Anna-Leena. "Singing of Incantations in Nordic Tradition." In Ahlbäck, ed., *Old Norse and Finnish Religions*. Åbo: Donner Institute, 1990. 191–205.

Simek, Rudolf. *Dictionary of Northern Mythology*. Translated by Angela Hall. Cambridge: D. S. Brewer, 1996.

Spengler, Oswald. *The Decline of the West*. 2 vols. Translated by Charles Francis Atkinson, London: George Allen & Unwin, 1926.

Stanley, E. G. *The Search for Anglo-Saxon Paganism*. Woodbridge, England: D. S. Brewer 1975.

Steblin-Kamenskij, M. I. *Myth: The Icelandic Sagas and Eddas*. Ann Arbor: University Press of Michigan, 1982.

———. *The Saga Mind*. Trans. Kenneth Ober. Odense: Odense University Press, 1973.

Steinsland, Gro. "Pagan Myth in Confrontation with Christianity: *Skirnismal and Genesis.*" In Ahlbäck, ed., In *Old-Norse and Finnish Religions and Cultic Place-names.* Tore Ahlbäck, ed. Åbo, Finland: The Donner Institute for Research in Religious and Cultural History, 1990. 316–28.

Strenski, Ivan. *Four Theories of Myth in twentieth-century history.* Basingstoke: Macmillan, 1987.

Ström, Åke V. "Indogermanisches in der *Völuspa.*" Numen 14 (1967): 167–208.

———. "Scandinavian Belief in Fate: A Comparison between Christian and Post-Christian Times." In Ruggren, ed., *Fatalistic Beliefs in Religion, Folklore, and Literature.* Stockholm: Almquist & Wiksell, 1964. 63–68.

Strömbäck, Dag. *The Conversion of Iceland.* Translated by Peter Foote. London: Viking Society, 1975

Strutynski, Udo. "Germanic Divinities in Weekday Names." *Journal of Indo-European Studies* 3, 4 (1975): 363–84.

Sturluson, Snorri. *Edda.* Translated and edited by Anthony Faulkes. London: J. M. Dent, 1987.

Tacitus. *The Agricola and The Germania.* Original translation by H. Mattingley, revised by S. A. Handford. London: Penguin Books, 1970.

Taylor, Richard. "Fatalism." *Philosophical Review* 71 (1962): 56–66.

———. *Metaphysics.* 2nd ed. Englewood Cliffs, N.J.: Prentice-Hall, 1974.

Thorpe, Benjamin. *Northern Mythology: From Pagan Faith to Local Legends.* Ware: Wordsworth Editions, 2001.

Timmer, B. "Heathen and Christian Elements." *Neophilologus* 29 (1944): 180–85.

———. "*Wyrd* in Anglo-Saxon Prose and Poetry." *Neophilologus* 26 (1941): 24–33 and 213–28.

Turville-Petre, G. *Nine Norse Studies.* London: Viking Society, University College, 1972.

———. *Origins of Icelandic Literature.* Oxford: Clarendon Press, 1953.

Van den Toorn, M. C. *Ethics and Moral in Icelandic Saga Literature.* Assen: Van Gorcum, n. d.

Saga of the Volsungs. Translated by Jesse L. Byock. Berkeley: University of California Press, 1990.

Voluspa: The Sybil's Prophecy. Edited, introduced, and annotated by Hermann Palsson. Edinburgh: Lockharton Press, 1996.

Vries, Jan de. *Altgermanische Religionsgeschichte.* 2 vols. Berlin: Walter de Gruyter, 1956–57.

———. "Die Bedeutung der Volkskunde." *Germanisch-Romanische Monatsschriften* 20 (1932): 27–39.

———. *The Problem of Loki.* Helsinki: Suomalainen Tiedeakatemia Societas Scientianum Fennica, 1933.

Warren, Wilham F. *The Earliest Cosmologies.* New York: Eaton & Mains, 1909.

Watkins, Calvert. "Studies in *Indo-European Legal Language, Institutions, and Mythology.*" In Indo-European and Indo-Europeans. Edited by George Cardona, Henry M. Hoenigswald, and Alfred Senn. Philadelphia: University of Pennsylvania Press, 1970. 321–54.

Wax, Rosalie. *Magic, Fate, and History.* Lawrence, Kans.: Coronado Press, 1969.

Weber, G. W. *Wyrd: Studien zum Schicksalsbegriff der altenglischen und altnordischer Literatur. Frankfürter Beitrage für Germanistik* 8. Bad Homburg: Verlag Gehlen. 1969.

Weyergraf, Bernd, ed. *Waldungen: Die Deutschen und ihr Wald.* Berlin: Akademie der Künste, 1987.

Williams, Michael Allen. *Rethinking "Gnosticism": An Argument for Dismantling a Dubious Category.* Princeton, N.J.: Princeton University Press, 1996.

Winterbourne, Anthony. *The Ideal and the Real: An Outline of Kant's Theory of Space, Time and Mathematical Construction.* Dordrecht: Kluwer Academic Publishers, 1988.

Wood, Cecil, "The Viking Universe." In Firchow et al. *Studies for Einar Haugen.* The Hague: Mouton, 1972. 568–573.

Wood, Ian. "Pagan Religion and Superstitions East of the Rhine from the Fifth to the Ninth Century." In George Ausenda, ed. *After Empire.* Woodbridge, England: Boydell Press, 1995. 253–67.

Zadra, Daris. "Symbolic Time." In *Encyclopaedia of Religion.* Edited by Mircea Eliade. Volume 14. New York: Macmillan, 1987. 193–98.

Zimmer, Heinrich. *Myths and Symbols in Indian Art and Civilization.* Edited by Joseph Campbell. New York: Harper and Row, 1962.

Index

aegis, 161 n. 31
Aesir, 64, 65
Akhnaton, 150 n. 44, 166 n. 24
Akkadian myth, 54, 101
Alfred, 89, 97, 161 n. 17, 164 n. 27, 169 n. 69
Allen, James, 149 n. 24
Angebert, Jean-Michel, 168 n. 53
Arab concept of fate, 52
Aristotle, 47
Asgard, 22, 61
   supposed origins in Troy, 65
ash tree, 77
Askr, 77
Assmann, Jan, 22, 30, 35, 71, 72, 73, 150 nn. 42 and 44, 166 n. 24
Assyrian mythology, 82
Athanassiadi, Polymnia, 148 n. 8
atonement, 37–38
Atrahasis (Babylonian myth), 55
Atropos, 84, 85
Augustine, 47

Babylonian myth, 54, 61, 85, 160 n. 3
Baetke, W., 144
Baldr, 71, 126, 140
Bauschatz, Paul, 53, 76, 87, 90, 91, 94, 114, 142, 160 nn. 8 and 12
Beard, Mary, 15
Bede, 124–25, 135, 166 n. 15
belief, 26, 144
   terms in Old Norse, 22
Bel-Marduk, 34
Beowulf, 40, 138
Bhattarcharji, S., 76
Bifrost, 65

binding
   and fate, 92–94
   and magic, 38, 69
blot, 37
Boethius, 89, 97, 143, 161 n. 17, 169 n. 69
Bogoras, Waldemar, 153 n. 12
Bosley, Keith, 80, 158 n. 51, 159 n. 56
Branston, Brian, 28

Cahen, Maurice, 128, 129, 166 n. 28
Cahn, Steven, 110, 114, 163 n. 2
Casey, Edward, 99
Cassirer, Ernst, 24, 26–27, 44, 45, 47, 48, 49, 50, 62, 142
Causality
   and fate in Norse mythology, 16
   and time, 75–76
Celtic influence, 31
Chaney, William, 30, 127, 166 n. 23
Christian ethics, 41, 137
Ciklamin, Marlene, 75
Clement of Alexandria, 136
Clotho, 84, 85
Cohen-Mor, Dalya, 154 n. 25
Coifi, 166 n. 15
conversion
   in Iceland, 130–32
   varieties of, 127
Coomaraswamy, Ananda, 159 n. 61
Cosmic Tree. *See* Tree
cosmogonies
   and eschatology, 68, 70
   "horizontal" and "vertical", 62–63
Creation, Epic of, 85

183

184 INDEX

Cumont, Franz, 28, 37, 122, 123, 129, 134, 151 n. 49, 167 n. 30
Cynewulf, 161 n. 25

Dalley, Stephanie, 154 n. 32
Dante, 159 n. 60
Dietrich, B. C., 56
Dihle, Albrecht, 143
Diogenes Lærtius, 119
divination, 112
djet (eternity), 72–73
djet-pillar, 89
Dronke, Ursula, 31, 34, 37, 151 n. 53
Dyroff, Adolf, 157 n. 16

Edda
  and non-Christian tradition, 21
Eddic mythology, 24, 33
Egyptian paganism, 29–30, 35, 89, 169 n. 63
  and cosmos as drama, 72–73
  influence on Northern mythology, 71
  language and logic, 29, 74, 149 n. 24
  signs, 86, 97, 151 n. 54, 157 n. 34
Eliade, Mircea, 40, 45, 46, 61, 68, 152 n. 61, 153 nn. 8 and 11, 156 n. 16
Elliott, R.W., 151 n. 54, 162 n. 43
Embla, 77–78
Enright, D.J., 86, 95
Erhardt-Siebold, Erika von, 100
Ethelbert, 124, 125
Exeter Book, 118

fatalism, 102
  and logic, 108–9
Fate
  as allotment, 52, 95, 100–01
  "book of", 76
  and causality, 105
  as challenge, 58, 88, 102–0
  and Christian providence, 136, 144–45
  in Ancient Egypt, 79, 97
  and fortune, 89, 93
  in Germanic culture, 90
  and language, 86
  and necessity, 50, 55, 86, 93, 150 n. 41
  and the past, 76
  as personified, 56, 116
  and the present, 87
  and spinning. *See* spinning
  as supratemporal, 49, 115
  and time, 55–56, 87
  and turning, 80–81, 87, 97–98
  and weaving. *See* weaving
  and the wheel, 97, 161 n. 29
Fates, Greek, 92, 100–101
Faulkes, Anthony, 148 n. 12
feuds, 138–141
Fimbulwinter, 75
Fletcher, Richard, 120, 122, 125, 133, 134, 148 n. 18, 167 nn 38 and 44
Flowers, Stephen, 1 43, 144, 169 n. 71
Foote, Peter, 37
Fowden, Garth, 166 n. 12
Frede, Michael, 148 n. 8
fylgja, 39

Gamkrelidze, Thomas, 158 n. 43
Gardiner, Sir Alan, 159 n. 58
genealogy and time. *See* Time
Germanic consciousness
  and soul, 143–44, 169 n. 71
Germanic paganism
  as cult, 122–24
  as true religion, 23
Gilgamesh, Epic of, 54
Gimbutas, Marija, 153 n. 14
Gislason, Jonas, 165 n. 3
Glosecki, Stephen, 156 n. 16
gnosticism, 136, 168 n. 53
god
  terms for, 128, 166 n. 28
Greek mythology, 38
Greek ontology and logic, 73
Green, D.H., 128, 145, 146 n. 8, 168 n. 61, 169 n. 67
Greimas, Algirdas, 154 n. 35
Grimnismal, 35
Guenon, René, 159 n. 55
Günther, Hans, 102, 130, 134, 163 n. 51, 167 n. 32
Gurevich, Aron Ya, 68, 156 n. 4
Gylfaginning, 24, 65

Haack, Susan, 110
Hagenlocher, Albrecht, 145, 164 n. 26
Hamel, A. G. van, 102
hamingja, (guardian spirit), 39
Havamal, 138, 165m.31, 168 n. 56
Heimdallr, 79
Hel, 22
Heliand, 51, 144–45
Hesiod, 78, 155 n. 38
Hesperides, 35
Hindu myth, 82
Höfler, Otto, 26, 122, 148 n. 16
Homer
 myth in, 94–95, 150 n. 41, 158 n. 42
 terms for fate, 56, 92–94, 101, 161 n. 32
honor
 in Old Norse, 141
Hubert, H., 44, 49
hubris, 16, 88
Huginn, 39–40
Hultgard, Anders, 147 n. 5
Hume, David, 16
Hutton, Ronald, 148 n. 15

Indo-European influence in myths, 102
Indra, 34
Irish settlers, 31
Irminsul, 35, 80
Ivanov, Vjaceslav, 155 n. 37

James, William, 121
Jammer, Max, 152 n. 1
Jonssen, Finnur, 21

Kalevala, 78, 80, 157 n. 23
Kant, 16, 18, 47, 147 n. 14
Kienle, Mathilde von, 116
Koran
 and the Holy Tree, 159 n. 55
Kratz, Henry, 151 n. 50
Kuhn, Hans, 167 n. 41

Lachesis, 84, 85, 95
law, primal. See *ørlog*
Lawson, Jack, 114
lex talionis, 139, 168 n. 56
Lindow, John, 140

Lithuanian myth, 55, 88, 96, 99, 155 n. 37
Lochrie, Karma, 118, 164 n. 27
logic
 and fatalism, 110–11
loom-riddles, 99
Lukasiewicz, J., 110, 163 n. 14
Lyungberg, H., 126

magic
 and Egyptian sign, 151 n. 54
 and speech, 86
Mannhardt, Wilhelm, 78
Markey, Thomas, 151 n. 46
Martin of Braga, 132
Mastrelli, Carlo Alberto, 77
Mauss, Marcel, 44, 49
Mayr-Harting, H., 134
Mazdaism, 75
Meletinskij, Eleazar, 68
memory
 and Germanic concept of time, 39
Mesopotamian myth. See Babylonian myth
Meyer, E. H., 61
Midgard, 61
Miller, W., 139, 141, 168 n. 59, 169 n. 65
Mimir's Well, 65
Mithraism, 34
Mittner, Ladislaus, 116
Μοιρα, 57
 as allotted portion, 57, 95, 101
monotheism
 in Egypt, 30
 and paganism, 23, 25, 126, 148 n. 8
Motz, Lotte, 81
Muninn, 39–40
myth
 definition, 15
 as symbolic thought, 24

Newton, Isaac, 43
Niðhoggr, 35
Niepokij, Mary, 33, 150 n. 36
Niflhel, 22
Niles, J., 25
Ninck, Martin, 161 n. 19
Njal's Saga, 98, 100, 161 n. 31

186 INDEX

Nordal, Sigurður, 19
Norns
   as birthhelpers, 84–85
   and Homeric myth, 92, 101
   and Roman *Parcae*, 57, 96, 101
   in *Voluspa*, 57
   as weavers of fate, 88, 96–100
Norse cosmogonies. *See* cosmogonies
Norse myth
   influence from Asia, 31
North, Richard, 24, 40
numbers
   mystical, 86, 134, 156 n. 16

oak tree cult, 77
Oðin, 34, 38–40, 79, 88
   and polytheism, 126
   and self-sacrifice, 38, 67, 93
   as shaman, 68
Olrik, Axel, 32
O'Neill, John, 80, 81, 159 n. 58
Onians, R. B., 92, 93, 94, 95, 97,
     100, 161 nn and 29, 162 n. 47,
     169 n. 63
ørlog (primal law), 88, 90–91, 161 n. 19
Osiris, 48, 79, 159 n. 54

paganism
   and belief, 22–24, 36, 121–25, 144,
     148 n. 18
   and Christianity, 22–23, 115, 131–32
   eschatology and Christianity, 135,
     141
   and ethics, 138
   and priests, 131
   Roman, 28, 121
   and temples, 151 n. 46
Palsson, Hermann, 147 n. 15, 164 n. 17
Parcae, 57, 84–86
Payne, F. Anne, 143, 162 n. 40
Perowne, Stuart, 148 n. 18
Persian myths, 32
Philippson, E. A., 158 n. 48
Plato, 50, 82
Platonism
   and conditional fate, 114
Polomé, Edgar, 38, 155 n. 38
polytheism, 23, 35

primitivism, 27
Prior, A. N., 110

Quine, W. V., 110

Radin, Paul, 147 n. 14
Ragnarok, 21, 48, 53, 64, 119, 128, 141
Re
   and Egyptian concept of eternity, 73
religion
   word in Old Norse, 130
Renfrew, Colin, 150 n. 37
Rig Veda, 23, 34
Ross, Margaret Clunies, 13, 63, 64,
     156 n. 16
Ruggren, Helmer, 154 n. 24
runes, 86, 151 n. 54, 162 n. 43
   and Oðin, 38
Rydberg, Viktor, 22, 65, 66, 70, 74, 81,
     157 n. 36

Saamis, myths, 85
Sagas, 15
   and magic, 38
Schach, Paul, 155 n. 42
Schjødt, Jens Peter, 68
Schlauch, Margaret, 150 n. 40
Schultz, W., 152 n. 3
Seebohm, F., 168 n. 57
shamanism
   Germanic, 39, 66
Sharpe. Eric, 133, 167 n. 42
Sibyl, 113
Sigrdrifumal, 138
Siikala, Anna-Leena, 151 n. 54
Simek, Rudolf, 40
Simpson, J., 146 n. 8
Simtu (fate), 54, 114
Sioux myths, 78
Skirnismal, 137
Skuld, 87
space, mythical. *See* Time
Spengler, Oswald, 13, 24, 39, 48, 51, 78,
     113, 153 nn. 11 and 22, 157 n. 27,
     158 n. 49, 164 n. 17, 165 n. 3
spinning
   and fate, 92, 94–96, 116

Steblin-Kaminskij, M. I., 14, 48
Steinsland, Gro, 130, 136, 137
Ström, Åke V., 90
Strömbäck, Dag, 130, 131, 132, 167 n. 36
Sturluson Snorri, 24

Tablet of Destinies, 54, 101
Tacitus, 37, 93
Taylor, Richard, 107, 108, 109, 110, 111, 112, 114, 137, 163 nn. 2, 9, and 14
teleology, 94
Therman, Erik, 102
Thor, 79
Tiamat, 54
time
  in Ancient Egypt, 72
  as cyclic, 53–54, 63, 69
  as destroyer, 54
  as genealogical, 39, 48–49, 75
  as irreversible, 62–63
  as linear, 74
  mythical v. historical, 48
  as Newtonian, 42–44, 152 n. 1
  in *Sagas*, 48
time and fate
  connection, 49, 53, 64
Timmer, B., 164 n. 26
tree
  cosmic, 77–78
  and creation of Mankind, 77, 91
  and Egyptian hieroglyph, 72
  as inverted, 82
  and mill image, 80
  and shamanism, 66
  as world-axis, 79–81
Turville-Petre, G., 21, 32, 33, 150 n. 31

Urðr (*Urth*), 87, 116, 142
Urd's Well, 22, 65
Utgard, 61

Vafþruðnismal, 53
Valholl, 64, 141
Valkyries, 100
Van den Toorn, M. C., 102
Vårdträd, 78
Venus of Willendorff, 48
Verthandi, 87
Visnu, 82
voluntas (will), 41
Voluspa, 19, 21, 33, 48, 56, 63, 70, 75, 87, 91, 144
Vries, Jan de, 23, 41, 146 n. 8

Wax, Rosalie, 17, 113
weaving and fate, 97–100, 116
Williams, Michael A., 164 n. 20
Wilson, David, 37
Wood, Cecil, 15
Wyrd
  and Christian God, 51, 89, 118, 161 n. 17, 169 n. 69
  as bridge to Christianity, 115, 117–19, 142–43

Yggdrasill, 34, 38, 46, 62, 65, 66, 76, 80–82, 158 nn. 46 and 49
Ymir, 34

Zeus, 34, 119
Zimmer, Heinrich, 21, 50, 154 n. 29
Zohar mythology, 82